Life, and Other Ways to Kill Time . . .

Life, and Other Ways to Kill Time . . .

by Mike Nichols

A Mario Sartori Book

Lyle Stuart Inc.   *Secaucus, New Jersey*

To Catherine Craddock, who started it all

My thanks to Ruth Nathan, Cathy Adams,
Kathy Strayer and John Forsyth for aiding
and abetting.
And, of course, my thanks to the gang at,
and the readers of, the Fort Worth
Star-Telegram.

Copyright © 1988 by Mike Nichols

Published by Lyle Stuart, Inc.
120 Enterprise Ave., Secaucus, N.J. 07094
In Canada: Musson Book Company
a division of General Publishing Co. Limited
Don Mills, Ontario

Manufactured in the United States of America

Library of Congress Cataloging-in-Publication Data

Nichols, Mike.
    Life, and other ways to kill time . . . / by Mike Nichols.
        p.   cm.
    "A Mario Sartori book."
    ISBN 0-8184-0462-0 : $15.95
PN6162.N5   1988
814'.54--dc 19   87-26728
                                                         CIP

Contents

FROM THE CRADLE

TO THE GRAVE

DOUBLE, DOUBLE TOIL AND TROUBLE

LOVE (OR A REASONABLE FACSIMILE)

IN THE NEWS, OF THE NEWS

THOSE SPECIAL OCCASIONS

LIFE AT LARGE

From the Cradle

Labors of love: Babies and bridges

"Honey, it's your turn to burp the Chrysler Building."

Someone has said that men—denied the miracle of birth—try to compensate for this and gain a bit of immortality through their inanimate creations: They write books, paint pictures, erect skyscrapers, build bridges and dams and such.

We'll overlook the fact that this theory seems to assume that women come up with all these babies on their own. Yet anyone who took seventh-grade biology knows that we men play a crucial role in procreation: We assemble the crib.

This theory intrigues me. I have often wondered (well, twice, to be honest) what God did to establish a balance between the sexes. This issue gets right down to the pro and con, the positive and negative, the yin and yang, the very Gladys Knight and the Pips of life itself.

Because, you see, God:

1. *Lets* women have babies. (This is the pro, positive, yin, and Gladys Knight of it all, in case you couldn't tell.)

2. *Makes* women have babies, which includes some downright unpleasantness during pregnancy and labor. He gave them a reproductive system so complicated that Rube Goldberg

should have been an ob-gyn. (You catch on fast: This is the con, negative, yang and Pips of it all.)

Note the symmetry in this arrangement.

So what did he do for men? Surely he evened things up by giving us:

1. Some good stuff.
2. Some bad stuff.

Well, the theory under discussion states that for some good stuff he gave us men an urge to jump out of bed and rush out to write and paint and build and blow big holes in the ground.

For some bad stuff, he gave us prostate trouble.

Personally, I think that writing must be a bit like pregnancy: It begins with a microscopic idea that with time grows and takes shape and comes alive. And often, when I get up in the morning and look at what I wrote the night before, sure enough — I become nauseous.

And I do think of these little essays as my children. I weep each time that they leave home to go off and appear in the newspaper. I rejoice each time that they come back home, especially when they bring no little libel suits to spend the night.

Here are more examples of how men have dealt with their ersatz motherhood:

Michelangelo, while painting the Sistine Chapel, became moody, self-conscious about his figure and convinced that he was no longer pretty. To cheer him up, Michelangelo's wife, Bettyangelo, let him go into town and buy a new smock.

When Lord Byron went over to his girl friend's house all aglow and told her that he had just been to his publisher and found out that he was going to have a poem in nine months, his girl friend quickly pointed out that she had been out of town that weekend.

Young Charles Dickens attended Lamaze writing classes before he delivered the manuscript of a bouncing baby *Oliver Twist*.

And the man who built Manhattan's World Trade Center must have wanted twins.

There are some definite advantages to this arrangement for men:

A Golden Gate Bridge won't give you stretch marks.

A Mona Lisa won't phone home at one A.M. to tell you she wrecked the family car.

A Hoover Dam won't wet the bed. Good thing, too. (Headline: "Thousands swept away as little Hoovie Dam has an oops!")

And the Chrysler Building never has to be burped.

No, a man can't have a baby. So maybe he *does* seek a bit of immortality through his inanimate creations, such as big, tall buildings.

But on the other hand, a baby won't be torn down to put up a parking lot.

Kitchy-coo and puberty, too

Recently I saw a TV news report on how modern mothers-to-be talk to their unborn.

Some experts, it seems, feel that a fetus benefits from having its mother talk to it. How I wish that this practice had been in vogue when I was among the womb-bound. But those were primitive times, when watches had hands and bathtubs had feet, when doctors made housecalls and crooks didn't, when "dope" referred to Uncle Floyd, who once lost a game of checkers to a duck. Floyd never finished the fourth grade. The duck never finished the third grade.

Mothers in those early times knew not the advantages of talking into their navel — that keyhole of creation. What a pity. For there are, oh, so many things that I wish my mother had told me before I made that first big change of address. Such as:

"Yes, son, there is life after birth. The first person you will see will be a strange man wearing a mask who will grab you by your ankles and hold you upside-down. For a moment this will make you think that the world is topsy-turvy. The older you get, the more often you will return to this conclusion.

"Later, as self-impressed as you will be when you master toilet-training, remember that this skill will never come up during a job interview.

"When you reach the sixth grade, believe it or not, you *will* survive the trauma of losing the spelling bee.

"However, there *still* aren't any *k*'s in 'Schenectady.' No one knows why.

"While you are held captive in church service on Sunday mornings, all the outdoor chores that you normally detest will suddenly seem to be unbearably enjoyable.

"Puberty is just an oil spill on the sea of life.

"Pimples are caused by music: You don't get them until the day of the senior dance.

"That girl in English class whom you will ask out because everyone in the boys locker room said she does . . . doesn't.

"The more distance you have to run to answer the phone, the less important the call will be.

"Never buy a used car from anyone named Slick.

"When you are eighteen you will love to drive. You will use any excuse to get into the family car and just drive. You will drive to the grocery store for a can of alphabet soup and buy it one letter at a time, necessitating 257 round trips. But twenty years later, you will hate to drive so much that when you run out of alphabet soup, you will call the store and have the grocer just read a can to you over the phone. When you ask him to spell out 'Schenectady,' he will tell you that the can contains no *k*'s. No one knows why.

"Women are all alike.

"Never generalize.

"Every slumping player whom the Texas Rangers trade will have a great season the next year.

"The meek shall inherit the Earth. But the lawyers will keep it tied up in court so long that the meek won't want it anymore.

"Everything makes you fat except water.

"Water makes you bald.

"Time flies. Paint runs. A new album skips.

"In this world, there are nine thousand, one hundred and

twenty-three different things that can go wrong. This has been documented. By the time you are thirty-eight, you will be going through the list for the third time.

"When you die, your cremated remains will be placed in an urn and set on the mantelpiece. Uncle Floyd will mistake the urn for a spittoon. Oops—I guess there are nine thousand, one hundred and twenty-*four* different things that can go wrong."

Of course, if my mother had told me all these facts before I was born, I probably would have just phoned up room service for dinner and stayed right where I was.

It beats Schenectady.

To the Grave

Death sentences: Some last words

Death.

The end.

The deep sleep.

The Stygian shore.

The way of all flesh. (Or is that 42nd Street?)

Death—from the Middle English "deeth" meaning, "You just try to collect *now!*"—was invented in A.D. 230 by a monk as a cure for old age. Before that, people just moved to Florida and lived in retirement communities.

Death has gotten a lot of bad press lately. Yet actually death is a great provider—it is nature's way of creating estate sales, it makes statesmen out of politicians, it gives us something to do with all that marble.

Without death, what would the National Safety Council keep count of on holidays? Without death, there would be no statues, putting millions of pigeons out of work.

There would be no epitaphs, no wills, no obituaries reading "Myron Musselmug, longtime person, died today after a short illness—his wife got sick of him."

And there would be no famous last words. Such as these:

—Oscar Wilde said, "I am dying, as I have lived, beyond my means."

—Joel Chandler Harris, American writer, upon being asked how he felt, said, "I am about the extent of a tenth of a gnat's eyebrow better."

—But playwright Henrik Ibsen, feeling disagreeable one day when his nurse pronounced that he was feeling better, said, "On the contrary!" and died.

—Beethoven, the deaf composer, said, "I shall hear in heaven. Clap now, my friends, the comedy is done."

—And Jean Rameau, French composer in the 1700s, said to his confessor: "What the devil do you mean to sing to me, priest? You are out of tune."

—George Hegel, German philosopher, was cryptic to the end: "Only one man ever understood me." Then Hegel added, "And he didn't understand me."

Understand?

—The Miss Manners award goes to Marie Antoinette, Queen of France. Upon accidentally stepping on the foot of her executioner, Marie said, "I beg your pardon, sir."

—On the other hand, don't turn your back on Ramon Narvaez, Spanish patriot. On being asked by the priest to forgive his enemies, Narvaez said, "I have no enemies. I have shot them all."

—As his soldiers were dodging bullets during a Civil War battle, General John Sedgwick scolded: "Come, come! Why, they couldn't hit an elephant at this dist—"

—English surgeon Joseph Henry Green said, pointing to his heart, "Congestion" and, taking his own pulse, "Stopped."

Dr. Green later was involved in the world's first posthumous medical malpractice suit. He was both plaintiff and defendant.

Although their last words are not recorded, some persons are notable for the mere "modus" of their passing:

—Charles VIII of France, escorting his queen into a tennis court, struck his head against the lintel. It killed him. The matches went on, but we hope that out of respect, the nets were lowered to half mast.

—Aeschylus, the Greek tragedian, was killed when a tortoise, dropped from the talons of an eagle flying above, landed on his bald head. At that time, falling tortoises were the third-leading cause of death among bald-headed Greek tragedians.

— And Fabius, a Roman magistrate, choked to death on a single goat hair in the milk he was drinking. His last words probably were, "Oooo, gross!"

— Pamphilius died while asking a boy what time it was. It was later than he thought.

— But Philomenes, another ancient, had the last laugh. He died laughing while watching a donkey eat the figs that had been provided for his own dessert.

And here are some not-so-famous last words:

— Alfie Sigerson of Toledo drowned when he slipped on a catwalk and fell into a vat of salad dressing. As he went under for the third time, he was heard to shout, "More croutons! More croutons!"

— Ollie O. Oxenfree, ninety-seven, was a lifelong little boy and devotee of children's outdoor games. As he died, at his bedside was his friend and longtime playmate, Junior Knerdel, eighty-nine. "Come closer," Ollie whispered to Junior. Then, feebly, Ollie reached out, slapped Junior on the arm and gasped, "Last tag!"

— Harpo Marx's last word was F-sharp over middle-C.

— Moose Johnson was quarterback for the Tulsa Missing Lynx of the USFL. One night, the stadium lights failed during a play, and Moose fumbled the ball. In the dark and din, an opposing player picked up Moose by his helmet and ran with him, dragging him and racking up ninety-nine yards, six points and four product endorsements. He then "spiked" Moose in the end zone.

The lights came back on as Moose lay dying. Cheerleaders shook black-crepe pompons over him as his teammates clustered around him for his final huddle.

"Who did it, Moose?" asked one.

"Where does it hurt, big fella?" asked another.

Both questions were answered by Moose's — and this column's — last words:

"The end."

Doomsday and how to dress for it

Repent!

For the time draweth nigh. The world will end tomorrow. Tomorrow 143 years ago, that is. Such was the belief of a 19th-century religious cult called the Millerites. Their leader, William Miller, went around predicting that on October 22, 1844, the world would end, bringing about the destruction of civilization, the negation of one million years of human progress and the death of every good and innocent person on the face of the earth.

Sheesh. And this guy wondered why he wasn't invited to more parties.

Nevertheless, it would be good for us from time to time to ponder how we would react if we thought that the world *would* end tomorrow. After all, we tend to take for granted that there will always be another tomorrow. If only our creditors felt the same way.

The prospect of imminent doom raises so many issues. So do this right now: Lock yourself in your bathroom, close your eyes and ask yourself these questions: What if a modern-day Miller said the world would end tomorrow? Am I prepared to meet my maker face to face? Wouldn't a phone call do just as well?

Am I ready for the Judgment Day, for the Earth to give up its dead? Aren't there few enough parking spaces as it is?

And how about what comes after: eternity? Eternity lasts a long time. Are there any coffee breaks?

Eventually, if you really concentrate, cloistered there in your bathroom, you might hear an unseen voice, an eerie, authoritative voice: "Hey, open up, Lois! Are you gonna be in there all day? The end of the world is tomorrow, and I really oughta shave!"

Reflective people would spend their last day on Earth introspectively, looking back upon their lives and asking: What kind of life did I lead? Was it a good life, noble of deed and act? Did I shun violence, honor the flag and bus my own tray? Was I hard-working, honest and prompt, or was I a government contractor?

Reflective people would devote the remaining time to getting their worldly affairs in order, forgiving their enemies, confessing their wrongs:

"Hey, Lois, remember that time in 1967 when we were playing Scrabble and I won by forming 'zqjzkxian' and insisting that it was a word, meaning 'of, relating to or being characteristic of zqjzkx'? Well, I lied. And later that night, you went into the kitchen and found the last of the Chinese take-out dinner missing. Remember when you confronted me with the evidence—bird's-nest soup on my tie—and I denied it and told you that the fridge musta been raided by an alien from the plant Zqjzkx? Another lie."

Ah, but the hedonists among you would devote that final day to as much riotous living as possible—wine, women and song. Or, for those of you who can't carry a tune—wine, women and charades. You would spend the time in desperate revelry at eleventh-hour penthouse orgies, perhaps not even pausing to go downstairs to feed the parking meter.

During your last few precious hours, you would not once ask yourselves: What is the meaning of life? Is there a cosmic plan? Do I really have to pay that parking ticket?

You hedonists would find that you had devoted your life to sex, gluttony and fast cars. So answer me this honestly: (1) What good did sex, gluttony and fast cars do you, in the final analysis? (2) Did your life of sex, gluttony and fast cars make the world a better place? And (3) Can I borrow your diary?

Yes, given a little notice, each of us would face the end of the world in our own way. But, of course, a modern-day Miller might be wrong again: We all might go to bed on October 21 expecting to wake up dead on October 22, only to open our eyes about seven A.M. and find the world still out there.

And boy, would we be disappointed then when we realized that we'd have to get up and go back to work.

Is death the living end?

In a national survey in 1972, 25 percent of those polled said they had had contact with the dead. In a follow-up survey in 1985, 42 percent said they had had contact with the dead.

Thus it seems that more and more We the Living are socializing with Them the Less Fortunate.

The Rev. Andrew Greeley, a priest who counts himself among the former and has a mortgage to prove it, helped conduct the latest survey for Chicago's National Opinion Research Center. He attributed the 17 percent increase to "a change in people's willingness to talk about such experiences."

Well, either that or the dead are simply starting to get out of the house more these days.

I personally have never had contact with the dead, although I've been out with women who need seventy-two hours' notice to be able to fog a mirror.

But I would dearly like to have contact with the dead, to pierce the veil, to know that there is life after liver spots, to know that death, after all, is just nature's way of getting me into a coat and tie one last time.

Here are some cases of contact with the dead:

—H.H. Wherfle was walking down his hall one night when he passed through an area of extreme cold. He had just encountered a "cold spot," which the dead sometimes use to get our attention, as it is considered more polite than clearing their throat. Wherfle knew that this was his late wife because the cold spot felt the same way her feet had felt in bed for thirty-six years.

"Hazel!" Wherfle called out. "Still got the bad circulation, eh? Tell me, what's it like being . . . dead?"

"It's wonderful," a thin voice said. "We have no pain, no suffering, and there's arts and crafts every Thursday."

The voice then faded away, and Wherfle never heard from

his wife again, although each year on his birthday he receives a handmade clay ashtray.

— Ed and Hilda Lish claim that each time they go on vacation, the ghost of the former occupant redecorates their house — new furniture, new drapes, etc. The Lishes say that the ghost is never violent or menacing but has terrible taste.

— After Murry Shimkus found that his wife had been sneaking around with every member of the law firm of Hudge, Hudge & Hudge, he swore he would never speak to her again. A week later Murry died after Hudge (the one on the end) put napalm in his shaving mug. To this day, each time her phone doesn't ring, Mrs. Shimkus is certain that it's Murry, keeping his word.

The 1985 survey also found that 60 percent of Americans have experienced extrasensory perception. Alas, I also have never experienced ESP, although once I was seized by a vague sense of foreboding, of pure dread and irrational horror, and the very next day received my Visa statement.

ESP takes many forms.

— In 1953 a man on the East Coast ate a Mexican dinner. Eerily, one hour later, his twin brother on the West Coast complained of gas.

— If you visit reader-adviser Sister Ruby, she will have you drink twelve cups of coffee. She will then read the grounds and predict that you will spend a sleepless night.

— The mystic Shandar is able to "see" without his eyes. While securely blindfolded, he once drove a car from San Francisco to New York without accident, although after a flat tire near Salt Lake City, he tried to loosen the lug nuts and twisted the kneecaps off the entire Osmond family.

Yes, according to the survey, four of every ten Americans have had contact with the dead and six of every ten Americans have experienced ESP. But what about us six of ten and four of ten Americans, respectively, who have not?

Well, we'll just have to start paying closer attention, won't we?

Things that go burp in the night

It was a dark and stormy night. Thunder rumbled, lightning flashed. Somewhere a cliché howled.

Five people had received the anonymous invitations to spend the night in the haunted house that Halloween. The invitations promised $1.63 and bus fare home to each guest who survived. All five accepted the challenge. This was an indication of either how good their nerve was or how bad the economy was.

The house was said to be haunted by the ghost of the previous owner, Elwood Dibley. His death had been quite unexpected. So had his wife, who came home early one night and found Elwood in the embrace of his secretary. He had Liquid Paper on his breath.

In a jealous rage, Mrs. Dibley locked him in the basement and starved him to death. She would stand on her side of the basement door and eat food, fanning the aroma under the door and calling out: "Pizza, Mmmmm! Elwood, some potato salad. Yummy!"

Dibley took five days to die. His last words were "Egg McMuffin."

The five guests were Rock Stone, the actor; Beatrice O'Barney, a spinster; Hank S., a free-lance blight on society; Latisha Yankleboch, a professional "escort" ("Hey, what's with the quote marks, Mac? I'm legit."); and Rumsford T. Blatherskite, who, because this column is running a bit long, got lost and never found the haunted house.

And then there were four.

The guests soon found that they were strangers to each other. And none of them knew who had invited them. Rock Stone found a note on a dusty table and read it aloud:

"Terror fills this house as soil fills a grave. When you least expect it, when the life force seems strongest within you, a cold and clammy hand will reach out and . . ."

"Yes?" said Beatrice, wild-eyed, hanging on Rock's every word. *"Yes?"*

"That's all. It ends right there."

Taking no chances, Beatrice screamed and fainted. As she fell, she hit her head on a hardcover copy of *The Oliver North Story.* She died of acute disbelief.

And then there were three.

Undaunted, Rock lit a candle and set off on his own to explore the house, leaving Latisha and Hank behind. As he left, he quoted a line from his latest movie, *Hamlet Meets Shaft:* "There are more things in heaven and earth, Horatio, than are dreamt of in your philosophy. Yo' mama!"

Ten minutes later Hank and Latisha found Rock in the kitchen, his head in the oven, the dial set on "homicide."

And then there were two.

Suddenly the house was filled with low moaning. "Oh, that ungodly moaning!" Latisha said. "My ex-husband used to make that very same sound every month when the Visa statement came."

She covered her ears and ran to her bedroom. She was not seen again that night. Inexplicably, two weeks later, she was found working in a K-Mart in Kankakee.

And then there was one.

Crouching now, alone and rigid with fear, Hank S. knew that the end was near. Edited highlights of his life began to flash before his eyes. His had been a dull life, so a newsreel and cartoon were thrown in for free. Then something cold and clammy touched him on the back of the neck, and he fainted.

When Hank came to at dawn, a silent, aged caretaker had unlocked the house. The caretaker gave Hank $1.63 and bus fare. Minutes later Hank was settling back in the crosstown express, speeding away from the scene of a living nightmare. He savored a deep sigh of relief and muttered: "Boy, I'm glad *that's* over."

Suddenly the smell of Liquid Paper filled the air, and an eerie voice whispered in Hank's ear:

"Psst. Wanna stop off for an Egg McMuffin?"

Past perfect:
A life sentence

I'm in a rut.

After all, I've been dping the same old thing — writing —
for . . . let me do some fast figuring . . . 3,687 years. At least
that's what I learned when I attended a local psychic fair
recently and asked two psychics to reveal to me the best past
lives that $6 can buy.

Please, let's keep an open mind. Perhaps there is something
to reincarnation. As it was explained to me, we begin our
incarnations at the bottom of the evolutionary ladder and rise
through the mineral and plant kingdoms (and indeed there are
mornings when I have felt remarkably like a lump of lead or a
particularly grouchy geranium) into the animal kingdom until
at last we become the fine specimens of humanity we are
today — strong, intelligent and overdrawn at the bank.

I was told that in other lives we may even have been of the
opposite sex. I like that. Just once I'd like to see how the other
half lives. Ah, to know the bliss of motherhood, the satisfaction
of homemaking, the joy of cramps.

Anyway, Mike Nichols, these were your lives.

—1700 B.C. In Memphis, Egypt, I was a scribe — a copier of
documents. Thus I was an early ancestor of the Xerox
machine. And I was probably just as misused, too, with workers coming to me on their lunch break and having me make
them copies of the football pool, recipes, news clippings and
library books. I hope I drew the line when some drunk at the
office Christmas party wanted to sit on me so that I could copy
his bare behind.

—11th century. In England, after the Norman Conquest, I
wrote up an inventory of the manpower and resources of a particular county. Maybe I reported directly to William the Conqueror. "Bill," I probably said in that familiar way I had,
"you've got 98,304 men, 45,239 oxen, 27,000 cubic meters of

fog, 13,000 liters of mead, and a Scotsman in a pear tree."

—Late 1400s. In France I was your basic Renaissance man: writer-architect-artist-scholar, grounded in the sciences, literature and mythology. Pretty impressive, eh? When I attend my twenty-year high-school reunion, I'm gonna put all that on my fact sheet and sorta smear over the date. *That*'ll show those jerks who voted me Most Likely to Have His Head Declared a National Wilderness Area.

But still, I'm in a rut.

The second psychic I consulted used psychometry: To divine your past lives, he asks to hold some possession that you feel close to. So he spent twenty minutes fondling my Visa card under the table. The two of them plan a spring wedding. I hope they'll be very happy. This is the past life he saw:

—Early 1400s. I was an American Indian: a bit of a mystic, working to raise the consciousness of others in my tribe. To broadcast my positive message, possibly I used smoke signals as sort of a wood-burning word-processor: "First, a correction: In yesterday's smoke signals, I identified Shona as the god of sun. Of course, *Wikum* is the god of sun. Shona is the god of *wind*. And Yarig is the god of partly cloudy with a 20 percent chance of showers, some locally severe. And now, some thoughts to think about: Each of us is a part of the cosmic whole, love is the answer, and never let a drunk Egyptian sit on your face."

Yes, I have been trafficking in words for 3,687 years now. No wonder my verbs are getting frayed at the edges. But the second psychic told me that after just a few more future lives, I won't have to come back to Earth in the flesh any more. I will be just a spirit, a blob of ectoplasm with no body. This will certainly save on dry-cleaning bills.

How I look forward to that glorious time, when I will at last get out of this writing rut and into heaven. I can see it now: The Big Boss will call me into his office, shake my hand, wave me toward a chair and welcome me to Eternity with these words:

"Take a letter."

A form obituary: Die-it-yourself

I once read of a fugitive who phoned in his own obituary to a newspaper in order to throw the authorities off his trail.

His ploy didn't work, but he had the right idea. At times, most of us wish we could throw this workaday world off our trail, leaving behind the debts, duties and drudgeries of our lives by faking our own death. We'd start anew in another town with another identity, maybe even dye our hair, grow a beard and add four inches to our height by strapping James Michener novels to our feet.

I'll bet that this fugitive failed in his attempt because he was not a highly trained professional obituary writer. Well, I was. In journalism school I majored in obits, with a minor in sports verbs ("Gators whip Dolphins," "Bulls stomp Colts," "Hairstylists coif Bears"). I wrote many an obit for this newspaper before I was demoted to columnist when I was found to be adding my own name to lists of survivors and attending the reading of wills.

I never inherited much, but I met some rich widows.

So for those of you who want to die and live to enjoy it, I offer here a do-it-yourself obit form:

(Your full name), (your full age), died Monday from injuries suffered when (your pronoun) fell onto an assembly line during a tour of the Hathaway shirt factory. Before the machinery could be shut down, (your last name) was critically button-holed and sent on to the Folding Department, where, the coroner later ruled, the cause of death was punctures from thirty-nine straight pins.

The next of kin have refused to pay the expense of embalming, pointing out that the accident had already left (your last name) Sanforized.

Funeral for (your last name) will be at two P.M. Wednesday at Jones Chapel. (Your pronoun) will be buried in Rose Hill

Cemetery with full military honors and matching slacks.

(Your last name) was descended from a pioneer family. (Your pronoun) ancestors came to Texas in a covered wagon in 1858. (Your pronoun) grandfather was a horse thief, bank robber and hired killer named Dead-Eye. He was shot down in 1889 by his wife, Mrs. Dead-Eye. At her trial, she testified that she didn't mind her husband's horse thieving, bank robbing and killing, but she would *not* tolerate a man who drinks the last cup of coffee and doesn't make a fresh pot.

She was acquitted.

(Your last name), a lifelong person, was a native of Fort Worth and was active in many organizations, most of which are under FBI surveillance. (Your last name) attended Central High School, where (your pronoun) took band, P.E. and several hubcaps.

Friends and colleagues fondly remembered (your last name). Said one: "Maybe heaven is a brighter place now that (your last name) is up there. Maybe those of us left behind are better people for having known (your pronoun). Maybe now I can keep some hubcaps on my car."

Surviving (your last name) are (your pronoun) (husband/ wife), (his/her first name) of Fort Worth; one son, Dexter, of Tulsa; two Siamese-twin daughters, Merry and Sherry, both of Dallas; eight cousins, six nieces, five nephews, four loan companies and Mike Nichols.

The family asks that expressions of sympathy be made in the form of cash donations to (your last name)'s favorite charity at (your post-office box in your new city).

End of obit. Now all that remains for you to do to start your new life after death is to phone in your obituary to your local newspaper. But when you ask for a reporter to take it down, don't bother to ask for me.

I died yesterday and am now living in an undisclosed city in Oregon.

Double, Double Toil and Trouble

A clean break with housework

A friend and I have agreed to a pact:

Let it be known that we, the undersigned, are two of those people who are not motivated to clean house unless threatened with the impending visit of a friend or relative. We do solemnly attest that there simply are better ways to spend our time than mopping, vacuuming and scouring the oven. Granted, everyone must clean house eventually. It's inevitable. Like death. But at least with death you don't ruin your manicure.

We each realized the futility of cleaning house recently while using a crow bar to pry cat hair off the sofa.

So Kathy and I, hereafter known as the Party of the First Dump and the Party of the Second Dump, agree that she won't clean house just because I am coming to visit, and I won't clean house just because she is coming to visit.

Thus do we agree to let the house-cleaning slide and not to be thrown into a Pledge-and-Pine-Sol panic by a phone call containing the words: "Hi. I'm gonna be in your area in a few minutes. I thought I'd drop by."

Further, when visiting, the Party of the First Dump agrees not to look at my bathtub, and I, the Party of the Second Dump, agree not to look at her son's room.

(Which, I might add, looks like the result of an earthquake at Toys R Us.)

Many people like us have mastered not-cleaning. When we spill something, we don't clean up the mess right away. We keep thinking that we will get around to it "in a minute." Eventually that sticky spot on the floor becomes the La Brea Tar Pits of the kitchen. Insects and small children get stuck in it, crying piteously and looking at us with faces full of freckles and compound eyes.

The cheese in our refrigerator has mold so dark and furry that little chunks of it break off and follow us around the house, rubbing against our leg and purring. They won't leave us alone until we give them a saucer of milk.

We, the undersigned, fully realize that some people are obsessive house-cleaners. They mop and dust and wax as if it were an act of love. In fact, after it is over, they lean back on one elbow, smoke a cigarette and say, dreamily, "Was it clean for you, too?"

Such people put hospital corners on the paper towels. They arrange the ashes in the fireplace by size, color and Social Security number. The commode is kept behind velvet ropes. Viewing hours are ten A.M. to five P.M. Monday through Friday.

But having a clean house is like having a new car: You are forever trying to avoid that first scratch or dent. You lurk in a corner of the room with a flashlight and an air-raid helmet, scanning the skies of the den, straining your ears to hear that first speck of dust crash and burn so that you can race out and pounce on it with a pair of tweezers.

Is this any way to live?

Conversely, we bachelors are the best at keeping house-cleaning in perspective. A bachelor does not consider his house to be cluttered as long as he can see the tops of the furniture.

He ignores the dirt on the floor as long as he can. Eventually he does do something about it: He plows it.

Finally, a bachelor deals with a filthy home thusly: He moves to a new one.

We, the undersigned, agree that this pact shall be duly binding, even after it is rendered illegible by pizza stains, dust, lint and greasy fingerprints.

In conclusion, we refuse to be sucked in by that old maxim: "Cleanliness is next to godliness," which was probably first said by a priest who had a maid. So we herewith agree to keep the house-cleaning in perspective.

We each accept the fact that the other's home soon shall look like the Apocalypse with carpet. But then, instead of wasting precious time on dull, repetitive chores such as mopping, vacuuming and scouring the oven, we can be out doing something fun and exciting.

Such as raking leaves or mowing the lawn.

List pens down life's load

I call it, simply, *The List*.

It is my trusty pocket memory. For twenty years I have carried with me a sheet of note paper on which I keep a running list of every chore or errand that I need to do during the next several days. I always keep *The List* in my back pocket, close to my heart.

See, in high school I began to distrust my memory. Some people have minds like steel traps. Mine is more like a sand trap. For instance, on history tests, I could never remember how long the Seven Years War lasted.

So, as a memory aid, I began keeping *The List*. Back then, it was mostly a reminder of which textbooks to take home each day. But now it includes important grown-up stuff, such as "pay water bill," "get cat food," "go to bookstore," "put up TV antenna," "fix loose shingles" and "call an ambulance."

Hmmm. I guess I should have "fixed loose shingles" before I

tried to "put up TV antenna."

The List is my feeble attempt to be organized, in control, to elevate life's unending list of petty aggravations to an unending list of petty achievements.

And it works. To *The List* I owe my dazzling success. (Huh? What's that? . . . My editor has just reminded me that I am *not* a dazzling success. Well, then, to *The List* I owe my dazzling mediocrity.)

I get such satisfaction each time I mark through an item on *The List*. Sometimes, if it was an especially dreadful or difficult chore, I do an instant replay and mark through it a second time in slow motion:

"Take . . . *that*, . . . 'clean . . . out . . . septic . . . tank.'"

Each day I have to remember but one thing: carry *The List*. Were I somehow to leave the house without my list, I would be lost. I would wander the streets, tugging on the sleeves of strangers and asking, "Hey, buddy, can you tell me what I was supposed to do today? Was it something to do with the car? Or the office? You got a spare list you can give me? Hey, come back! Stop! How long did the Seven Years War last?"

Of course, at times I resent *The List*. It can be such a ball and chain. "Do this. Do that," its items are always nagging.

"Me, me, me! Do *me* next," cries the item "tune car."

"No, no! You'll get all greasy! Do *me* next!" pleads "pick up dry cleaning."

Sometimes it seems as if chores must come from all over the world just to get on *The List*.

"And then do *me* after that!" whines "milk the reindeer."

See what I mean?

I can be seen several times a day whipping out *The List* and consulting it. No matter where I am, if I have my pants on, I have *The List* on me. If not, it's beside the bed, where I can find it with the flashlight when I wake up at four A.M. and remember that the car has to be inspected last month.

I would recommend a version of *The List* to everyone who wants to improve their own personal gross national product. You can even have some of my old ones to study. Especially if you promise to "milk the reindeer."

But my ultimate goal, of course, is to achieve a state of Finished List. And I have gotten close at times—just one or two items left — but something new always comes up.

Life will do that to you.

So actually, finishing *The List* is probably scientifically impossible, like creating or destroying matter, traveling in time or taking a bath without the phone ringing.

But at least my trusty little pocket memory has made me a model of efficiency. And I have promised myself that if and when I do ever get every single little nagging item marked off *The List,* I'll finally have time to get over to the library and find out how long the Seven Years' War lasted.

And I bet I'll do it, too. If I'll just put it on *The List.*

Not all quiet on the western front

Surely no war was ever declared at sunset.

It is, after all, such a peaceful time. Far and away my favorite time of the day. I always try to be at a western window — or, better yet, outdoors — when the sun punches out at the end of its shift.

I pull up a glass of tea and a lawn chair and settle back into a front-row seat to watch the world's longest-running show, letting the neighborhood provide the soundtrack — the lazy drone of lawn mowers, a radio playing somewhere, distant dogs barking, voices laughing or talking, the darling nine-year-old boy next door . . . hey, what *is* that kid doing? It sounds like he's prying rusty nails out of an old board using walrus tusks. While the walrus is still wearing them.

Anyway, as I was saying, with the sun doing an encore every day, you will get to see perhaps twenty-seven thousand sunsets in your lifetime, if you exercise, watch your cholesterol, and stay off cigarettes, whisky and the freeway.

Sunsets always cause me to reflect on beginnings, on the nature of things.

In the beginning, the sun was high on God's list of Things to Do Today. On the fourth day he created the sun in order that it might give light, divide day from night, and fade the paint on your Camaro.

But it was not until the sixth day that God got around to making man and woman. And then, thanks to the sun's light, Adam and Eve could see that they looked very chic in their designer skin.

"Good work, Lord," Eve said. "We look just like you."

"Yeah," said Adam, staring at Eve. "And anatomically correct, too!"

Yes, we owe much to the sun. Without it, Rembrandt would have had to paint by torch-light. Bach would have had to compose by candle. Dracula would be giving industrial-strength hickeys at high noon.

At dawn, the sun is the master magician, pulling day out of the black top hat of night. It then proceeds to make corn stalks prick up their ears, potatoes open their eyes, and lettuce turn their heads.

But to me, it is at sunset that God shines. If the world is God's masterpiece, the sunset is surely how he signs the canvas.

Sunset is a time to reflect on the day, on work well done, on good friends, on . . . what is that kid doing *now?* It sounds like he's got a flamenco dancer over there on a tin roof, popping corn in a hailstorm.

Where was I? Oh, yeah: I never met a sunset I didn't like. But I do admit that I grade them. Of course, I give the sun C-minus just for showing up every day. But an A-plus sunset has to have some clouds in the vicinity: fleecy clouds grazing in a blue pasture, herringbone clouds swimming in the overhead sea, curdled clouds clabbering a buttermilk sky. Most any kind of clouds will do. Just to soak up the pinks and golds and grays, like sponges.

Often at sunset, the sun is bright orange — a tennis ball, God's own Spalding served into the western court, sinking slowly over the net of the horizon. On other days it is as yellow as a yolk — an egg broken on the edge of this old skillet Earth.

When I am watching a sunset, I can think only good thoughts. I am peace. I am love. I harbor no ill will to any living creature. I am at one with . . . what is that kid doing *now?*

It sounds like he's cutting a tuba in half with a chainsaw. No, no, it sounds more like he's strangling a bull elephant with a piano wire. A G-sharp, I think.

Hmmmm. I wonder if science could develop a morning-after birth-control pill that works retroactively — nine years.

Yes, sunset is a serene time. A time when surely no war was ever declared.

But, kid, there's a first time for everything.

The grapes of wrath and other breakables

Early in *The Grapes of Wrath* — Steinbeck's almost-biblical tale of Okies seeking the promised land — there comes a grim rite of passage.

The Joads, like the corn in the fields, have been uprooted. They are moving: "Rose of Sharon brought out all the clothes the family possessed . . . and she packed these tightly into a wooden box and got into the box and tramped them down. And . . . she struggled through the door with the mattresses, three double ones and a single."

Then the Joads rouse Grampa and Granma and tell them that it's time to board the overloaded truck and rattle off to California to win the 1940 Pulitzer Prize.

When I am at the supermarket and see people begging for cardboard boxes, I recall that poignant scene. Then, at the tomato bin, I pause in mid-squeeze to observe a moment of silence for these latter-day Joads as they prepare to move.

It is while moving that people survey the accumulated belongings of a lifetime and ask themselves: Do I possess or am I possessed?

Take even a Spartan guy like ol' Hank Thoreau. When he packed up to move from Concord to Walden Pond, he was chagrined to find that he had accumulated thirteen pencils, two sacks of flour and forty-six platitudes.

Few people get through life without being called upon to help someone move. We all have friends who change jobs or get married or hear that the FBI is closing in. And so they move.

Helping a person move breeds instant camaraderie among that person's circles of friends. They might be strangers to one another, but when they join in a grand task for a grand friend, they form friendships that last, oh, until the time comes to move the grand piano.

Here are some tips for moving-day helpers.

—Help only the illiterate. Never, *ever* help well-read people to move. Before you volunteer, make them take a literacy test. If they score ninety or above, tell them: "Drat! I have to floss my nails and file my teeth that day."

This is because the literate will promise you: "Oh, I have just a few books." But somehow, the night before moving day, those "just a few books" will go into a mating frenzy and give birth to sixteen big boxes full of hardbacks. When you arrive, you will see the parent books lying about, exhausted, their pages dog-eared, their bindings cracked.

—And when people tell you, "Oh, we'll have it all packed by the time you get here," make them swear to it before a notary public. Then make the notary public swear to come help them finish packing before you get there.

—Always show up with some part of your body wrapped in an Ace bandage. This will provide an emergency excuse when the time comes for the truly heavy work and will allow you to be a supervisor instead. A supervisor holds doors open, orders the pizza and points out which of someone's toes the grand piano was just dropped on.

—Moving day defies time and space: The job will take twice as long as predicted, and there will be half as many boxes as needed. The contents taken *out of* a home of 2,000 square feet will not fit *into* a home of 4,000 square feet.

—Ranges and refrigerators will undergo a phenomenon called "major-appliance bloat" between the time they are purchased and moved into a home and the time they are moved out of it. A 30-inch range that went *in* a 32-inch door will have swollen too much to go *out* that same door.

Here's a handy hint: Using a clean sheet of paper, a sharp pencil and a tape measure, determine the minimum measurement of all large objects and the maximum measurement of all doorways—with doors removed. This will tell you how much TNT to purchase and where to stick it.

—Don't let the feeble-minded (and I think we know who we are) try to fold the four flaps of a cardboard box so that they are interlocked. I closely watch others perform this simple sleight of hand, and still, when I must repeat it, everything becomes hazy and the floor tilts. Then I must be led away to a dark, cool corner, where I am given dish towels to fold and pack.

—Just before the now-empty home is locked up, assign someone to conduct a thorough search to guarantee that at least one valued item is left behind to necessitate a bothersome return trip.

—In a convoy of five vehicles, the middle one somehow will take a wrong turn and never be seen again. And it's always the car carrying the ice chest.

—The vehicle carrying the three large, overactive dogs will *never* get lost.

—Each rental truck or trailer comes equipped with a dolly, furniture pads and a factory-trained gremlin. You won't see him, but you'll know he's on the job when helpers start screaming:

"How did *this* get broken?"

"I *know* I put the lid on that paint can."

"How could we misplace a whole refrigerator? It was clearly labeled 'kitchen'!"

—When the moving party arrives outside the new home, the key to the door will be missing. Three hours later it will be found inside a jar of grape jelly inside a box labeled "bedroom."

But eventually it will all be over—every vehicle emptied, every box placed where it can best be in the way during those first trying days in the new home. There will have been only minor damage and injury, only minor threats of divorce.

The helpers will start to sneak toward their cars and trucks, swearing under their breath: "The next time I help move someone, it'll be as a pallbearer."

But then—gotcha!—someone will holler, "Hey, wait, everybody! Come back! Ma and Pa have looked everywhere and can't
find them:

"We musta gone off and left Grampa and Granma Joad
behind!"

"The lost sweater": A yarn of woe

It's so sad to see a once-firm mind begin to take on the consistency of Jell-O Instant Pudding.

The other day I went to my closet for a sweater. You know
the one: fuzzy, white, makes me look like a pipe cleaner. And
lo, there it was: missing. Now I may be many things (beginning
alphabetically with adrift, agog and a kook), but I *am* orderly.
That sweater is *always* in that closet.

Until now.

Question: Where and when did I last see the sweater?
Answer: On or about Sunday, on or about my upper body,
which can usually be found between my lower body and my
head, which I now fear I also am losing.

Sure, this mystery seems trifling, yet I take it personally. At
age 38 will I have to redefine myself existentially as Mike-
Who-Loses-Sweaters? This is more than a matter of fifteen
ounces of wayward Orlon acrylic. It's a matter of principle. I
just don't lose things. Ergo, it is *not* lost.

So where is it? With scientific detachment, I've watched
myself grasping at straws as the search continues. Isn't it odd
how, when there is just *one* logical place where a thing can be,
and it isn't there, there suddenly becomes a *second* logical
place it can be? So I looked in the dresser. Not there. So there
must be a *third* logical place it can be. And then a fourth.
Then a fifth.

Soon I had checked the washer, dryer, clothesline, car and garage and strip-searched the dirty-clothes hamper.

As they say, that sweater didn't just get up and walk off by itself. However, while going through the clothes hamper, I did find some jeans that have been buried in there so long that they are capable of crawling and taking a few faltering steps.

(Note to self: Try to remember to do the laundry between census years.)

I looked inside the TV, outside the house, under the bed and over the rainbow.

Nothing.

I could understand losing a sweater in a big, crowded place: a dormitory, a shopping mall, Oprah Winfrey's refrigerator. But I live alone. My house is small. Why, you can stand in a certain spot in my house and see into all the rooms. People who have actually done this usually go away disappointed.

More straws: Maybe, while wearing the sweater recently, I went bonkers and began to live out my fantasies, leaving the sweater somewhere in the process and waking up with selective amnesia. In that case, there's nothing to do but wait for Jane Pauley to call and say I left the sweater on the floor beside her hot tub.

And yet I'm pretty sure that I haven't disrobed away from home lately. I mean that unfortunate incident at the Safeway—when I got nekkid in the express line and was arrested wearing only a grocery list—is behind me now. Honest.

More straws: Irresistibly, again and again, I went back to look in the closet, as if the sweater would magically reappear if only I looked enough times.

Bah! Superstition. Why don't I just move into a cave and worship trees?

Still more straws: I called in yarn-sniffing dogs. The TV weatherman found no trace of the sweater on radar. The men who found the *Titanic* tried sonar. A medium, Sister Rose, tried a seance. The closest she got was making contact with a smoking jacket once worn by Francis X. Bushman.

During my day-long search, however, we *did* find a few long-lost things, including my old baseball mitt, a TV dinner that I abandoned in 1978, Jimmy Hoffa, Amelia Earhart and

Joan Collins's innocence.

But no sweater.

Yes, it's sad to see the mind start to go at a tender age. But I've learned my lesson: The next time I lose a sweater, I won't even bother to look for it.

I'll just hope that Jane doesn't let Garry Trudeau wax his car with it.

Passing grade: The driver's test

If you've been out on the streets lately, amongst the licensed drivers, you know this only too well:

A driver's test does not prepare people to be drivers any more than a history test prepares them to be Thomas Jefferson, or an English test prepares them to be a dangling participle.

Now I admit I haven't taken a driver's test in years (as part of *mine,* I had to parallel park a team of oxen), but I think that the test should be made more relevant. After all, driving is the most complex, dangerous act of daily life. In what other endeavor can you start out for the 7-Eleven down the block and end up on the six o'clock news with a '78 Pontiac stuck in your braces?

A typical driver's test consists of three parts:

— The vision test. But passing this part proves only that you can read ADSFWERQYP on an eye chart. It does not prove that you can read and understand highway signs, which, of course, make less sense than an eye chart. So the test should go like this: While driving on the freeway, cover one eye and decipher a typical highway sign. Such as: "Right lane exit left to downtown via uptown off onramp over underpass." If you did as the sign says, congratulations: Your vision is 20-20, but you are now in suburban ADSFWERQYP.

—The road test. This includes skills such as passing, stopping and cornering while a surly Department of Public Safety examiner wearing Cool Hand Luke sunglasses and hob-nailed boots scowls at you and gives you points for traits such as self-assurance:

25 — very confident

10 — nervous

5 — you just wet your pants

0 — you just wet his pants.

But this part should also include:

Concentration. You must keep your mind on the road at all times and not be preoccupied with thoughts of, for instance, your love life. In fact, you lose ten points if you are caught absent-mindedly kissing your radar detector. And twenty-five points if your lips are clocked doing 57 mph in a school zone.

Patience. You must be able to sit idling in five o'clock rush-hour traffic in August in an un-air-conditioned car without suddenly pulling (1) your hair, (2) in front of me, (3) the pin of a grenade.

No rubbernecking. You must be able to pass the scene of an accident without slowing down and gawking. After all, if you've seen one wreck involving a cattle truck and Prof. Hubble's Traveling All-Girl Topless Tuba Band & Yogurt Parlor, you've seen them all.

—The written test. These questions deal with traffic rules and statistics, such as, "How much braking distance is required to stop a car traveling at 60 mph? Answer: 272 feet. Less, if you hit a topless tuba player."

But there should also be a few questions to help determine the applicant's attitude. I mean, is this person morally fit to operate a hard and unyielding motor vehicle within a mile of my own personal body:

Arrogance. When you get behind the wheel of a car, do you suddenly become God? If so, could you please bestow peace on Earth, goodwill to men and make me two inches taller?

Purpose. A motor vehicle should be used to:

1. Get from point A to point B as safely and courteously as possible. Or,

2. get from point A to point B while picking up lots of chicks and drinking lots of beer with your bare backside stick-

ing out the window.

(Traffic update. All roads to point B have been closed for repairs. Traffic is being detoured to point C, which is experiencing an outbreak of typhoid. But folks there have pretty well forgotten about the typhoid, what with the cyanide tank cars derailing and the hatchet murderer escaping and all.)

There. Those folks who cannot pass such a driver's test should not be behind the wheel of a car. It would be better for us all if those folks just moved to some place where they can walk everywhere.

Let me suggest point C.

Can't hear me?
I'll type LOUDER

It has finally happened.

For years I had defined middle age as being just one year ahead of whatever age I was. Well, I think I rear-ended middle age the other night.

I was at a quite proper social gathering (no felons allowed) where a band was playing. With a vengeance, it was playing. As it was about four bars into "Pretty Woman" I realized that I have grown unfond of music that is so loud that persons who are trying to talk in its presence must resort to semaphore or cave drawings to communicate a thought as simple as "Do try the shrimp. It's very dead."

Don't get me wrong—I still love music. Any music. Music is one of my five favorite things in life. The other four are Heather Locklear.

But I no longer like music—live or recorded—that is so loud that it makes my tonsils rattle such that you could lower a microphone into my throat and hear the bells of St. Mary's. Most bands today seem to be playing for the listening pleasure of the hearing-impaired deceased of Neptune.

As a result, party dialogue often goes like this:

Person A: "Huh?"

Person B: "Huh?"

Person A: "Could you speak up?"

Person B: "I said *'huh?'!*"

Person A: "Oh, yes. I tried the shrimp."

Person B: "Huh?"

There are certain predictable reactions to having to talk over loud music.

— You fake it. You smile a lot and nod, throwing in a "yes" and an "Is that so?" now and then. This is risky. At a party in 1978, an ill-timed nod, a misplaced "yes," and I found that I had volunteered to take part in a medical experiment involving cattle prods, rabid bats and an insurance salesman.

— You read lips in Braille. This is not recommended unless reader and readee are well-acquainted.

— You lean ever nearer the ear or mouth of those with whom you desire meaningful converse. You raise your voice. Those awful cords begin to stand out on your neck. Soon the room is filled with tiny meteor showers of spit.

Then the inevitable happens: You are over in a dark corner shouting tenderly into some sweet young thing's shell-like ear just as the music stops. The sudden silence catches you in mid-shout· ". . . not lying to you, baby! My wife *told* me I could fool around with other women."

— Next you try to retreat from the source of the music. Back you go. Back, back. From room to room. Then outside. Eventually you are in the kitchen of the house next door, where the neighbors shoot you as an intruder but where at least the shrimp is fresher.

Younger people, of course, have no need for the spoken word while loud music rends the air. I remember. Vaguely.

They communicate with body English. For instance, if their bodies sway in time to the music with both hands held aloft, it means that they are having a major religious experience. If boy and girl look at each other with nausea writ large upon their faces, it means that they have found true love. And if five thousand of them break into a spontaneous riot in which dozens are trampled to death, it means, "Far out! Let's do this again real soon."

But we middle-aged folks have come to frown upon trampling as an acceptable form of expression outside of the NFL. We prefer a more dignified form of communication.

So come on, party hosts and bands. Music need not be loud to be good. Let's turn it down a tad, OK? Then at last the rest of us will be able to hear what we're saying.

Now, if only we could think of something interesting to say.

Case closed: Don't overpack

For years my motto while packing for a trip always had been: Be prepared.

Toward that end, I had always stuffed a Boy Scout into each suitcase. Preferably one who was working on his Claustrophobia and Fear of Darkness merit badges.

Yes, I overdid it. I packed suitcases with tons of items that I *might* need but never did: books, batteries, bandages, alarm clocks, galoshes, flares, C-rations, plasma, pins (straight, safety and bowling) and ties (twist, bow and railroad).

After lugging around such suitcases for years, I can now tie my shoelaces without bending over. Thus either my arms are getting longer of the ground is getting shorter.

So during the last few years I have tried to pack less and less each time I travel. And the next time I take a trip, I plan to wean myself to just one piece of carry-on luggage. I will work this minor miracle by obeying my Ten Commandments of Packing.

1. Thou shall not pack for every imaginable contingency. Sure, the old "be prepared" motto is difficult to overcome. But let's face it, if you haven't needed, for instance, a flashlight around your house in the last year, why assume that you'll sud-

denly need one during just a week away? After all, they have electricity in the Bahamas, too.

Every Tuesday, as I recall.

2. Thou shall not pack enough clothing to outfit the Mormon Tabernacle Choir. Try to hold it down to the Budapest String Quartet.

Clothing is the worst excess of many travelers. Simplify! Example: Pack just one pair of sensible shoes. Leave behind your sensible spats.

Pack one pair of knee-high black socks, each of which can serve many purposes. For instance, a long black sock can double as a necktie, a belt, a glove, a shoeshine cloth or a garrote to use on your tour guide when he informs you that you have just twelve minutes to see Rome.

3. Thou shalt make the best use of thy space. Pack things within things. For instance, think of the shoes you pack as empty containers that cry out to be filled. So come on, stuff those Thom McAns with something. Anything. (Sour cream, however, is not recommended.)

And if you simply must pack your volleyball, deflate it first. And tightly roll your jeans before you pack them. Do *not*, however, also starch them beforehand. Otherwise as you are strolling through Toyko or London some day, your legs will curl up.

4. Thou shalt economize on toiletries and personal grooming articles. Don't pack the submarine-size tube of Crest. Don't pack a hair drier powerful enough to thaw a polar ice cap. Don't pack enough face cream to grease a '56 Pontiac.

5. In your room at Best Western, as you pack for the trip back home, thou shalt not pack any motel towels. Too bulky. And besides, once you get those towels home, how are you going to explain that big BW monogrammed on them? Unless you legally change your name to Barbara Walters.

6. Thou shalt not cram a pharmacy into thy suitcase. Pack one Dramamine tablet, one Alka-Seltzer tablet and one Tums tablet.

If you need more than these, you're probably dying anyway. Maybe you ate the Salmonella au Gratin at the Jacques in the Box in Paris? Ah ha! You were warned about that. You're in big trouble now. Unless you later had tea at Lourdes.

7. Thou shalt not pack anything that will cause a customs

official who openeth thy suitcase to giggle and shout to his co-workers, "Hey, Mort! Brenda! C'mere! Wouldst thou looketh at all *dis:* one Boy Scout, four hundred choir robes, a pair of sensible spats, and patent-leather, open-toed sour cream!"

8–10. Sorry. Thou shalt have room for only Seven Commandments of Packing.

Dead weight:
Rest in peace

Are you an overpacker?

So am I. That makes us kindred souls, doesn't it? I can't help it. I figure that when you travel, you never can tell what you'll need. And so I tend to overdo it.

Thus each time I pack for a trip, I must force myself to remember a centuries-old graveyard that I visited some years ago in Calais, France.

There, amid the rows of lichen-covered tombstones, stands another cold, gray slab.

It is heavy with the weight of human folly.

It is a monument to overpacking.

It is my old Samsonite suitcase.

You see, that first trip overseas, I went prepared. Remember, you never can tell what you'll need, right? So I took one big camera bag and two heavy bulging suitcases—the kind that Samsonite makes from some hard pebbly gray material that is not native to this solar system.

On the other hand, my traveling companion, John, carried all his worldly goods in one small tote bag. So naturally I began to feel sorry for him. Thus in Calais I offered to let him carry one of my suitcases—the light one, weighing in at a dainty seventy-seven pounds.

Well, I could see the gratitude on his face as he grabbed its handle, gave a mighty heave-ho and then staggered into a nearby shop, flipping through his French-English dictionary.

"One medium truss, please," he gasped. "To go."

But alas, he garbled a diphthong, unwittingly pledging his troth to the shopkeeper's bearded daughter.

Later, after the engagement party (catered by Gillette), John insisted that I toss out forty or fifty pounds of unnecessary items. I told him that everything that I had packed was necessary, thank you very much.

"Oh, yeah? How about this Topeka phone directory and these duck decoys and this softball trophy?"

"Hey, you never can tell."

"Uh-huh. And how about this washboard?"

"That's in case we can't find a laundromat to wash our clothes."

"Dumb. Real dumb. Toss it out."

"Oh, OK," I whined. "Anyway, I have an extra one in the other suitcase."

"And how about this large, flat rock?"

"That's in case the washboards break."

Finally, I gave in and agreed to jettison some of the less-essential essentials. Oh, it was agony, deciding which of those necessities to part with. But I even agreed to cram them all into one suitcase and just throw away the whole kit and kaboodle, knowing full well that soon after, I'd probably need a kaboodle and have to go out and buy an inferior European one that would require metric tools.

But while looking for a trash bin to dispose of the suitcase and contents, we passed this old graveyard near the English Channel. We noticed all the heavy, gray slabs of stone standing in rows. I think that the idea came to each of us at the same time.

We left my big, gray suitcase there—standing on end—in a row of headstones. The tomb of the unknown packer. It looked right at home.

Requiescat in pace (which means "rest in peace," or, if friend John had tried to pronounce it, "Kiss me, my fuzzy French pastry!").

Yes, I am an overpacker. I admit it. It's a terrible affliction. And some day I'm going back to France. Back to Calais. Back to that graveyard. And when I do, I'll see if that old, gray slab of Samsonite is still there.

If it is, I'm going to open it and get out my large, flat rock. Because when you travel, you never can tell.

Variety is the strife of life

Let's call it the Mustard Syndrome.

It is decision overload, caused by having to make too many picky-picky choices in daily life. It was brought to my attention recently by a friend. Suzette had gone to the store. "I went after a jar of mustard. Simple enough, right? Wrong. I never saw so many varieties of mustard. There must have been thirty kinds. I was overwhelmed."

And Suzette has a four-year-old daughter who no doubt some day also will suffer from decision overload but who right now just wants me to put her name in the newspaper.

Sorry, April. I can't do that.

Yes, we in America today simply have too many options. Shopping for a car? What make, color and size? Automatic or manual? Four- or eight-cylinder? Disk or drum brakes? Diesel or gas? Shopping for a VCR? Beta or VHS? Mono or stereo? Cable-ready or not? Two heads or four? Front load or top load?

Whew. Take a break and clear your head. Here—have a Coke. Oh, do you want new Coke, Classic Coke, Diet Coke, Caffeine-Free Coke, Caffeine-Free Diet Coke, Cherry Coke or Diet Cherry Coke?

I had a team of scientists over to the house last weekend to study the Mustard Syndrome. After seventy-two hours of intense discussion, they told me (1) "Yup, this is a problem, all right"; (2) "someone oughta do something about it"; and (3) "hey, send out for more pizza, OK?" However, one of them,

Dr. Huxley Phiggles, author of "Social Stratification Among Yeast," could not decide between mushroom, olive, pepperoni, anchovy, hamburger, Canadian bacon or plain cheese and now just sits under a tree all day, mumbling and trying to pick spots of sunlight off the ground.

The others have since applied for a $500,000 federal grant to build a cyclotron capable of splitting a mozzarella atom.

In most such cases, of course, there are no wrong choices. These are *not* life-threatening decisions. Still, each one requires brainwork. And eventually the brain short-circuits, and one day you are found hiding under the bed, sucking your thumb, curled into the fetal position.

Ah, the womb. You didn't face many decisions there, did you? You had to decide to be one of just two sexes. The diet was simple and unvaried. And it was too dark to read, too cramped to dance and too humid to write on the walls. So you passed the time by kicking the tar out of your mother, who later got even with you by taking your temperature in such a way that you could hold the thermometer and whistle at the same time.

What we need to combat the Mustard Syndrome is an agency that would make these piddling decisions for us. The agency could hire young people whose decision-making processes have been numbed by attending heavy metal concerts. It would work something like this:

"Hello, Decisions R Us? This is Suzette Hensley. Help! I'm at Safeway trying to buy mustard. But there are just too many kinds. Mild yellow, stoneground, Polynesian, tarragon, spicy, coarse grated, mild English, Dijon, Country Dijon, German style, with white wine, with jalapeños, with onion bits, with green peppercorns, with horseradish. I can't decide. Come pick one for me!"

The kid from Decisions R Us arrives and mindlessly picks a mustard for her.

"Oh, thank you. How much do I owe you? I just know that if I had to make one more decision today, I'd bite a brick."

"Glad to help. The fee is $5. How do you want to pay that—cash, personal check, Visa, Mastercard, Diners Club, American Express, traveler's check, postage stamps, cashier's check, bank draft or electronic transfer from your acc-"

Crunch.

Got a hang-up
about solicitors?

Let us wax philosophical for a moment.

Assume that every thing—animal, vegetable, mineral—and every action—from butterfly sneeze to nuclear explosion—is part of a grand design, that we are all cogs in the cosmic machine and that all creatures great and small have a reason for being.

Then why are phone solicitors?

I mean what are they *for?* There must be a reason for them, perhaps even a good reason. But I have yet to find it.

Oh, I know why some things exist. Mechanics are to fix our cars. Teachers are to make us smart. And bank tellers are to tell us, "Next window, please."

But why are phone solicitors?

I'm at home a lot, working. So I get them all: siding and storm windows, charities, investment schemes, carpet cleaners, portraits, dating services, exterminators.

Let me stress that I respect their right to call me. Our founding fathers gave phone solicitors certain unalienable rights, among them life, liberty and the pursuit of my Visa card.

But I do resent their tactics. With lungs made by Hoover, they take a deep breath and deliver a seamless spiel that gives me no polite place to jump in and say no. They ask not *if* I am interested but *when* they can send out a representative, not *if* I want any but *how many* I want.

So if I had to guess, I'd say that phone solicitors exist to make my life miserable. But that's a vain notion, isn't it? Creating thousands of phone solicitors just to torment one man is excessive. That's not nature's way. No, nature would simply give me an abscessed tooth.

In nature there is no accident, no waste. In the ecological balance, everything is related. Take a typical food chain, for instance: vegetable matter-worm-bird-fox-Avanti Fur Salon.

So phone solicitors, too, must have a niche, some *raison d'être*.

I have searched for clues in Genesis. It says that the firmament was created to divide the waters from the waters and that the light was created to divide the day from the night. It says that man was created to have dominion over the fish and the fowl and the beasts and that woman was created to tell man which wine to order with each.

But there is no mention of solicitors. So they must not have been invented by the time of Genesis. Or else we would read of them trying to talk Adam and Eve into having their fig leaves steam-cleaned.

I have also searched in Ecclesiastes: "To everything there is a season and a time to every purpose under the heaven . . . a time to kill, and a time to heal; a time to break down, and a time to build up."

No mention of "a time to call folks up when they're taking a bath and try to sell them dance lessons."

"I have only one leg," I always lie. The solicitor then consults with her supervisor and offers me a 50-percent discount.

I have partaken of the great philosophers. They explain all about life and death and why each is more fun in a Hawaiian shirt. But not why we have phone solicitors.

Sartre, however, comes close. In examining the related phenomenon of junk mail, he reasons that junk mail exists to provide cheap fuel for our fireplaces. But this logic breaks down when extended to phone solicitors, because most cities have restrictions against starting a fire by rubbing two solicitors together.

Perhaps I am overlooking the answer because it is so obvious. Perhaps Mother Nature gave us phone solicitors to help the rest of us build character, to teach us patience, determination and compassion. In short, to help us to improve ourselves.

But I think she could have accomplished the same thing with a good Dale Carnegie book.

And at least *that* way we wouldn't have to get out of the bathtub.

Does this have a familiar ring?

At any given moment in America, I estimate, one-third of us are languishing on the telephone—on hold. Retail stores especially are bad about putting us on hold until half past eternity.

Often, to pass the lonely times while I am on hold, I wonder just why my call is not getting through, for instance, to the housewares department. I try to visualize the scene there.

Perhaps, due to a change in ownership, the store is now staffed by a tribe of South American natives who have never seen or heard a phone. No doubt they are dressed for success—three-piece suits, bones in their noses. Around their necks they wear primitive necklaces made of alligator teeth and business cards.

As the phone begins to ring, the natives gather round it at a safe distance. Curious, frightened. No one dares to touch the jangling phone. Finally the tribal chief, Mombasa, pokes at it with a stick. This knocks the receiver off the cradle. The natives then hear my tinny little voice: "Well, *finally!* Hello? . . . Do you have a Corning Ware two-quart casserole dish? . . . Is anybody there? Hello?"

Mombasa points a trembling finger at the phone and shrieks: "Shangibubu!" ("Devil Box!") The witch doctor cries: "Jumbakimbawah?" ("Corning Ware?") His receptionist cries: "Casserole dish? Aaa-eeeee!" ("Casserole dish? Aaa-eeeee!")

Mombasa then sends a runner to the deli counter. The runner returns with a luncheon special. The chicken is sacrificed to appease the Devil Box. The cole slaw, rolls and Diet Pepsi are divided among the tribal elders.

Then all the native salespeople circle around the phone, which is still emitting my weak, pleading voice. They dance the Devil Box Dance, accompanied by the Devil Box Chant (available on RCA records and tapes).

From that day forth the natives worship my voice as a god.

They bring it gifts of silk, pearls and gold but no casserole dish.

Of course, not all phone systems ring as your call is being transferred. With these, all you hear is a hollow, eerie silence. This always makes me fear that my call has been misrouted into the electronic twilight zone, between dimensions, and that the next voice I hear will be that of Amelia Earhart or Jimmy Hoffa.

Often I am kept on hold so long that I brace the receiver against my ear and go on about my business: reading, writing, etc. And an Ohio man once was kept on hold so long that he and his wife used the opportunity to conceive a child and smoke a cigarette afterward. The man finally got through to a salesperson but, alas, had to hang up because by then the kid needed a ride to kindergarten.

Being put on eternal hold becomes a sort of perverse game. After several minutes, I hang up and redial the main number, only to be put on hold again. This cycle can go on all afternoon. Days pass. The operator comes to recognize my voice. We introduce ourselves. We chat. Soon we begin to see each other socially. But it doesn't work out: I'm *Time,* she's *Newsweek;* I'm Coke, she's Pepsi; I'm 6-foot-2, she's 5-foot-none on high heels but 12-foot-6 on her husband's shoulders.

Just about here American retailers will probably protest that they are simply understaffed. Yet when I'm in a store in the flesh, I see plenty of salespeople standing around making paper airplanes out of service contracts or wrestling shoppers to the floor and making wax impressions of their credit cards.

So it's time we started helping each other out. Next time you are browsing in, say, the housewares department, and the phone rings and no salesperson can or will get it, get it yourself. Sure, you might not be able to answer the caller's questions or complaints, but you can provide that poor consumer with a much-needed human voice.

And who knows: You might even make a sale and be entitled to a nice commission. You'll have to work that out with the sales manager.

You'll recognize him by the cole slaw on his chin.

Oh, and his name tag will read "Mombasa."

Reach out and chain someone

OK, everybody, *freeze!*

Sit down at your desk while I read the following proclamation: I hereby declare this to be *National Everybody-Stay-by Your-Phone-During-Normal-Business-Hours-Because-Someone-Like-Me-Who-Might-at-Any-Moment-Begin-to-Weep-Into-the-Mouthpiece-May-Be-Trying-to-Call-You Day.*

For everyone who has ever played teletag and gotten sick of being "it," this could finally be our day to get some work done.

I recently was involved in a project in which a roving gang of street-toughened editors forced me at pencil-point to make literally hundreds of phone calls, one after another. I averaged *three* successful calls an hour. By "successful" I mean that I reached the person I wanted or otherwise got the information I wanted.

I began to suspect a conspiracy. But do not think that this suspicion is the result of a persecution complex (although I have several, listed in alphabetical order in a booklet that will be on sale in the lobby as you leave). No, the frustrations of teletag have reached a critical level and affect all of us.

For all we know, lasting world peace has been within grasp several times when Gorbachev had a change of heart. But each time he picked up the hotline, he was told, "I'm sorry. President Reagan is out of town until Monday. Could the presidential manicurist help you?"

Let's have a show of hands out there. Raise your hand if you have ever been kept "on hold" so long that you started doodling and would have finished a full-sized cubist version of the Mona Lisa, but your Bic ran dry after the third nose.

Raise your hand if you've tried to reach Mr. Dingle so many times that his secretary and you have become friends. In fact, you got a nice card from her in December. In it she wrote,

"Merry Christmas and Mr. Dingle is still in a meeting."

Very few business calls are successful because the work day of the average American businessperson, I have discovered, is divided into three parts:

From 8 to 12: "He's in a meeting."

From 12 to 2: "She's out to lunch."

From 2 to 5: "I'm sorry—he has gone for the day."

The only exceptions allowed are:

From 10 to 11: "She has just stepped away from her desk for a moment."

From 2 to 3: "He's on another line. Can he return your call?"

From 4 to 5: "She's no longer at this extension. I'll try to transfer you, but I've never done it befo- (click; hmmmmmmmmm)."

Where do they all go? How do they know when to disappear? Personally, I think that all the people we need to call on a given day somehow find out about it the day before, perhaps via an alert broadcast by civil defense:

"Teletag alert. This is *not* a test. The following persons are in danger of being reached by telephone tomorrow and should take appropriate countermeasures: Aaron, George; Abbott, Sheila; Ackert, Paul . . ."

And then all those people are evacuated to a large, phone-proof enclosure, perhaps the Grand Canyon. There they get real still. Someone whispers, "Shhh! Stop snickering! They'll be trying to call us soon."

Then, along about dark, after we have slashed our wrists and bled all over our Yellow Pages, these people put on party hats, have a happy hour and relive highlights of the business day.

"Boy, Blithers, I thought I'd die laughing when that guy tried to call you and your switchboard started him at extension 101 and worked him all the way through extension 317. He was already whimpering *before* the operator told him, 'I'm sorry. I have been informed that Mr. Blithers left the firm in 1947.'"

What can we "it's" in the game of teletag do about this conspiracy?

Well, we could hot-wire a bulldozer and fill in the Grand Canyon.

Or hope for the time when all citizens are issued a pager-

beeper at birth. That will happen as soon as scientists figure
out a way to make a pager that is tiny, has no sharp edges and
looks good in strained carrots.

Better yet, the solution is for all persons to chain themselves
to their desks from 8 to 5 today. What a noble experiment! A
teletag king's X. Efficiency will soar, ulcers will go begging.
The gross national product will swell so much that we'll have to
start launching cash into orbit to keep it from cluttering up our
offices and homes.

So on the count of three, everyone chain yourself to your
desk. Give the key to the mail clerk, who will place it in an
envelope and put it in interoffice mail, where it will be safely
lost until 1993.

Remember, you can go to lunch tomorrow. You can go to a
staff meeting tomorrow. You can go have those twins tomorrow.
But *today* you stay near the phone so that I can reach you if I
need to.

As for me, I think I'll just "step away from my desk for a
moment" and go to the South Seas.

St. Claude is outta sight

Everyone needs a patron saint.

The Irish have St. Patrick. Lovers have St. Valentine. And
travelers had St. Christopher until he picked up a hitchhiker
who took his car and clothes and left him standing naked
beside the Ventura Freeway.

When last seen, Christopher was trying to flag down passing
cars, shouting, "Stop! Help! I'm a saint. Really I am! Really!"

But what about us souls whom the whole world seems to
ignore and to look right through? We are the great Legion of
the Unseen, and our patron saint, of course, is St. Claude, the

patron saint of invisible people. That's Claude as in Rains — the original Invisible Man in the movies.

Personally, I find that there are three situations when I am at my plate-glass best.

— On the road. Other drivers are always pulling in front of me suddenly and without warning, causing my brakes to squeal in such a way that dogs within a ten-mile radius begin to howl "Feelings."

Perhaps the offending driver is blind, I tell myself charitably. But no, a quick inspection of the car tells me the driver is not blind. Because although in Texas the blind are allowed to drive, their cars must be equipped with white curb-feelers.

The driver is not blind. Yet he did not see me. Ergo, I must be invisible. And so must my car. Thus we of the Legion of the Unseen clearly have the power to infect our cars with our invisibility. And making a two-ton car invisible is no mean feat, let me tell you. In fact, until magician David Copperfield had reached puberty, the best *he* could do was make a two-ton car translucent.

— In stores. I can never get anyone to wait on me. So the operative word here is indeed "wait." Let's say I'm in the pet-supply department. I want an extension cord for my electric eel, Larry. I stand around in plain sight of the clerk. He looks right through me. Yet he waits on other customers with fawning alacrity.

I smile my best consumer smile. Nothing. I flash cash. Still nothing. I stroke my Visa card provocatively. Even more nothing.

Finally I go to the sporting-goods aisle, get a can of Coleman fuel, return to the pet-supply department, douse my body with the flammable liquid and set fire to myself by rubbing two wooden parakeet perches together.

As the smoke alarm goes off, and I go up in flames, the clerk finally notices me and says, "Hello, sir. How are you tonight? Marshmallows are on aisle 13."

— In restaurants. I can usually get seated, but I can never get a waiter to take my order. I raise my arm. I arch all available eyebrows, clear all available throats. I signal him with semaphor flags and flares. I grow thin and weak from hunger. My whole life begins to pass before my eyes. Oddly, in most scenes I see myself as Mahatma Gandhi, sitting cross-legged as I fast to force the British to make social concessions to Indians: better working conditions, ethnic tolerance and free water-skiing on the Ganges.

Sometimes even other diners don't see me. Some think the chair is empty and sit on my lap. I don't always object to this, especially if the diner is young and pretty and doesn't slurp her soup. Once when a comely lass sat on my lap, I began blowing on the back of her neck. She was halfway through dessert before she caught on. She finally turned around, summoned the waiter and complained that a window must be open somewhere.

Yes, it's time that we — the vast Legion of the Unseen, led by St. Claude — organized. Our mascot will be the Cheshire Cat. Our bylaws will be written with water on Saran Wrap. For our charter meeting, we'll rent a banquet room at the convention center. Be there, OK?

But how will you find us? Oh, just look for the room that has no one in it.

That'll be us.

Love (or a Reasonable Facsimile)

Of love and light, magic and malaria

Tomorrow will mark the 189th anniversary of the death of the legendary lover Casanova. When he died on that long-ago June 4, women all over the world lowered their lips to half mast.

So today let's pause to give some thought to love. There are many kinds of love. There is the love between a man and a woman, the love between a mother and her child, the love between a narcissist and his shaving mirror.

But let's focus on romantic love, because it's more magical, more overpowering, more likely to result in lifelong bliss or a trip to the free clinic.

Where to find love. Love, like a lost sock, often is found in the last place you'd think to look for it. Yet actually love can be found anywhere, although there is no recorded instance of it ever having been found in Iowa. You may find love in the office, at a party, in the supermarket. In 1967, Hadley K. and Juanita R. found love in the produce department at Safeway. Both were a bit disappointed, as they had been trying to find the broccoli.

But with the impetuosity of lovers, they went ahead and got married and spent their honeymoon in the express line. At a tender moment, the smitten Hadley was heard to coo to Juanita, "When the light hits you just right, you look just like four no. 2 cans of cling peaches in heavy syrup."

How to recognize love. Symptoms of love include disorientation, sweaty palms, rapid pulse and loss of appetite. Those of you just back from the tropics will recognize these symptoms as similar to those of malaria.

How to tell love from malaria. If you get better, it was malaria.

How to tell love from like. If you dial a person's phone number and the line is busy and you hang up, deciding to try again the next day, that's like. If the line is busy and you keep redialing every 11 seconds, eventually wearing your fingertips down past the wrist until you're dialing with your elbow, that's love.

If you finally get an answer, and the voice says, "Hello. Acme Taxidermists," that's a wrong number.

If that's *not* a wrong number, your musk ox will be ready after four P.M. Wednesday.

How to tell love from lust. Love and lust, like a dentist and a proctologist, are related but not necessarily interchangeable. If two young people on a Friday night date are still together at two A.M. Saturday, it's lust. If they're still together at noon Sunday, it's love. If they're still together at noon Monday, their braces are locked and they're both late for work.

What can trigger love. For women, it's subtle things: a man's smile or his spirituality. For men, it's more obvious things, such as whether a woman's figure corresponds with the layout of the roller-coaster track at Six Flags.

How to tell mature love from immature love. Mature love is not possessive. Think of an ice cube. Hold it loosely in the palm of your hand, and it will stay put. But grasp it too tightly, and it will squirt out of your hand, bouncing off the wall and landing under the bed, where it gets covered with lint, and melts. When you look under the bed for it, sure enough — there's your lost sock.

Yes, love is wondrous. Having been National Lovesickness Poster Child six years in a row, I know much about love. I know that we fall in, but we must climb out. I know that when love walks in the front door of the heart, reason tiptoes out the back door of the mind and is later seen on a street corner, mumbling to itself and carrying a shopping bag full of old string and tin foil. I know that . . . I know that . . . that . . . I know that that's all I know.

Don't misunderstand me. I make light not of love but of those of us who keep trying to get it right. Love, after all, is the greatest of life's gifts. Why, Casanova devoted his entire life to love.

And look where he is today.

Of moosery and Ms.-ery

I know just how he feels.

Perhaps you read recently about the bull moose in Vermont that has fallen in love with a farmer's Hereford cow. A mixed marriage if ever there was one. I mean what *will* their families say? It's doomed from the start.

I, too, am always falling — nay, *leaping* — in love with Ms. Wrong. I can't take any credit for this. It's just a knack I have.

Through the years, these Ms. Wrongs have been attracted to me much as a tornado is attracted to a mobile home. And with much the same result.

Inevitably we eventually find that we are oil and water, fire and ice, null and void.

The Vermont farmer said the star-crossed critters just stand close to each other and stare, cow- and moose-eyed. Well, maybe a bit more than that. "They've nuzzled like they're kissing, but I ain't seen no action," he said.

And he won't, either, unless the moose is wearing a better cologne than I have been able to find.

The cow's name is Jessica. Now personally I have never fallen deeply in love with a Jessica (although I *have* fallen deeply in like with two Tessies and a Bessie).

But the day is young.

Scott Darling, a state Game and Fish Department biologist, said that during the mating season, a normally proud, elusive moose becomes so smitten that he doesn't notice that dozens of two-legged spectators have gathered to watch his wooing.

Hey, me too.

With eyes aglaze and palms asweat, I will hold hands at a board meeting, play footsie at a summit conference, wink at a wake (and wake at a wink) and go gaga at a go-go.

"They do get pretty dopey-acting when they're in this breeding mode," state Game Warden Donald Gallus said in that poetic way that state game wardens have.

For the bull moose, "this breeding mode" lasts just a few weeks. That still gives the farmer time to resod the pasture and replant the trees that have been knocked down by the 700-pound bull moose's tender overtures.

Hey, me too.

But for me — a 180-pound bull columnist — the mating season lasts all year, twenty-four hours a day. It never closes. I am the 7-Eleven of ill-fated love.

This sort of thing has happened before up in moose country. Gallus said that in 1977 a moose invaded a Vermont dairy, fell in love with the whole herd and threatened any person who tried to milk the cows. The moose even chased two men up a tree.

Likewise, in 1966 I threatened my best friend when he tried to give *my* girl friend *his* letter jacket to keep warm with. He was still in the jacket at the time.

I even chased him up a tree.

He is still up that tree.

Where he lives happily with my girl friend.

They are expecting a little letter sweater in the spring.

Yes, for the moose and myself, the phrase "fatal attraction" is redundant.

So, alas, I know what fate awaits poor Mister Moose. He will awaken one morning after a night of dreamy dreams of his beloved Jessica — dreams of springtime strolls along the Champs Elysées in Paris, of moonlight gondola rides down the Grand Canal in Venice, of shopping for wedding rings at the feed store, only to find a note pinned to his antlers saying that she has left him — thrown him over for the Merrill Lynch bull.

Women just can't resist a man with a big portfolio.

Hobsnobbing: It's a date

Crème de la crème, here I come.

I just read about a dating service that caters to only the upwardly mobile. Well, I am not very upwardly, but on a good day I am mobile. And naturally I am determined to worm my way into any group that won't have me.

Yes, Gentlepeople, Ltd. of Cambridge, Mass., matches only the well-heeled and well-educated (no butchers, bakers or candlestick makers). These are folks who have two children from their first marriage and two Porsches from their second and who stand around at cocktail parties quoting James Joyce over and over until little bits of foam begin to appear at the corners of their mouth.

"I don't find the word 'snob' offensive," Gentlepeople gentlefounder Zelda Fischer said. But, she said, "I wouldn't turn away an intellectually curious trades person." Such as, one assumes, a plumber who can play Shostakovich on the bathroom plunger while discussing Sartre's philosophy of grease clogs.

Predictably, "Money is very important in all this," Fischer said. The membership fee for six months is $2,500. And soon will rise to $5,000.

I'm sure that couples who meet through Gentlepeople spend wonderfully romantic nights together in front of the fireplace, comparing portfolios. They probably gaze at each other over some vintage wine that was bottled before Adam was wearing fig-leaf BVDs ("In the beginning" was a very good year) and whisper:

"Oh, my dearest Osgood Wellington Osgood IV . . ."

"Call me IV for short."

"Oh, IV, I get tingly all over when you whisper 'AT&T, 2,000 shares.'"

"And my darling Hillary, when I hold you close and look into your eyes, I see the most precious thing in all the world."

"Oh, what, IV, *What?*"

"Myself!"

Then they have a big wedding, after which the bride and groom stay home while their accountants go on the honeymoon.

Fischer turns down about 20 percent of her applicants. She screens them carefully with questions, probably such as "Who is Faust?" "What is relativity?" "Why is opera?" Also, "In part two of Joyce's *Ulysses,* Molly is abducted by a one-legged albino midget who tickles her with a herring. Why a herring?" and "Did you know you have some foam on your upper lip?"

Yes, I simply *must* get into this exclusive set, where I can meet a brilliant and successful woman who will while away many meaningful hours with me, sharing the finer things and pretending to understand abstract art.

Ah, but how can I come up with the $2,500 fee? I mean, have you seen my last W-2 form? (It's on display in the lobby as you leave.) I guess I *could* get the money be selling my pickup. Five times.

But better yet, I'll open a dating service of my own—one that won't accept any person who earns more than $20,000 a year. I'll screen them carefully, of course, with my own incisive questions:

Do you put peanuts in your Dr Pepper?

Have you watched "The Three Stooges" in the last year?

Is your idea of landscaping to buy a pair of pink lawn flamingos?

Do you carry around in your wallet a photo of the first deer you ever shot?

Do you carry around the first deer you ever shot?

Whose face is on the $10,000 bill?

Five *no's* and one "Salmon P. Chase" and they're outta here.

With the profits from this dating service, I can join Gentlepeople.

One satisfied Gentlepeople member said of that $2,500-soon-to-be-$5,000 fee, "It's a terrible thing to say, but perhaps the fee sorts the wheat from the chaff."

And, boy, aren't we chaffs glad!

Night moves:
Watch closely

Now they tell me.

Tim Perper, author of *Sex Signals: The Biology of Love,* has been studying the courtship techniques of perfect strangers (who are perfect because they *are* strangers). He has concluded that two-thirds of the time, it's the woman who makes the first move.

I've been looking for such first moves now for (let me check my watch . . .) twenty-two years and have seen very few. The last time I was in a situation where the woman made the first move, she made it to Akron.

Now they tell me. These first moves are very subtle. They can be detected only by sociologists using seismographs, infrared cameras and specially trained dogs.

To conduct this research, Perper and his wife, Martha Cornoug, spent more than nine hundred hours in singles bars. (The wonder is that they emerged with their wedding vows and livers intact.)

They found that courtship is a five-step process: "approach, talk, turn, touch and synchronize." The woman starts it by placing herself near the man, making him think that their meeting is a chance encounter. They talk. She then turns her body toward him. This causes him to turn his body toward her, so that they are almost facing each other. Perhaps his nostrils twitch. Then the woman makes contact, lightly touching his elbow or picking lint off his shirt. At last, they synchronize, such as lifting their glasses at the same time.

(Is this getting too racy for you?)

Now they tell me. I have always found courtship to be a *six*-step process: be introduced, avert eyes, hem, haw, panic and run to the restroom.

The one in Akron.

And I have always thought that when a woman picked lint off your shirt, she was picking lint off your shirt.

Silly old me.

Perper said the woman expects the man to "get the hint" eventually and take charge of the situation. If the man does not do this share of signaling, the woman will move away, and the man will be left with a full moon, empty arms and a lint-free shirt.

Perper said, for instance, that if a woman cuddles against a man, he's expected to put his arm around her. If she puts her head on his shoulder, he's expected to kiss her. If she takes off all her clothes and anoints her body with peanut butter, he's expected to furnish the grape jelly.

Well, OK, I added that last one myself. *Someone* has to spice this up. I can hear readers turning to Ann Landers.

But those examples are pretty obvious signals. And even apparently obvious signals can be misinterpreted. Once at a party, a comely lass winked at me severely and pushed me into the hall closet with her, finally coming to rest among the galoshes with her tongue wedged in my ear. I took this as an introduction. I asked her if she comes here often.

Later, after she had slapped my face into the next time zone, I found that she had merely gotten something in her eye and stumbled.

Perper also found that a woman singles out a man not so much for his looks, humor, wealth or power, but for his ability to respond the way she wants him to. This should be great news to me, because I seem to have left my looks, humor, wealth and power in my other jeans. But this is *not* great news. Because courtship that is based on picking lint and touching elbows is far too subtle for me. We big dumb men need something obvious: Women should bring us roses, write us poems and send us their room keys.

On second thought, forget the roses and poems.

Yes, *now* they tell me. In the great river of life, it's the women who do the fishing.

But I'm getting too old to see the bait.

The single file:
Solo and so what

I know that there are some single folks in the audience today. I can hear you talking to your pets.

And we people who live alone do that, don't we — talk to our pets, mumble to ourselves, argue with the television.

Several of us singles were sitting around the other night, pondering our condition: the advantages, the disadvantages, how to give someone of the opposite sex an obscene hug and convince them that it's the Heimlich maneuver.

Here, I think, is the main advantage of being single: never having to consider anyone else.

Here, I think, is the main *dis*advantage of being single: never having to consider anyone else.

What else is being single?

Single is falling asleep by counting the cracks in the plaster ceiling over your bed. How you wish that someone was there at your side, to help you count.

Single is dining out alone. At a table for one you feel quarantined from the whole world. So you eat as fast as you can, perhaps while pretending to be absorbed in a book. Actu-

ally you are reading—tucked into the open pages of Plato's
Republic—the singles ads in *Dallas Observer:*

"Outrageously attractive, brilliant woman, 22, seeks old-
fashioned, romantic gentleman. I am very physical and
affectionate but vulnerable and slow to trust. Let's put on suits
of armor and cuddle. Suzi."

Single is buying fresh produce at the market and then having
to eat like a plague of locusts to finish it before it goes bad.
Why can't farmers grow half-heads of lettuce?

Single is not knowing where your next argument is coming
from.

Single is having friends who are always trying to fix you up
with someone. That someone invariably looks like the result of
nuclear testing on a Mexican dinner.

(And you don't know what you'd do if your friends ever
stopped trying.)

There are two basic camps in the great singles army—the
so-far single and the suddenly single. The so-far singles have
never been married. The suddenly singles have arrived at their
dubious condition through divorce or death or, on a really bad
day, both.

Both camps spend their time alternately blessing and
blaspheming their singlehood. Me, I bless on Monday,
Wednesday and Friday and blaspheme on Tuesday, Thursday
and Saturday. On Sunday I write to the above-mentioned Suzi,
telling her that I made all A's in metal shop and was the 1967
all-conference cuddling champion.

Some people live the single life very successfully. They have
friends of all known genders, have many interests, seldom are
lonely, enjoy their economic and emotional independence and
view singlehood as a lifestyle to be led, not fled.

These people are sick.

Others don't fare so well. They mope, they sleep too much,
they hang out in bars until they stop feeling single and start
seeing double. They will tell you that loneliness, misery and
frustration are not all they're cracked up to be.

They have yet to learn a valuable lesson: that happiness must
come from within, not without, that no one else can make you
happy. Although I suspect that Jane Pauley could make me
smile real big, perhaps to the point of unconsciousness.

All singles know some marrieds who equate wedlock with hemlock. "You have so much freedom!" some say to me with drool on their chin. "Tell us about the catered orgies, Mike. Tell us about the one-night stands!" "So who stands? . . ." I reply, flaring my nostrils, my ellipsis thick with unspoken debauchery.

Then I go home to talk to my pets, gobble a head of lettuce and count the cracks in the ceiling.

Read 'em and weep, Kilroy

If only Kilroy were here to see it all:

Bubba Loves Shannon. Mark-n-Natalee 4-ever. Cathy (heart) Shane. Laura + Chuck.

Yes, love is alive and well and living on a retaining wall at the high school near my home. The graffiti clings to that wall like ivy. The concrete is covered with layer upon layer of names and initials: a Babel of pairings and pinings.

But, alas, no evidence that "Kilroy was here." But then he would be more than forty years old now, wouldn't he—far too old for such foolishness, right? Kilroy, you recall, was that mysterious little graffiti gnome born of World War II. Back then, it seemed, everywhere GIs went, walls sprouted that simple drawing: often of a nose hanging over a horizontal line, but always accompanied by the words "Kilroy was here."

As for today's teen-aged graffitist, science has now isolated the enzyme that compels kids to go out and buy a can of spray paint, find a flat surface and tell the world of a love that will last forever or until the paint dries, whichever comes first.

So there is much to be read at that high school, there on Cupid's bulletin board. *Missi-n-Sean. Michelle-n-Erik. Robin-n-Kevin.* Everyone is there except Ken-n-Barbie, who apparently were too short to reach the wall.

But the most-intriguing name I saw was that of the fair Cindi. As Roxanne was to Cyrano, as Josephine was to Napoleon, so Cindi is to Larry. Oops. And to Rick. Hmmm. And to Jeff. Yes, I found at least three boys confessing their enchantment with the fair Cindi. This Cindi person must be one fine fox. (Did I phrase that correctly?)

Note that the fair Cindi is of the *i* school of spelling. There is a lot of that going around now: Mindi, Becki, Staci. In *my* day (defined as falling after the Cold War but before hot pants) she would have been Cindy. With a *y*. Back then, a boy knew where he stood with a Cindy-with-a-*y*.

But now you'll find Cindi's, Cyndi's and Cindee's. I wonder: Does each spelling denote a different personality? Are Cindi's perky and bouncy while Cyndi's are quiet and studious and Cindee's are sullen and prone to commit heinous crimes using farm implements?

I also found that today's graffiti has little of the anger of the Vietnam era. And much of the graffiti that I saw would be enigmatic to someone of Kilroy's years. *Surf Nazis. We are here to stay. '68 Buicks never die, they just get wrecked. Who killed Bambi?*

And on an overpass not far away is painted: *The fire still burns.* Today, who knows what esoteric meaning that message has?

But in *my* day (further defined as falling after the Limbo but before Rambo) a passing motorist would assume that such a message had been put there to remind some forgetful commuter who was prone to go off and leave the stove on.

And for parents who are concerned that today's kids are not learning how to reason clearly, I saw this: *Sex is sin. Sin is forgiven. So let's beg.* The author of that little syllogism no doubt will someday make a fine logician.

If he has any strength left.

How these night writers have bared their souls there on that retaining wall! Witness the poignant *I (heart) someone . . .* and the world-weary *Love is a tragedy.*

Such angst, such weltschmerz.

Indeed, some pairings have been marked out. But not with flimsy spray paint. No—with thick white housepaint that has trickled haltingly down the wall.

And so indeed the course of true love runs, but not smoothly.

Yes, if only Kilroy were here . . . oh, let's face it, if Kilroy were here, he too probably would be swept away and some night spray paint the following:

Kilroy was here. And he (heart) Cindi.

Hits and Mrs.:
A Laurel lie

Those of you who know me may be surprised to learn that after thirty-eight years of bachelorhood, I have at last taken a wife.

She is charming. She is intelligent. She is completely imaginary.

See, on a recent trip to Bangkok, Thailand, I grew weary of taxi drivers asking me if I was single. When I said yes, they'd whip out a brochure for a local massage parlor, such as "Madam Mai Ching's House of Joy. Featuring only cleanest girls, prettiest boys. Ask about our group rates. With each visit, free bowl of curried duck feet."

When it wasn't taxi drivers, it was a moonlighting lady tour guide who kept offering to meet me after hours for a cozy dinner and a private tour of the erotic etchings at the Sacred Temple of Divine Enlightenment And All-Night Mah-Jong Parlor.

Now, granted, my libido could jump-start a '56 DeSoto. In gear. But I'm an old-fashioned kind of guy. I could never make love with a woman of the opposite sex unless (1) we had a strong intellectual bond; (2) we shared a deep spiritual kinship; (3) she brought the Cool Whip.

Thus in Bangkok I found it simpler just to start saying that I am indeed married, that my wife is back at the hotel, resting. Naturally, to be more convincing, I needed to *believe* in this wife. So I fleshed her out.

I shall never forget. It was spring when I met Laurelei. She was lovely. Sensitive, cerebral, with a face like an angel and a figure so full of angles and arcs that I was at once reminded of my final exam in geometry.

At the time, Laurelei was teaching a course in Sartre at Columbia by day, playing first cello in the New York Philharmonic by night and mud-wrestling in Jersey on weekends.

On our first date, we looked deeply into each other's eyes and discussed symbolism in Melville. She said that Moby Dick symbolizes evil; I said Moby Dick symbolizes a large pale whale. Playfully, she gave me a love tap on the head with her copy of *War and Peace*. How I loved the way her eyes flashed as she watched me slump to the floor!

Thus began our courtship. Much smitten, I would write her long, passionate love letters. Deeply moved, she would send them back to me, corrected.

Life was good, life was full.

We would go on quiet walks through lush, green meadows. How we would frolic hand in hand, laughing merrily as we realized that we had wandered into an artillery range. One shell crashed into our picnic basket, denting a cake that Laurelei had baked.

And so we were wed. We spent our wedding night discussing James Joyce's *Ulysses*. Afterward, she sighed, leaned back on one elbow and asked, dreamily, "Was it obscure for you, too?"

For relaxation, Laurelei has lately been translating some ancient Hebrew scrolls into English. But she has discovered that they are only some of Moses' old grocery lists and is now translating them back into Hebrew.

Our life together has been truly idyllic. But of late there is trouble in paradise. I sense that Laurelei and I are drifting apart. She watches Dan Rather, I watch Peter Jennings. I drink Perrier, she drinks Evian. I pretend to understand Picasso, she pretends to understand Pollock.

These days, in unguarded moments, she gets a wistful look in her eyes. It's the same look that Sweeney Todd would get when someone would say, "Just a little off the top, please." And one night last week, as she slept, I saw her smile faintly and heard her mutter, "Oh, Billy Buckley, take me to the place where ecstasy knows no bounds!"

Next morning I confronted her with this, but she became defensive, stammering that she simply must have fallen asleep while watching the PBS test pattern.

Yes, I have taken a bride. But Laurelei, if you are reading this, you'd better shape up, woman, or else the next time I go to Bangkok, *you* stay home.

Love lines:
Ad nauseam

Ladies, are you lonely and looking?

Looking for Mr. Right, that is, in the personal classified ads? The personal ads have gone respectable and now can be found in many publications, from *New York* magazine to this very newspaper. You know the kind of ads I mean:

Handsome, witty, affectionate, sincere neurosurgeon seeks lasting relationship with an old-fashioned lady who has traditional values and enjoys porch swings, art museums and group sex with mollusks.

Now, ladies, I suspect that this ad is a pack of lies. All except that bit about mollusks.

I know how we Mr. Rights think. We're a sneaky bunch. Don't trust us. These ads usually are written on lonely Friday nights, when the old hormones kick in. At such times men are apt to breathe heavily and play fast and loose with their modifiers.

Here's one of the first personal classifieds on record, placed in a London newspaper of the 1500s:

Single white male king, 40ish, is tired of relationships that don't last. I am pleasingly plump, jolly, but, alas, a

widower. Would you enjoy cozy nights around the castle
with fine food and wine, watching the executioner sharpen
his ax? Do visions of wealth and power fill your pretty little
head? Then let's take a whack at it. Reply with a wallet-
size oil painting of yourself to Henry. P.O. Box VIII.

So, as a public service, ladies, I'll tell you how to interpret
some key phrases and read between the lines in men's personal
ads:

Slender, neat and clean Libra seeks that special lady. Let's
share quiet times in my world, full of flowers, soft music,
satin, mahogany.

Slender: He'd have to swallow an olive just to cast a shadow.
Clean: During each night of a full moon he must be hosed
down.
Quiet times in my world, full of flowers, soft music, satin,
mahogany: Ladies, this man is an undertaker.

Sports-oriented Pisces. Nonmaterialistic and outdoorsy.
Knows how to treat you like a lady. Affectionate.

Sports-oriented: He has a tennis racket, knows which end of
it you putt with.
Nonmaterialistic: He lives in a packing crate.
Outdoorsy: The crate is in a vacant lot.
Knows how to treat you like a lady: On the *Titanic,* he
would give up his seat to a woman.
Affectionate: He has one wife, two mistresses, three fiancées,
and several mollusks call him "Sugar."

Fun-loving, financially secure man seeks a woman to enjoy
foreign cuisine and take long walks. Well-read, never far
from a book.

Fun-loving: He has a dribble glass.
Financially secure: The dribble glass is paid for.
Enjoys foreign cuisine: He lives on French fries and Scotch
whiskey, and goes Dutch treat.

Takes long walks: He doesn't own a car.

Never far from a book: Being 5-foot-none, he often stands on an unabridged dictionary.

Successful executive, equally at ease on the town or on safari, very giving. 42, 188, 5–10.

Equally at ease on the town or on safari: He wears a silk loincloth.

Very giving: He has one of the Top Ten social diseases.

"42, 188, 5–10" are his age, weight and height, right? Wrong. They indicate his IQ, weekly wage and how many years in prison he served after his *last* date.

I hope that these insights are helpful to you, ladies. Remember, you can trust *me*. After all, I have never been more than just close friends with a mollusk.

The first 100 are the hardest

The Jafarova marriage is off to a promising start.

In fact, husband Ilyas and his blushing bride, Khatyn, celebrated an anniversary recently in their mountain village in the Soviet Union. When they got married, Ilyas was nineteen, Khatyn only fifteen. Mere children. But so far, so good.

The Jafarovas have been married 100 years.

One hundred years with the same person! A century of his snoring and of her hearing burglars downstairs. A century of her telling him to roll over and hush and of his reminding her that they don't *have* a downstairs.

A century of "for richer, for poorer, in sickness and in health, to love and to cherish, 'til twin beds do us part."

(In case you are wondering about the traditional mineral

that is given on such advanced wedding anniversaries, the
fiftieth is gold, the seventy-fifth is diamond and the hundredth
is petrified wood.)

This newspaper printed only a photo of the Jafarovas, dancing on their hundredth anniversary as some of their two hundred descendants watched. To supplement that photo, here is
an exclusive interview with this remarkable couple.

American reporter: Up in these Soviet mountains, longevity
is common. Folks often live to be 100. But such longevity in
both life *and* love is indeed amazing to us back in the Land of
the Coronary and Mental Cruelty. Tell us your secret.

Ilyas: Ah! Our long life we owe to our hard work and simple
food. That and the fact that in Mother Russia, people must get
written permission for any change in health: one signature to
get sick, two to die. For 76 years we have been on a waiting
list.

Khatyn: And our long marriage we owe to mutual tolerance
and respect. That and a mutual deafness, I in my left ear,
Ilyas in his right. So he stays to the left of me, and each has
not heard a word the other has said since 1947.

Ilyas: Huh?

Reporter: Khatyn, does Ilyas still tell you he loves you?

Khatyn: Hardly ever. Maybe three times a week.

Reporter: Is that correct, Ilyas?

Ilyas: No. I tell her constantly. Maybe three times a week.

Reporter: Ilyas, what changes have you seen in Russia in
your 119 years?

Ilyas: Before the revolution, the workers were poor and
hungry. But communism reversed that trend. Now the workers
are hungry and poor.

Khatyn: I remember our first home — a two-room cottage.

Reporter: Were you happy in it?

Khatyn: Yes. So were the other nineteen couples. We had to
sleep in shifts. I slept Mondays and Thursdays. Ilyas slept
Wednesdays and Sundays. Our first child was conceived eleven
years later.

Ilyas: By telepathy.

Reporter: After 100 years, I suppose you two know each
other pretty well?

Ilyas: Yes. I can always tell when my Khatyn is restless to gossip with Natasha, the miller's wife. She has done this each day for many years. But the joke is on Khatyn: Natasha died in 1931. Hah!

Khatyn: Hmmmm. I *thought* Natasha seemed distracted lately.

Ilyas: Then Khatyn will come home and bake. But she does not see so well now, and sometimes she uses too much yeast. In fact, old Grapotkin and his wife hollowed out a loaf of Khatyn's pumpernickel and are living in it.

Reporter: Are they happy in it?

Ilyas: Yes. So are the other nineteen couples.

Khatyn: And I, too, know my Ilyas well. I can read him like a book. A dirty book. Every day, when Sonya, the beautiful milkmaid, comes around, Ilyas says to her, "A quart of skim, Sonya." but he is thinking, "Ah, lovely Sonya, if only I were a young man of ninety again!"

Reporter: What personality differences have you two adjusted to in 100 years?

Ilyas: Khatyn is always hopeful. She's like the optimist who, as he fell ninety stories, plummeted past the second story thinking, "So far, so good."

Khatyn: But my Ilyas, ah, such a pessimist. He goes around all day looking up, afraid that he will be hit by a falling optimist.

Reporter: I understand that you two have two hundred descendants.

Khatyn: Yes. Five generations. Our youngest child, Dimitri, already can tie his shoes. And he is barely seventy.

Ilyas: No, Khatyn. Our youngest child is little Gregor, and he is sixty-six.

Khatyn: No, Ilyas. Gregor is 104, and he is your aunt.

Ilyas: No, Khatyn, my aunt is 113, and she is the Brothers Karamazov.

Reporter: I hate to interrupt, but someone is knocking. Why, it is Sonya, the beautiful milkmaid.

Ilyas: A quart of skim, Sonya.

Khatyn: (Whap!) That does it, Ilyas! I've warned you about coming on to that low-fat floozy. I should have listened to my girl friends. Back in 1885 they *warned* me it would never work out.

Ilyas: Oh, no! Our first fight. And right here in the capitalist running-dog press. Forgive me! Come back, Khatyn.   Where are you going?

Khatyn: Goodbye, Ilyas. I'm moving back home with my parents!

Past Perfect

White Levis had the wearwithal

Hanging on the rack there at the Goodwill store, they beckoned, calling to me like a siren to a sailor, like a maiden to a unicorn, like a Twinkie to a dieter.

'Twas a pair of white Levis! Now if you are of my era (defined as falling after "Louie Louie" but before Duran Duran), you remember such jeans. Once they were a vital part of the uniform of high-school boys. Resplendent in white Levis, penny loafers, a paisley shirt and a splash of British Sterling, you could swim wide rivers, climb tall mountains and defeat mighty armies, although your white Levis probably would require washing afterward.

And now, twenty years later, here was a pair tugging at the sleeve of my memory like a beggar: "Hey, Buddy! Remember 1967? Remember *The Graduate?* Remember 'Hey Jude'? Remember Lovetta T.?"

Of course! I had forgotten Lovetta T. I'm sure that I was wearing white Levis that Homecoming night that she and I had that unfortunate misunderstanding involving her angora sweater and my hangnail. When the riot squad arrived, I pleaded temporary insanity, brought on by trying to memorize irregular verbs for Spanish class.

How could I resist these jeans now? They were in excellent condition, a perfect fit and just $2.99. Their material was as soft as rolled-and-pleated bucket seats, as pale as gym-class legs, as thin as a freshman book report.

I went into a changing booth, slipped them on and looked in the mirror. Instantly they became a size 34–32 time machine, speeding me back to my teenhood. "The corner of 18 and acne, please," I said, "and step on it!"

White Levis were perfect for cruising a Sonic Drive-In diner in a '63 Super Sport. Funny how we boys would spend all of our savings and anything we could extort from our parents to soup up a car so that it would go 127 mph with the emergency brake on. Then we'd drive it through the Sonic parking lot so slowly that it was 30 seconds passing a given carhop.

They were perfect for wearing to drive-in movies, where, no matter what was showing on the screen, the double feature was always "Raging Hormones" and "Stop or I'll Scream!"

They were perfect for sleeping through math class, staying awake only long enough to pass a note back to Lovetta T. telling her how sorry I was about the sweater and would she go out with me Friday. When she passed the note back to me, it was on fire. I took this to mean that she had made other plans.

White Levis went well with science class, where, for extra credit, each day for a month you'd volunteer for an experiment in which you grasped the two leads from a hand-cranked generator. You not only earned an A, but to this day you can jump-start a car by just placing your hands on the hood.

They went well with cheap dates. Ah, those romantic nights on the miniature golf course, boy and girl strolling along, putter-in-putter. "Look, Inez," you'd say, nuzzling her neck as she teed up on the par-three seventeenth, "there's a full floodlight out tonight. When the light hits you a certain way, you look just like the Arc de Triomphe."

"Oh, Howie, I love it when you talk French!"

Yes, white Levis went with any occasion: filling your worst enemy's locker with raw chicken parts, trying to imagine the principal and his wife "doing it" or smuggling hamburger patties out of the lunchroom to use as tire patches in auto shop.

As I did a U-turn from the past and headed stylishly toward the cashier to plunk down my $2.99, I wondered where Lovetta

T. is today. I'd like to think that she, too, is in a Goodwill store somewhere, trying on an angora sweater and traveling back in time, remembering that awkward, skinny guy—the one with the white Levis.

And the hangnail.

It was love at first gear

An open letter to a '51 Pontiac, wherever it might be.

We never quite forget the big firsts in our life, do we? And you were my first car.

I would go on to own more than a dozen cars, trucks and motorcycles. But you left a soft spot in my heart forever, a warm spot in my memories and an oil spot in my parents' driveway.

You were big and heavy, with 16-inch tires, a long hood covering a flathead straight-8, and a trunk that I could have sublet to a family of Gypsies. With your metal windshield visor and grille of chrome teeth, yours was a stern visage. But to this teenager, you were a madonna in mud-flaps, a Venus in Valvoline.

It's an American tradition to pair young boys with old cars. And from the beginning, our relationship was a marriage of inconvenience.

I paid $50 for you in 1965, remember? And during the daylight hours, you were worth every dollar of that. During the day, I could count on you to get me to school, to a summer job, to baseball practice.

But you apparently belonged to some rigid auto religion that didn't believe in doing work after dark. You would never start at night. And with that sixth sense that is standard equipment on clunkers, you *knew* when I really needed you to start.

This was usually about 11:52 P.M., after the second feature at the drive-in. My date had to be home by midnight. Any time she was late, her dad would put his arm around my shoulder, say "Now, son . . ." in a fatherly way and force-feed my penny loafers to me.

Your starter switch was located on the dash. It looked like a door-bell button. Every Friday and Saturday night, I would clench my teeth, close my eyes and push that button (anyone home?), only to hear the most dreaded sound in all the world:

RRRRrrrrRRRRrrrrRRRRrrrr . . . rrr . . . rrr . . . rr . . . r-r-r. . . .

Then I'd get out and rush over to the car that was parked "next-door" and knock timidly on the fogged front window. "Oh, *there* you are," I'd say as some dreamy-eyed fellow teen rolled down the *back* window. As he got out of the car to get his jumper cables, he'd make a growling noise not unlike yours:

RRRRrrrrRRRRrrrrRRRRrrrr . . . rrrr . . . rrr . . .   rr . . .   r-r-r. . . .

But he'd give me a boost, you'd fire right up, and I wouldn't have to ask the Gypsies to get out and push.

I did everything I could to make you reliable, O Pontiac of my past. I brought you offerings: a new battery, starter, solenoid, voltage regulator, generator. I took you to a mechanic. He suggested a faith healer. I took you to a faith healer. He suggested that I drive you through the car wash at Lourdes.

Then, predictably, I resorted to the superstition of car-owners: I prettied you up. I put fake whitewalls on your tires. I washed you, anointed you with Turtle Wax. Then I took you back to the drive-in.

RRRRrrrrRRRRrrrrRRRRrrrr . . . rrrr . . . rrr . . .   rr . . . r-r-r. . . .

I added more chrome. Floor mats. Seat covers. Back to the drive-in.

RRRRrrrrRRRRrrrrRRRRrrrr . . . rrrr . . . rrr . . .   rr . . . r-r-r. . . .

And so it went until, finally, in a weak moment, I threw you over for that cute little MG. Did you ever forgive me? I've often wondered what became of you. You probably rolled out your last miles as someone's "second car" and then were crushed and recycled, perhaps reincarnated as thousands of tin cans.

In fact, I think of you each time I see a tin can. And who knows, maybe we'll meet again some day. If some night I try to open a can of peas or carrots, only to hear my electric can opener go

RRRRrrrrRRRRrrrrRRRRrrrr. . .   rrrr. . .   rrr . . .   rr . . . rr . . . r-r-r. . . .

I'll know that we're together again.

Sputtering down Memory Lane

Sometimes, to fall asleep, I count not sheep but the cars that I have owned.

My early vehicles totaled three coupes, two sedans, one truck, one hearse, one van, two foreign cars, one tractor, two motorcycles and a scooter in a pear tree.

Yes, I had owned fourteen vehicles by the time I was twenty-two. In my fickle youth, I was the Henry VIII of motordom.

But I have since settled down and been married to the same truck for sixteen years.

Cars are vital totems in our culture, aren't they? We worship the mobility they give us. While we own one, we alternately pamper and abuse it. After it is gone, we remember it vividly. Often our memories are pegged to the car that we owned at a given time.

"Remember when our little Trixie was born, Ma? We had that old Nash back then." And, "Remember when our little Trixie first went astray, Ma? We had the Olds sedan." And, "Remember when our little Trixie was taken from us in her prime, Ma? We had that green Plymouth. The vice squad had a black-and-white Ford."

I've never owned a new car. But I've learned much by keeping old cars running. For instance, the Pontiac taught me that I—who barely passed freshman German—can swear fluently in nine languages when a wrench slips, causing me to scrape a matched set of knuckles, given to me at birth by my parents.

And the Chevys taught me the joys of lying on my back under a car and hefting a starter off the ground and into the flywheel housing. The first attempt is done with much energy. But by the fourth attempt, the muscles in my arms have the consistency of guacamole, and I am openly weeping into the repair manual.

This knowledge must not be allowed to fall into the wrong hands. Such as those of Latin American governments.

"Won't confess, eh, Valdez? You won't tell us that you killed El Presidente's personal banana-peeler? Fine. Guards, take Valdez out, flog him, pull out his fingernails and put him on the rack."

A week later.

"*Still* won't talk, eh, Valdez? Very well. Guards, take him out and make him put a starter on a '68 Impala!"

"No! Not *that!* I'll talk. I did it! I killed him. Also, I cheat on my taxes, my sister has some unpaid parking tickets, and in 1959 my mother stole a crust of bread!"

Thinking back over my cars, I see that some of them represented phases that I was going through.

I went through my Chevy Super Sport phase. Three times. I wanted something fast, low and brightly painted. Why didn't I just go out with Trixie instead?

And the MG was my sports car phase. It had the cutest little engine. You'd look at it and just want to hug it and coo "Godluvit!" Hah! That engine was cast-iron evil. Fickle. Spiteful. Oil pressure that fluctuated with the stock market. Twin carbs that had to be synchronized by Zubin Mehta.

Sooner or later, many young men suffer a sports car phase. In severe cases, they wear tweed coats and ascots. This can now be cured with antibiotics.

The old orange hearse represented my no-chlorophyll phase. It was one of three cars that never budged out of the backyard. They could lie very still for months at a time. And if called upon, they could lie twice as still. They turned the rectangle of grass under them a sickly yellow. By pushing them around in the backyard at regular intervals, I never had to mow the lawn.

Yes, as I finally drift off to sleep, I wish there were some way that I could have all of those old friends back with me now. I'd buy a round of drinks for us all—warm milk for me and a quart of Havoline 10W-30 for each of them.

Better make that *two* quarts for my truck. It's leaking pretty badly.

Barking up the family tree

Recently my mail box coughed up an offer from a publisher who was eager to provide me with *The Nichols Family Heritage Book* for just $30.

This handsome volume would contain the genealogy and coat of arms of every Nichols family in the land. All that I—as a practicing Nichols—had to do was remit $30.

No way. Many a fine person has borne the Nichols family name, but I won't pay good money just to confirm what I already suspect: My family tree (like yours, I'll bet) has more than one case of root rot.

—My earliest known ancestor was Brunhilda Nycholes, a poor Dark Ages woman who eked out a living selling ekes. But one day she was accused of being a witch. At her trial, she was given that era's version of due process—when she was tossed into the Lake of Justice: if she floated, she was a witch; if she sank, she was innocent and would be fondly remembered.

Brunhilda floated. But the mob found out why just as she was about to be burned at the stake. "Look!" someone yelled. "She has a wooden leg! No wonder she floats! Free her!" She was cut loose. Gratefully, she gave everyone in the mob a 10-percent discount on her fall line of ekes.

For Brunhilda, life was good, life was full again. Then, two days later, she was killed by an arrow fired as a neighbor was cleaning his crossbow. "I didn't think it was loaded," he testified.

—Sir Theo Nychols was a knight serving King Arthur. Well, let's be honest—Theo was head waiter at the Round Table. He created our family coat of arms: a gratuity rampant on a field of Formica with the credo *Circum omnia naso* ("I recommend the pepper steak").

—Jasper Nichols was a door-to-door salesman who, in March of 1836, knocked on the wrong door and found himself inside the Alamo, surrounded by four thousand loitering Mexican soldiers.

Men learn things about themselves in time of war, and so it was with Jasper. He learned that he could not bear to look into the jaws of death. Or even into the gums of discomfort. In vain he tried to convince Col. Travis that he was classified 5F: "In the event of war, I become a Swiss citizen."

—Dublin investor Paddy "Spud" O'Nichols, seeking to profit from Ireland's huge potato industry, cornered the market in sour cream in 1845. But then came the Great Potato Famine of 1846. Paddy was ruined. He was soon a laughingstock. When he walked down the street, children snickered and dogs growled. When he walked back *up* the street, children growled and dogs snickered.

Paddy was down but not out. Soon he met the unsuspecting O'Shaunessy family. He persuaded them to give him their life savings for his sour cream. He told them that it was Elmer's glue and that there would always be things that needed to be stuck to other things. Soon it was the O'Shaunessys who were ruined.

Do you think that Paddy had learned his lesson? Hah! In the midst of the potato famine, he took the O'Shaunessys' life savings and cornered the market in Baco-Bits.

—Vincent van Nichols was a minor artist whose career roughly paralleled that of the great master—you guessed it—Toulouse-Lautrec. Like Toulouse-Lautrec, van Nichols immortalized dance-hall girls on canvas.

Once a lovely dancer sat for a portrait by him. Her name, coincidentally, was Toots O'Shaunessy. But when he showed the painting to her, she was mortified. He had portrayed her as having stringy hair, a harelip, stubble, three moles (one for each nose), and a figure like a sack of unabridged dictionaries. She demanded an explanation. Van Nichols shrugged and said, "You moved."

The hapless dancer never got over the shock, and forever after she would boogie when she was supposed to woogie.

Yes, as I said earlier, no way. I want no family-heritage book in *my* house, begging to be thumbed through by anyone who happens to drop in.

Especially when a family of O'Shaunessys is living next door.

For 10 years, letter perfect

Poor guy. He was just trying to get in the last word.

Ten years later, he's still trying.

Recently, my friend John "Scuzzy" Forsyth and I realized that we have been writing each other a letter a week for ten years now. From each of us, that's more than five hundred letters, more than a million words, more than $90 in postage. Each of us is the first to admit that the other ain't worth it.

Yet on we write.

We met years ago after our respective journalism professors had abandoned us on the doorstep of the *Star-Telegram* newsroom. The accompanying notes had read, "Chain him to an unabridged dictionary and keep him away from sharp objects."

Then, ten years ago, Scuzzy moved on to the *Tulsa World*. I stayed here, filing away at my chain. From Tulsa, he dropped me a short note just to say hi, I made it, this place sure is strange. Regards, Scuzzy.

I mailed a reply. Well, he hadn't counted on that. He mailed back a short note, thinking that this surely would be the end of it.

Only recently did I learn this—that he had wanted only to get in the last word. I was hurt. I wrote and told him so.

Which oughta be good for another ten years or so.

Sometimes, when Scuzzy and I visit in person, we use the occasion to hand deliver the next letters. And once in a while, if Scuzzy is in Fort Worth but pressed for time, he'll drive by my house, pausing just long enough to lob a letter into my mailbox.

This is not normal, other friends have told us. But like many people who make a living by forcing innocent words to do their bidding, we just enjoy talking by typewriter.

And, now, in the eighties, by word-processor. We resort to the pen only when on the road. We have written from trains and planes. From most of the states and several foreign lands, stretching from Vancouver to Vienna. In 1982, passing through Calais, France, I checked General Delivery at the post office. There was a letter from Scuzzy.

He was still trying to get in the last word.

Our letters reveal that we, like most people, spend half our time wishing *for* change, half our time wishing *against* change. We talk about journalism. We try to figure out women. We solve the world's problems. We try to figure out women. We swap yarns. If there is any room left over, we try to figure out women.

Letters outraged and letter outrageous. Letters profound, letters profane. Letters so heavy with sadness that they surely caused the mail carrier to list to one side. Letters so buoyant with euphoria that they surely caused the mail carrier to fairly float along the sidewalk.

Therapy at 22 cents a session.

From Tulsa, Scuzzy moved on to work at other dailies. He added "author" and "publisher" to his resume. He continued to live life. A series of our exchanges might include tidbits such as:

He: This week I had a date with Carolyn.

Me: This week I started reading *All About Aphids.*

He: This week I had a date with Sherry.

Me: This week I finished *All About Aphids.*

He: This week I had a date with Linda.

Me: This week I started rereading *All About Aphids.*

(Oh, sure, I envy ol' Scuzz his full, eh, social life. But on the other hand, of the two of us, which one knows all about aphids?)

Picking at random a stack of his letters, I find other sides of this "phenom de plume."

He tells of job satisfaction:

"Did I tell you about the guy that the (Austin) *American-Statesman* hired who went out for lunch and never came back *on his first day!?* I've considered it myself. Consider it every day, except that I don't get a lunch break."

And metropolitan life:

"The big topic in Mentone (pop. 50) now is Newt Keen getting shot. Happened only five or six years ago. A prowler shot him in the mouth. Newt told me that gettin' shot didn't bother him as much as the prowlers drinking all his beer."

He offers medical reports:

"Bad news from the doctor. He said I'm in perfect health. 'No, this can't be, Doc. Tell me my heart is chicken-fried, find some cream gravy in my aorta, some pudding in my pancreas! I can't feel this poorly and be well.'"

Because I am a couple of years older then Scuzzy, I'll probably be the first to go, destined to be found someday slumped over my orthopedic typewriter. I know old Scuzz will attend the funeral. He'll shuffle into the mortuary, approach the visitors book and with palsied hand sign it: "Dear Nichols: How are things with you? Well, I don't have much to report this time around except . . . *last tag!*—Regards, Scuzzy."

"Finally!" he'll cackle triumphantly. "I got in the last word!"

(Until I drop him a note with an Eternity postmark: "Hi, I made it, this place sure is hot, wish you were here. Regards, Nichols.")

Reason doth spring a leak

Spring, the sweet spring, is the year's pleasant king;
Then blooms each thing, then maids dance in a ring,
Cold doth not sting, the pretty birds do sing:
Cuckoo, jug-jug, pu-we, to-witta-woo!

Thomas Nashe of England committed that bit of poetry in the 1500s, causing all of Europe to vote to hold the Renaissance in Italy next time.

But spring will do that to you.

Spring will cause people to act as if they have what clinical psychologists define technically as "bait for brains." At this time of year people simply are no longer responsible for their actions. I know: I am probably less responsible than any two people I know. On the first day of spring I am seized with a sudden urge to walk in the rain, to dig in the dirt, to talk to strangers, although I never accept candy from them.

I will go lie on a hillside and stare up at the sky, picking out shapes among the fluffy, fanciful clouds. ". . . And look at that one — doesn't it look like a tea cup? No, *there* — to the right of the ducky and to the left of the bunny. Yeah, that's it. And *that* one there — it looks like a dope addict mugging a nun as thirty-four passers-by refuse to get involved."

I guess I've been reading the newspapers too much.

My glands, at times sluggish in winter, jump to their feet on the first day of spring, do some quick jumping jacks and shout, "OK, gang, let's all go over to the TCU campus and watch for the first pair of shorts of spring."

From that point on, I will fall in love with any woman located roughly east or west of the prime meridian.

And, yes, at this time of year people do begin to think in verse, to write letters in verse, to make out grocery lists in verse, to write holdup notes in verse:

> *I'm withdrawing some dough*
> *With a gun, as you see,*
> *And I ain't gonna show*
> *Three forms of ID.*
> *To-witta-woo!*

Spring will do that to you.

In spring people take renewed interest in nature's many miracles: a leafy tree, a delicate flower, a parking space downtown. In short, people take notice of the beauty about them. And, as Keats said: "A thing of beauty is a joy forever. Unless you're the one who has to dust it every day."

Ah, to rise up early in the morn, go out to the front lawn and feel the giddy sensation of good green grass beneath your bare feet! Cool, soft and . . . *yeeech!*

It appears that your neighbor's dog did rise up earlier in the morn than you did.

In spring, even great big burly men with black hairy beards and hearts to match sprout smiles that have no visible means of support. Young and old alike begin to daydream, to stare out a window and sigh, their eyes glazed like a doughnut. Suddenly they have the attention span of moss.

People begin to call in sick. And if they do go in to the office, they find excuses to get back outside. Personally, I sneak over to a phone at a vacant desk, dial up my boss, disguise my voice and make a phony bomb threat, causing the entire building to be evacuated so that everyone can go outside. But first, of course, I divert suspicion from myself.

"Hello? First, let me say that I am definitely *not* Mike Nichols. I don't even know him. And second,

A bomb I did hide
In a nook oh, so dark,
So send us outside
To play in the park.

Oh, and one more thing."

"Yeah, Nichols?"

"To-witta-woo!"

Spring will do that to you.

Helter-swelter:
The heat is on

Let's take a survey. All of you who are tired of the heat, raise your hand.

Ah, I see by the needle marks on some upstretched arms that some of you have been shooting ice-cold Lipton directly into a vein. Face it: Each summer you get hooked on the stuff. You have a tea bag on your back.

Yes, we are being held hostage by another Texas summer. Texas summers are Mother Nature's way of showing us that although she is kind and gentle most of the year, in August she is a vicious little tramp.

Here's a fun way to spend a hot summer day. Go down to the K-Mart and see fat people in shorts. As far as the eye can see, a sea of cellulite. Fat people in shorts is Mother Nature's way of making the rest of us wish that we were blind.

But it's natural that folks wear as little clothing as the law allows during the summer. Ironically, our founding fathers originally had drafted an Eleventh Amendment that guaranteed everyone the right to strip down in the summer. Then ye olde Martha Washington showed up at the Constitutional Convention ye olde buck nekkid. One day later, the amendment was repealed. Two days later, Ben Franklin invented the muumuu.

Nowadays, we keep cool by worshipping the air-conditioner. We huddle around it, coo to it, pamper it, bring it offerings, even as it giggles quietly to itself and sucks all the electricity out of the tri-state area. When the compressor kicks in, the lights dim just like they did the day that Killer Putski got the chair. In a panic, we rush to the air-conditioner and start feeding it dollar bills.

But if your home has little or no air-conditioning, in August you suffer mightily. Your home becomes the Right Guard Proving Grounds. You hold impromptu races for beads of sweat as they trickle down your leg. You play Connect the Dots with your prickly heat. You sneak into closets with a straw and suck the cool air out of dark corners. As a last resort, you press your body against cool surfaces, such as tile floors. You lie belly-down in the kitchen and get real still. It looks like nap time at the alligator pond.

Or maybe you find excuses to go to the mall, where it's cool. Soon you are arrested for wading in the Orange Julius machine.

Or you spend a lot of time in cool supermarkets. Perhaps too much time: In the summer, children often are conceived there, in the frozen food section.

"Where did I come from, Mommy?"

"The A&P, dear, between the fish sticks and the Tater Tots."

But some folks, of course, thrive on heat. They worship the sun. In backyards and on rooftops across Texas the beautiful people disrobe and bake their skins. Their only relief from the heat comes when the crews of traffic helicopters hover over-head, lean out the window and drool on them.

Of course, sun worshippers pay for their bone-deep tans. Their skin becomes as dry and wrinkled and cracked as parchment. Soon archaeologists come from all around to read their bodies like the Dead Sea Scrolls.

"Hmmm. Professor Perkins, this verse on the arm seems to end abruptly."

"Not to worry, Professor Davis. It continues down here on the back of the leg. But, say, *this* is odd—I'm running across bits of breaded fish and frozen potato!" In the summer, black-marketeers from the Yukon try to get rich off Texans' frantic need to cool off. Every day at the border, U.S. Customs agents search smugglers and find Baggies of cold air strapped to the inside of their legs.

Eventually, the heat begins to get to people. They become short-tempered. Example: When George Washington told Martha to for God's sake please put some clothes on, she nailed his wooden teeth to the floor.

Yes, summer is a bummer. But be of good cheer: In just a few weeks, the first freeze of winter will be here. No more heat and sweat. Just a nose that runs and pipes that won't.

Oh, and put your arm down now. Your deodorant walked out on you last week.

Fall (as in asleep, apart and behind)

There are so many things that I need to be doing these days. But I just can't be bothered right now. It's fall.

My old truck needs a tune-up, and the roof of the house needs to be patched. Well, I guess I can always walk anywhere I need to go, and if it rains, I can sleep outside, where it's drier.

Because I just can't be bothered right now. It's fall.

I see that the front page is full of bad news: drugs, inflation, disease. The world is at an all-time low: South African whites are shooting South African blacks, Iran is bombing Iraq, and, for all I know, by now the Amish and the Quakers are sticking their tongues out at each other.

But I just can't be bothered right now. It's fall.

And I read recently that even as we speak our bodies are speeding east at 14 miles a minute as the Earth rotates. We are also going 18.5 miles a second as the Earth revolves around the sun. Plus, the whole shebang is speeding through space at 12 miles a second. In one day our bodies travel 2,655,360 miles. Some day soon I plan to turn in a travel voucher for all that and try to get this newspaper to pay me its usual 21 cents a mile.

But I just can't be bothered right now. It's fall.

Ah, fall. Surely the world was created during six days at this time of the year.

Adam: "What a gorgeous day, Eve! Hey, let's drive up into New England this weekend and see the fall foliage. Maybe we can stay at that cozy little inn in Vermont where we stayed last year."

Eve: "But let's not take Cain with us this time, Adam. Last time we were there, it came to pass that Cain rose up and slew the bellhop, and you had to leave an enormous tip."

Spring and fall are the carrot on the stick of the seasons.

Mother Nature wisely arranges them as our reward for having endured winter and summer.

Summer and winter are mean seasons. Big bad bullies with long black beards and a scar across one cheek who saunter in, pound on the table and growl, "I'm summer, and you're taking orders from *me* now. Let's see you *sweat* . . . You call *that* sweat? Come on: Faster! *Faster!*"

By August your heat rash has spread so far that Vice President Bush has to fly over it in a helicopter, frown for the press and promise you immediate disaster relief. Fire fighters then are airdropped in to spread calamine lotion on your thighs.

But fall is inspiring. Football, Halloween, sweaters. Fall is especially inspiring to writers. It makes us drag out our figures of speech by their ears and trot them across the stage of the printed page.

"Ready now, all you metaphors? Stand up straight and speak clearly."

— Fall is the Svengali of seasons. It waves its wand and pulls pumpkin pies and turkeys out of ovens. Using no wires, it levitates our lowest moods. Using no mirrors, it makes our cares vanish and saws our air-conditioning bills in half.

— The day dawned gray and windless, as if the sky intended to hold its breath until it turned blue.

— The leaves begin to drift to earth — autumn's circulars, advertising the colors of the new fall fashions, showing what all the best-dressed trees will be wearing this season.

— A restless rain drums its . . . its . . . A restless rain drums its . . .

(Off-stage prompt: "Fingers on the roof tops!")

Oh, yeah: A restless rain drums its fingers on the roof tops.

— It was a stained-glass sunset, with shards and slivers of pink and gold.

— The harvest moon rose, a bright copper penny minted but once a year.

— Needle-nosed hummingbirds are flying south, taking stitches in a blue-denim sky.

— The leaves, wearing their Josephean coats of many colors, laugh softly as a breeze tickles their funny bones.

— The clouds are chubby-cheeked, like cherubs — great billowing Botticellis in the vaulted gallery of the sky.

I know I really should apologize for all that. But I just can't be bothered right now. It's fall.

Fall also makes folks want to rise up early in the morn and go for a brisk tramp in the woods. (We writers have to use the noun "tramp" in this context or else get a nasty letter from the Writers Guild.)

And from chimney tops everywhere wafts the crisp, invigorating smell of wood smoke. (We writers also have to use the verb "waft" there or else people from the Writers Guild will come and tramp on us.)

"Hey, look, Mr. Jones! That crisp, invigorating smell of wafting wood smoke: Your house is on fire!"

"So what? I just can't be bothered right now, son. It's fall."

Well, enough about this wonderful time of year. I really should get back to work. Gotta earn a living to keep the wolf from the door. Or at least out of the living room—he always forgets to wipe his feet.

But I just can't be bothered right now.

After all—you guessed it—it's fall.

In cold blood:
Winter on trial

It's time again for headlines such as these: "Cold cripples East," "Snow snarls traffic," "Nun slips on ice, breaks her vows."

Look at those verbs: *cripples, snarls, slips, breaks.* Yes, we are again caught in a cold-blooded crime wave perpetrated by the Godfather of seasons: Old Man Winter.

When you get your heating bill each January, do you want to move to Tahiti and take over payments on Gauguin's little grass shack? Does cold, gray weather depress you so much that you once tried to impale yourself on Willard Scott's pointer? Then you, too, are a victim of winter. If only we could put winter on trial for such crimes. [Fade to a state courtroom. Shhhh! . . .]

Bailiff: "The people of Texas versus Old Man Winter, alias Jack Frost."

Judge: "O.M. Winter, you are charged with 1,081 violations of statute 432, section 17, subparagraph 4, row 11, seat 5: being a pain. How do you plead?"

Winter (looking rather like Marlon Brando with icicles): "Not guilty."

Prosecution: "The state will prove that the accused is a habitual criminal who, on or about December 21 to March 20 each year, causes 131 bones to be broken in falls, 879 fenders to be dented and 71 couples to divorce over the setting on the electric blanket.

"Call W.W. Potts to the witness stand. . . . Mr. Potts, tell us in your own words what the defendant did to you."

Potts: "I was driving on icy streets when my car skidded like a four-door hockey puck and crashed into a Sears store. It took the rescue squad two hours to hack me out of Women's Lingerie."

"Step down. Call R. Loomis to the stand."

Loomis: "I was fixing a busted water pipe. The wrench slipped, causing me to skin four of my favorite knuckles. I turned to my wife and said, 'Pshaw, M'dear (or words to that effect). Methinks Winter has struck again. Hand me a tourniquet please.' "

Winter: "It's a lie! I was out of town that weekend!"

Judge: "Silence! Another outburst like that and you'll be held in contempt. Say, it's getting nippy in here. Bailiff, turn up the heat."

Then Alma Tidwell testifies. In 1957 she bundled up her son so well to go out to play in the snow that when she unbundled him that night, no little boy was ever found—just two coats, some thermal underwear, three sweaters, two mufflers, four mittens, earmuffs, and a ski mask used in a liquor-store holdup.

Judge: "B-b-bailiff, get s-s-some more heat in h-h-h-here!"

The defense then calls witnesses on behalf of Old Man Winter.

Mort Nubbish: "I'm a plumber, and I think Winter is a

great guy. Busted pipes put my kids in private school and a new Caddy in my driveway. Hey, when do I get paid, anyway? I get $40 an hour as a character witness."

Roy Crunk: "I run a gas station. Winter means business for me: stalled cars, dead batteries, antifreeze. Yes sir, I think the defendant is a prince."

(Crunk is dismissed to jump-start the judge's pacemaker. Crunk charges $20, but he also wipes the judge's glasses.)

Winter himself then takes the stand: "Nobody understands me. My ma—Mudder Nature—had four boys. Spring and Fall, they're wimps. And me, I got a bad temper. But I can't help how I am! I just can't!"

As Winter rants, snow begins to fall from the ceiling. Soon members of the jury are huddling together for warmth. As they retire to deliberate, several have become engaged. They quickly return with a verdict.

Judge: "Old Man W-w-w-winter, you have been found (sniffle) guilty. This court s-s-sentences you to be deported (achoo) on the first day of spring."

Winter (shouting): "OK for youse guys for now. But just wait 'til June, when my *other* brudder, Summer, gets here. When you're so sweaty that you gotta carry a body squeegee, you'll wish I wuz back. It's a bum rap, I tell ya! Hey, somebody get me Melvin Belli! *He* can have me back on the streets by the end of autumn."

The Arts

Novel is groan with the wind

"Let me go! Let me *go!*" Autumn hissed breathlessly, half-hoping that Trey would do no such thing. There on the marble staircase, Trey held her roughly, ripping her bodice.

Then he silenced her protests by covering her mouth with his.

(Yup, you guessed it: I have decided to cash in on the popularity of romance novels. You know the genre. On the cover there's usually some Southern belle in an off-the-shoulder blouse who is squirming in the embrace of a dashing young man named Branden or Grant. Bosoms heave. Lips part. Royalties soar. Yes, sir, that's for *me!* So let's go back to my first effort—a sizzling epic of greed and lust titled *Mortgaged Hickeys.*)

Autumn yielded to Trey's kiss, her auburn tresses cascading down, hiding the pounding of her hostage heart. Just how much do I really know about this Trey Talmadge, she thought. First, he has a terrible overbite. Second, he is standing on my foot. Third, he is president of First National TransMercantile InterDixie AntebellumCorp Bankshares, the bank that is threatening to foreclose on my plantation.

She loved the old plantation and would do what she must to keep it. Her father, the Colonel, had won it playing bingo at the Jeff Davis American Legion hall. At one time it grew hundreds of acres of cotton. But it had changed with the times: Now it grew hundreds of acres of polyester.

So Autumn had to listen when Trey offered to delay foreclosure. "What will it cost me?" Autumn said icily, with perhaps more defiance in her voice than she felt. "Autumn, my blossom," he said in his easy drawl, caressing her with his eyes, "we'll work something out . . ."

His ellipsis was lewd.

Her cheeks flamed. Her nostrils flared. Suddenly Autumn stopped, searching her mind: Had she forgotten any clichés? Oh, yeah: Her eyes flashed.

"You know, you're beautiful when you're in debt," Trey said, smiling a knowing smile.

The two of them then drove down to Trey's bank and signed the necessary papers delaying foreclosure. Trey then gave her a complimentary calendar and ripped her bodice.

Headstrong, beautiful Autumn McKenna had been educated back east at an exclusive women's college, where she majored in swooning, with a minor in thank-you notes. She had even been married once. And she had been faithful to her husband. On at least three occasions. But now she was through being used by men. From now on, *she* would do the using.

And she had begun with Buck, her foreman. Buck would come to her late in the night, his voice thick with desire and a chaw of Red Man. Buck was crude and rough-hewn: He didn't know a chardonnay from a Charolais. Which is why he once tried to pull the cork from a bull and spent several weeks in traction. But he was virile and obedient. He stood 6-foot-6 in his stocking feet. Oddly, he stood 6-foot-7 in *her* stocking feet, but that's another story (*He-Men in Hanes,* $3.95, Bantam).

Autumn trembled as she felt the gloom of night creep over her. It was a sultry night. The air was sultry. The trees were sultry. The linoleum was sultry. She drank a glass of water. It was sultry.

She desperately wanted so much from life: love, happiness, a really comfortable pair of mid-heel pumps. And she knew that she could have it all someday, if she'd just watch the Kinney sales.

But then, without warning, tragedy stepped out of the shadows. Not thinking, Autumn had arranged simultaneous trysts with Buck *and* Trey. Both men showed up in Autumn's boudoir at the same time. They glared at each other.

"Oh, yeah?" sputtered the inarticulate Buck. Trey, the eloquent sophisticate, quickly put Buck in his place: "Yeah!"

Men are such children, Autumn thought as the two suitors began to circle each other, hate writ large upon their hard faces. But she knew how to handle men. Among Autumn's myriad charms was The Pout. She always won the blue ribbon at the annual All-South Invitational Pout-Off. Hers was a pout that made men want to poke their eyes out just so they could read her lips in Braille.

So now she began to pout. Just a little one at first. Still Buck and Trey circled. She shifted into hyperpout. But the two men would not be denied their primitive rite.

"Be careful, boys, don't break the étagère," she pleaded before swooning. Banker and hired hand fought with the only weapons they knew. When Autumn came to, Trey and Buck lay dead, Trey fatally horse-whipped, Buck choked to death with a *"next window, please"* sign.

Autumn felt hot tears well up in her smoldering eyes as she realized that this turn of events left her without an escort to the fall cotillion.

Later—it seemed years Autumn was dimly aware of strangers in her room. They were four ambulance attendants, come to carry away the two bodies. Regaining her composure, she followed them, sweeping down the marble staircase as only she could.

Suddenly, just as the two stretchers reached the yawning front door of the mansion, one of the ambulance attendants stooped, walked deferentially back to Autumn and ripped her bodice.

Then, with eyes that bespoke a sad gratitude, Autumn McKenna turned and swept back up the marble staircase.

You just can't beat the beat

Of all the things that I am a pushover for (including cats, base-ball and any woman who doesn't pour Drano down my shorts), I am perhaps a pushover most of all for music.

Music, methinks, is the thing that humanity makes best. Better than it makes love, war or excuses. Music convinces me that there are geniuses among us, that there is a soul.

Darwin believed that the art of music was developed by our half-human ancestors ("I give this song an eight, Ogg—like I dig the beat, man, but it's hard to evolve to"). In fact, Darwin believed that our earliest ancestors developed the art of music before they developed the art of speech.

(Sometimes I wish that they had stopped while we were still ahead.)

He said we continue to be influenced by music because it stirs the mud of our "racial memory" with long-forgotten asso-ciations of primordial life—when each day dawned fraught with fear, when the individual strove against great odds to sur-vive amid ignorance and intimidation only to be mauled or stabbed in the back. It was, in fact, much like the modern office.

Today, music hath soothing charms. Armed with two speak-ers and a volume-control knob, we are invincible. Come on, world, do your darnedest!

What? You say someone just parked their car on one of my favorite feet? So what? I have Billy Joel on the radio.

What? You say I gave my sweepstakes ticket to my neighbor, and he just won his choice of any three NATO countries? So what? I have Willie on the tape deck.

What? You say my wife just left me for her secret lover and said they'd write when they finish redecorating France, England and Spain? So what? I have Ray Charles on the turntable.

I like most all music. Mine is a promiscuous ear: I will leave hard rock for "Rock of Ages," leave "Rock of Ages" for Rachmaninoff, leave Rachmaninoff for Roy Acuff and leave them all to go back to hard rock.

And once, in a tuba-induced frenzy, I accepted a polka as my personal savior.

Sometimes, we must hear music with our entire body, every organ an ear. At such times, unless restrained, I will break into a clumsy, stiff-legged two-step that archaeologists have carbon-dated and labeled the Karloff Shuffle.

It is not pretty.

Music is less fattening than food, less destructive than drugs. Yet so powerful and seductive is its influence that someday we may be tested for its use in the workplace.

Employer: "Blatherskite, your urine test shows that you have listened to Bach within the last forty-eight hours."

Employee: "Yeah, boss? Well, you know that test isn't 100 percent accurate. I know a guy who once tested positive for Billy Idol when all he had done was listen to a little oregano."

And music is the cheapest therapy on earth. I think that psychologists could place a phonograph in their chair and tip-toe out to the park while the client on the sofa just relaxed and listened to Segovia or Springsteen.

Many's the time that I've been depressed, weighed down by the problems, both petty and profound, of life as we know it, by the dark, ugly side of this high-tension, dangerous game of humor.

At such times I see the world on the brink, swaying uneasily between Plato and Pluto, between Steppenwolf and Steppenfetchit, dancing to an apocalypso beat. Crime is up, wages are down, and I don't know where my next punchline is coming from.

Things look hopeless.

But on the other hand, have you heard the new Huey Lewis album?

Yes, I believe that musicians are the true healers of our time.

Thank goodness they still make house calls.

Help cure the critically artistic

Kind and generous reader, have I ever asked you for money?

Well, sure, there was the time my typewriter burned to the ground. And, yes, there was that time a blackmailer threatened to go to the tabloids with those doctored photos of me, some cole slaw and the Radio City Rockettes.

But this is different. I'm asking you to open your hearts and checkbooks not for me but for crazy artists.

Because a study published in the April issue of *Psychology Today* has reinforced the connection between creativity and madness. Yes, it seems that creativity often separates the insane from the sane, the demented from the merely mented. The fifteen-year study focused on thirty members of the prestigious University of Iowa Writer's Workshop and found that 43 percent suffered manic-depression, compared with only 10 percent of a comparison group.

"Manic-depression may facilitate access, in creative individuals, to a richness and intensity of experience that is not shared by the rest of us," the study concluded.

So I'm establishing a fund to help writers and other crazy artists. No money will go to me (although I may incur certain operating costs). Won't you help find a cure for the heartbreak of writer's block? Won't you help alleviate the mental suffering of a director who can't decide whether to film *Hamlet* or *Porky's XIX: Teddy Fails His Wassermann?*

Yes, artists are not like normal people. Where your Vincent Van Gogh would cut off his ear for the girl he loved, you—a normal person—at most would nick your chin while shaving and send the girl a love letter written in styptic pencil. Where you—a normal person—would look at an ordinary inner-city street scene and see a certain ordered calm, a writer would see abject misery, dark intrigue, $1.2 million in paperback sales and a guest appearance on Johnny Carson.

Manic-depression in artists goes way back, of course. When Euripides — an early Greek poet whose family was too poor to give him a first name — found that "beauty" did not rhyme with "festering," he pouted for days. Finally he gave up poetry and when last seen was selling major appliances at Sears.

Beethoven would have fits during which he was convinced that his piano was following him. Oddly enough, he was right. Beethoven had a first name — Ludwig — but hated it and once offered it to Euripides. But Euripides had nothing to offer Beethoven in return except 20 percent off a Kenmore washer.

Beethoven's now-classic reply was: "Huh? Could you speak up?"

Rodin was inspired to create *The Kiss* — his sensuous sculpture of two naked lovers kissing — after witnessing a train wreck. The sight of mildew had the same effect on him. So did gravy stains. And fence posts. And clams. In fact, *everything* that Rodin saw reminded him of two naked lovers kissing. Except two naked lovers kissing, which reminded him of Pittsburgh.

Or take James Joyce. A very, very great writer. And thus very, very crazy. If some night you had James Joyce over to the house (this would be back when he was alive, of course), why, there's no telling what shenanigans he might pull. He might track mud on the ceiling. He might go to your sock drawer and paw through your argyles, cooing, "And how are all my little children tonight?" He might roll his eyes and demand: "Bring me cottage cheese, normal person. I want to gargle."

And you'd have to humor him. If you upset him, he might go write a sequel to *Ulysses*.

So dig deep, generous reader. Remember that all money, minus operating costs, will go to help wipe out creativity in our lifetime. Send your contributions to this address:

Fund for Crazy Artists
c/o Me
A Shoebox at the Back of My Closet
Third Villa on the Left
The South of France

I thank you. Euripides thanks you. And my secretary, Miss Bridgit "Operating Costs" Lamour, thanks you.

All washed up
as an artist

Yes, it was ugly. But was it art?

I contend that it was, and it was to be my key to fame and fortune. Soon I'd be dining on caviar and truffles. Soon I'd be driving a new Jaguar, its radiator filled with Perrier.

But then tragedy struck. Not once, but twice.

My rise and fall began thusly. Recently a public-relations agent for Clorox came to this office. I seek public relations, said she to me. Clorox, it seemed, was test-marketing ACT. ACT is a revolutionary laundry detergent. Clorox's research scientists had worked months and spared no expense in determining that ACT would be spelled in capital letters.

I think that she even stood on tiptoes when she spoke the very word.

Then she unpacked a white cloth and several jars of foodstuffs — jelly, mustard and their ilk. A picnic, perchance? Would we spread a feast in the sylvan glade of the newsroom and nibble contentedly ("Have some more ilk, m'dear?") as we watch the sun set over the parking garage?

But, no. It was not to be. She merely invited me to express myself. So I expressed. Upon the white cloth I squirted mustard and ketchup. With my fingers I brushed on grape jelly and spaghetti sauce. I splattered ink and orange marmalade and, yes, Gerber baby food.

If Clorox wanted to conduct a smear campaign, they had come to the right boy.

Soon the formerly white cloth was a subtle shade of yeech. When some of my colleagues did gaze upon it, lo, they did almost gag. That's when I realized the magnitude of what I had done.

I had committed art.

But not just any art. *Abstract* art. And that's the best kind. Because abstract art is culture's Rorschach test. All things to all people. Some see in it the soul laid bare. Others see in it the summit of humanity's esthetic sense. I saw in it a penthouse with hot and cold running maids.

All I had to do was frame it and title it. A new career! I was already imagining the rave reviews of art critics.

"Cultural circles are indeed a-spin over the unveiling of newcomer Mike Nichols's *Sunrise on Strained Peas.* Already he is being heralded as the art world's Pablum Picasso. Cyril Brokas of the Museum of Modern Art was moved to say: 'It sings! It soars! Its subtle use of condiments is reminiscent of Jackson Pollock's *Woman With Horseradish.*'

"Nichols's bold interplay of bright colors and restrained finger strokes is most evident in the teasing manner in which the grape jelly's purple is juxtaposed against the mustard's yellow, which experts have interpreted as either the sun or jaundice. But no one can doubt the symbolism rampant in the foreground: The Ragu is technology, the marmalade is Old World values, and the ketchup speaks volumes about man's inhumanity to tomatoes.

"Bertram Bisbee of *Brush and Gush* magazine said: 'Viewing *Sunrise on Strained Peas,* I saw startling new spatial relations and symmetries, a subtle tension between splash and splotch. I wept. It is angry yet calm. It is daring yet timid. It is absurd yet inane.'

"The painting's overall effect is frenetic: a hitherness that borders on a thitherness and that, in time, may achieve a yonness.

"For this first painting, Nichols's medium was a wild and unsettling mixture of incompatible and spicy foodstuffs on handkerchief. It is hoped that the medium of his followup painting will be antacids on napkin."

But then the Clorox PR agent broke in upon my reverie. Now, said she, we will cut the cloth in half. Egad, my masterpiece rent asunder! She told me that I would keep one half—as a control sample—and that she would spirit away the other half and wash it in ACT. She departed, saying she would return just one day hence to show me that ACT had removed all the stains.

I proudly displayed the remaining half of the cloth on my desk. In a few hours, my colleagues were grumbling about the sight and smell of it.

Sour grapes, chided I.

Yeah, they agreed, and the marmalade isn't too fresh, either.

Sure enough, the next day the PR agent brought back the other half of the cloth, washed woefully devoid of the stains that I had worked so hard to elevate to art.

Some patron of the arts *you* are, Clorox.

I consoled myself with the fact that I still had *my* half. Still enough to set the art world on its pierced ear. But fate was not done with me. During the night the cleaning lady came by my desk, saw my masterpiece and threw it in the trash!

Oh, well, to an abstract artist, I guess that's the supreme compliment.

Hamming it up in Peking "Pork"

Will Ting Lo ever find the father of her child? Will Chung Woo ever come out of his coma? Will Wong Yin ever get the handball concession at the Great Wall? Will I ever get to the point of this column?

During a recent visit to Peking, I was sitting in my hotel room one night, watching TV. Suddenly I realized that what I was watching was a soap opera, Communist Chinese style. Granted, the dialog was in Mandarin, but the program still had the unmistakable marks of a soap: four people a-betraying, three people a-dying, two people a-pregnant and a partridge in a bamboo tree.

Here, as near as this Westerner could make out, was the plot of *As the Sweet and Sour Pork Turns.*

Poor Ting Lo (sustained close-up of Ting Lo). Poor, *poor* Ting Lo. She is going to have a baby. She does not know who the father is. Her sister, Ting Hai, is also going to have a baby.

She does not know who the mother is. In school, Ting Hai earned very poor marks in biology.

Ting Hai cries. She cries as she pedals her bicycle through the crowded streets of Peking. She cries until her bicycle bell begins to rust (close-up of bell). The bell used to go "jingaling, jingaling." Now it goes "jingaling, jingar-r-r-g-g-ghhphhht." Ting Hai may have been lousy at biology, but she is an accomplished crier, having majored in sobbing with a minor in chin-trembling.

Meanwhile, Chung Woo, whom we also met in the first paragraph but who was later disgraced and forced to go live in an unfurnished footnote, has torn a hangnail while opening a fortune cookie and slipped into a coma. Doctors call in a specialist—old Wing Fat, the Chinese mystic. As Chung Woo's family (close-up of family) watches, Wing Fat (close-up of Wing Fat) reads the entrails of a chicken (close-up of entrails—yeeech). Wing Fat looks up and declares the chicken to be one sick bird.

The scene shifts. The newlyweds, Zhao and Chao Liu, wish to have a baby. But they are told by the local party official: "China needs no more tiny Chinese persons. China already has one billion people, most of whom are always ahead of me in the express line. You must obtain permission of the party to have a child. This takes time. It takes three months to get permission to have sex, six months to get permission to enjoy it.

"My advice is this: Go stand in a cold shower for three months."

Zhao replies: "But it takes twelve months to get permission to take a shower."

Meanwhile, Wong Yin is trying to get the handball concession at the Great Wall. Wong Yin speaks: "Think of it— handball rentals, shoe and glove sales, headbands, Gator-Ade. If business is good, we'll have to open branch Great Walls in malls and suburbs."

Wong Yin is not an attractive man. At a distance, he looks like a small serving of stir-fried prawns. Up close, he looks like a large serving of stir-fried prawns.

Meanwhile, the peasant Lee Wang has stolen a priceless Ming vase. He is willing to sell it to an unscrupulous collector for 100 yuan ($26 American). One hundred yuan is a year's earnings for Lee Wang. It would buy two oxen. Or ten thousand sticks of gum. Lee prefers the gum. You can't blow bubbles with an ox.

Lee Wang speaks: "I have done wrong. But I am poor. I am so poor I can't pay attention. It is an old joke, but it's all I can afford until the rice harvest is in."

Lee Wang has more worries: "My daughter, Tai, has taken on decadent Western ways. She listens to rock music. She wears blue jeans. She comes home with Ronald McDonald on her breath."

The episode closes with a timely thought by Confucius: "The lotus blossom never dances with the spit sink."

No one knows what he meant.

Will Ting Lo find the father of her child? How about Chung Woo and his hangnail? Will Wong Yin open his first Great Walls R Us?

Tune in tomorrow, comrades.

Or else.

How about "a jot of sleepless writers"?

Just as drug addicts have a monkey on their back, just as junk-food junkies have a potato chip on their shoulder, we in the writing business have a language on our brains.

We are word junkies.

Of late, my particular craving has taken a piteous form—I make up collective nouns.

I started out on the soft stuff. I still remember the first time someone came up to me—it was at a party—and whispered, "Psst. Hey, buddy, want 'a brace of orthodontists'? Or how about 'a fleet of runners'?"

Why not, I asked myself, giggling as I accepted the phrases with a vague thrill of wickedness. Weeks later, I still told myself that I could stop any time I wanted. But then I got on the harder stuff. Now I lie awake at night, tossing and turning, churning out collective nouns.

An addition of math teachers.

A brood of sulkers, a body of anatomists, a bale of bondsmen, a block of tacklers, a baker's dozen of triskaidecaphobics (try to say *that* thirteen times real fast!).

A clique of safecrackers, a claque of domino players, a collection of duns, a corps of apples, a cast of skiers, a clutch of hot-rodders, a camp of effeminates, a caucus of crows, a convoy of prisoners.

A drove of truckers.

By two A.M. I am wide-eyed and sweaty. If only I could quit this cold turkey. Turkeys? Hmmm. Flock . . .

A flock of Christmas-tree decorators.

A gob of sailors.

A herd of orators (and an unheard-of ghostwriters), a horde of misers, a host of maître d's.

A litter of messy people, lots of house-builders.

A mess of litterbugs, a critical mass of scientists, a holy mass of priests, a mite of maybes.

A pack of movers, a pride of egotists, a pile of hemorrhoid-sufferers.

A rookery of chess players.

A set of tennis players, a score of composers, a string of cellists, a stable of rational people.

At three A.M. I get out of bed and begin to pace. As I stumble down the hall, I see the bathroom scales. Against my will, I begin to think of weights and measures.

A pound of blacksmiths, a peck of kissers (or typists). Crabgrass by the yard, podiatrists by the square foot, joggers by the running foot. A cord of stranglers, a gram of crackers, a grain (.06 gram) of farmers, a scruple (1.2 grams) of moralists, a hundredweight of centenarians, a gross of slobs.

By four A.M. my mouth is dry. I go to the kitchen for a glass of water. There I see—too late to look away!—containers.

A bowl of keglers, a plate of denture wearers, a spoonful of lovers, a pan of critics, a dish of beauties.

A sack of quarterbacks, a sock (or a box) of pugilists, a rack of sadists, a scoop of reporters, a case of detectives, a drawer of artists, a kit of kaboodlers, a can of plumbers, a thimbleful of seamstresses, a sty of ophthalmologists, a trunk of elephants, a crib of cheaters, a bin of past participles, a Tubb of country singers, a chest of topless waitresses.

Oh, if only I could begin to get drowsy. Just a little . . .

Just a little? A shortage of Napoleons, a scarcity of Vincent Prices, a minimum of corsages, a bit of drillers, a sprinkling of ironers, a dribble of basketballers, a slice of golfers.

A pinch of mashers, a dash of runners, a dab of perspirers.

By five A.M. I know that I must clear my mind. I lie very still and try to think of something else. That, I am sure, would help a lot. . . .

A lot? A rash of allergists, a shower of brides, a downpour of meteorologists, an outpouring of bartenders, a beaucoup of hecklers, a slew of killers, a raft of rivermen, a heap of gravediggers.

By now, the sun is rising. Another night of tossing and turning, of counting the wasted minutes. If only I could count sheep instead. Wait! *Sheep?*

A baaa-tch of lambs . . . a rod (5.5 yards) of rams . . . a staff . . . of . . . a staff of shepherdzzz-z-z-z . . .

No holds Bard: Prose and cons

The annual Shakespeare in the Park festival begins Tuesday. So this is a good time to review that old controversy: Who—if anyone—really wrote all those plays?

Some scholars contend that the works attributed to Shakespeare were actually written by Jonson or Bacon or Marlowe.

Lesser nominees include the Duke of Rutland, the Earl of Oxford and The Duke of Earl.

These scholars usually raise three questions: How could Shakespeare—a commoner—write so knowingly about the arts and sciences and the aristocracy? Why is so little known about someone who was so prolific? And lastly, if Shakespeare was really who he said he was, why would he never turn around when neighbors sneaked up behind him and shouted, "Yoo hoo, Vivian!"?

Suspicious behavior indeed for a man with nothing to hide.

Let's look at some theories.

—Ben Jonson was actually Shakespeare. And boy, was Anne Hathaway mad when she found out. Here she had married this man who called himself Shakespeare and who signed all his deposit slips that way. She loved the guy because he was a good father, a law-abiding citizen and gave a really good foot rub.

Then suddenly she had to rethink everything and wonder what *else* this impostor had lied to her about. Is all the world *really* a stage, she wondered? Are there, in fact, more things in heaven and earth than are dreamt of in Horatio's philosophy? Had Willie lied about the foot rubs, too?

And who was this Vivian the neighbors were always shouting to?

—Anne Hathaway was really Shakespeare. Now it was Shakespeare's turn to be mad. Think how *you'd* feel if you came home and found out that the woman you loved was really yourself. When the two of you danced, who would lead? The theory that Anne Hathaway was Shakespeare is based on the observation that of the two of them, Shakespeare looked better in leotards.

—Some experts are convinced that the real author didn't want to be known in his or her own time but did want to be known to posterity and so left clues in the text. So these experts examine the plays for anagrams and ciphers. One expert who believed that Shakespeare was not the real author used complex computations to decipher this message: "Shak'st-spur never writ a word of them." However, a pro-Shakespeare cryptologist used the same text to decipher *this* hidden message: "He didst so, nyah-nyah-nyah."

—Marlowe was really Shakespeare. Ah, but how about the

fact that Marlowe was killed in 1593, before some of the plays were written? Scholar Nigel Twigg-Gwinley has an answer: To escape debt and start a new life, Marlowe faked his own death. He even attended his own funeral disguised as John Milton, who was blind and didn't notice the difference.

And now some theories in support of Shakespeare.

—Stanford's Lars Utterly, drama professor and varsity marbles coach, believes that little is known about Shakespeare's life because the Bard was a painfully shy person. For example, Utterly believes that Shakespeare was an avid gardener but was too shy even to talk to his house plants, preferring instead to pass them notes. One such note later turned up in London and was performed at the Globe Theater as *A Midsummer Night's Philodendron.*

—Some numerologists think Shakespeare even helped write the King James version of the Bible: It was printed in 1610, when Shakespeare was forty-six. "Shake" is the forty-sixth word from the beginning of Psalm 46. "Spear" is the forty-sixth word from the end of Psalm 46. Of course, using that method of reasoning, I can prove that I wrote *Love Story.* But that's the chance I take.

Yes, such theories can be carried to ludicrous extremes. This should teach us to endeavor to advance only those theories that are plausible and constructive. Toward that end I leave you with this closing thought.

Everyone knows that Mark Twain was really Samuel Langhorne Clemens. But was Clemens actually the Brontë sisters with a mustache?

The write stuff:
Some timely tips

Do you ever wish that you did something else for a living?

Personally, I wish that I had learned to play the guitar so that today I made a simple living making music. But alas, I didn't and I don't.

Perhaps some of you even wish you were a writer. Yes, learn to write, and soon your name will be a household word, along with those of Dickens, Updike and Maalox. Publishers will snatch up everything you write: sentimental letters, pithy grocery lists, deeply moving deposit slips. (A time card once filled out by Hemingway soon will be a major motion picture, directed by Steven Spielberg and starring Sally Field as three hours of overtime.)

As a highly paid professional I've written, oh, dozens of words, some of them the very same words found in the classics (my *the's* and *an's* have been compared to those in *Silas Marner*). And now I'm willing to tell *you* everything that I know about writing. In fact, I'll tell you twice, so it will fill this space.

Thus you will be spared having to learn as I did. I learned to write the same way that I learned to swim. When I was small, my parents tied me to a typewriter and threw me into a lake.

—First, don't be intimidated. Look at it this way: The ancient Egyptian slaves built the pyramids using thousands of heavy stone blocks. You build a sentence using only twenty-six letters. Light, easy-to-carry letters, at that. But when it's all over, you have a nice, cozy sentence, and all the slave has is a 4,000-year-old hernia.

Now, gather up all the words you can find. Separate them into nouns and verbs. If you're a beginner, you can tell the nouns from the verbs this way: The verbs are active, always moving around, fidgeting and whispering to each other. The nouns just sit there and don't do much of anything. Sorta like your first husband.

Here are some tricks of the trade.

—Write about what you know best. Twain had been a riverman, so he wrote *Life on the Mississippi*. Dashiell Hammett had been a private detective, so he wrote *The Thin Man*. Mary Shelley had had a series of unfortunate blind dates, so she wrote *Frankenstein*.

—Suppose a writer writes "Jane shovels her food." Now we know that Jane does not really eat with a shovel. (Well, *don't* we?) No, this is a metaphor, something we writers use all the time. Practice your metaphors. Walk up to a Hell's Angel, clear your throat and say: "You, sir, are a low-down, dirty pit of slime." As he lifts you off the ground by your eyelashes, reassure him: "It's all right. That's a metaphor! I'm a writer!" When you get to the hospital, the doctors will say: "Gee, this writer is a battlefield of bruises."

This is yet another metaphor.

—Use strong, vivid verbs.

Good: The elephants made a noise and ran over forty-two innocent bystanders.

Better: The elephants trumpeted and trampled forty-two bystanders.

Best: The elephants trumpeted and trampled forty-two people I don't like.

—Symbolism. English teachers will love you for this. It gives students something to make notes about in the margin. For instance, the great white whale in *Moby Dick* symbolized Nature at once revered and reviled. Try using symbolism in *your* writing, too: "It was a hot, dry day in Iowa. State trooper Perkins was speeding down the dusty road when his car crashed into a great white whale. Perkins called his dispatcher: 'I got a three-oh-two here. That's right: a major accident involving Nature at once revered and reviled.'"

There. I've done *my* part. You now know how to write. Now if only some musician would teach *me* how to play the guitar. I'm sure I'd catch on fast as soon as someone showed me which end I'm supposed to blow into.

Quick, Watson: Follow that guffaw!

A valentine to the Sherlock Holmes stories, to mark their centennial.

Of all the cases in which I, Dr. John H. Watson, was privileged to assist my good friend Mr. Sherlock Holmes, none was stranger or took us into more exalted circles than *The Adventure of the Missing Sense of Humor.*

From my notebook, then, I see that it was upon an evening in December 1887 that Holmes and I occupied our lodgings in Baker Street, glad of a cheery blaze in the fireplace, for outside Mrs. Hudson was hurling soapflakes against the window, for atmosphere. Holmes was immersed in one of his malodorous chemical experiments when he suddenly handed me a vial of smoking liquid and bade me to drink. Obligingly, I swallowed. Two hours later I regained consciousness, suffering no ill effects other than a growth of fur over my body and a tendency to turn around three times before I lie down.

I found Holmes standing at the window, staring down at a carriage at the curb. "A caller, Watson. And one on serious business, I'll wager, to brave the elements at this late hour."

Moments later Mrs. Hudson ushered in a short, well-dressed woman whose face was hidden behind a veil. After Mrs. Hudson retreated, our visitor lifted her veil, and there before us stood none other than Her Majesty Victoria Regina, queen of the United Kingdom of Great Britain and Ireland, empress of India and part-time cocktail waitress at the Hey, Sailor Bar.

"We are honored, Your Majesty," Holmes said with his usual chivalry. He bowed; I licked her hand. "Pray be seated and tell us how we may serve you."

"Mr. Holmes, I have lost my sense of humor. Prince Albert, my royal consort, said only this morning, 'Vicki, old girl, you're no fun anymore. Give us a little laugh.' He then tickled the royal ribs. Nothing. He told me the one about how many

Frenchmen does it take to change a lantern wick. Nothing. He tried joy buzzers and dribble glasses. Still nothing. Finally I said, 'We are not amused,' and had him locked in the Tower of London.

"Find my sense of humor for me, Mr. Holmes, and your reward will be ample — a knighthood, a castle in Wales and, if you act soon, a bonus set of ginsu steak knives."

Holmes said he would be honored to accept the case and told her the one about the traveling crumpet salesman. She stared at him blankly, said, "We are not amused," and with that departed our humble rooms.

"A singular case, Watson. I sense here the handiwork of Moriarty, the Napoleon of crime. This is his specialty. I cannot prove it, but I am convinced that it was Moriarty who stole Wordsworth's sense of rhyme in 1843, causing the poet to write: 'I wandered lonely as a cloud/that floats on high o'er vales and hills/when all at once I saw a crowd,/a host of golden pyracanthas.' Moriarty also stole Wellington's sense of direction in 1812, causing the duke to attack downtown Liverpool."

As was customary when Holmes was pondering a new case, during the remainder of the night he played his violin and smoked his pipe. When this grew tiresome, he played his pipe and smoked his violin.

Before dawn next morning Holmes woke me: "Come, Watson, the game is afoot! Eh, do you mind?" indicating once again the smoking liquid. I drank and soon was straining at the leash he had secured to my neck. Then, to put me on the trail of the missing sense of humor, he emitted a queenly guffaw. With a howl I loped off on all fours, sniffing across the slumberous great city.

I soon picked up the trail. "Good boy, Watson. We progress apace. Look: a recent smile." A few blocks later Holmes said, "Closer still, Watson! Listen: a giggle has been here. And hark! Up ahead: a chuckle. It's still fresh, too. Yes, the royal sense of humor definitely has passed this way."

Unerringly I followed the trail into an empty warehouse in the East Docks.

"Good evening, Holmes," said an evil voice in the darkness. "I've been expecting you."

(To be continued.)

Will Holmes have the last laugh?

The conclusion of The Adventure of the Missing Sense of Humor.

Holmes lit his lantern, revealing to us Professor Moriarty — murderer, extortionist and all-round naughty person. Moriarty spoke to Holmes in a sinister tone.

"We meet again, eh, Holmes? You've come about Queen Victoria's missing sense of humor, of course."

"Of course. You have it, of course."

"Of course. In my safe."

"Of course. By the way, Moriarty, I notice that recently you have been in Peru, that you just arose from bed and that you have taken up smoking."

"Bravo, Holmes. How did you know?"

"Elementary. You are riding a llama, and your pajamas are on fire."

With a cry of alarm, Moriarty galloped off to have his burns treated. As he disappeared, Holmes called after him: "Beyond that, I observed little, other than that you are left-handed and have been a ship's carpenter, you are a Virgo, your favorite book is *Love Story,* your favorite color is green, and your idea of a perfect evening is sharing a romantic candlelit dinner, followed by torturing someone really special."

When we returned to our Baker Street lodgings, I asked: "What will you do now, Holmes?" But he was in his most reticent mood, and I knew better than to pry at such times. The effects of Holmes's strange brew lingered with me. After I had fetched him his pipe and slippers, he tossed me a bone.

Holmes was already gone when I rose betimes next morning. When he returned in two days it was evident from his improved spirits that his investigation was going well. "You will be relieved to know that Her Majesty will live to laugh again," he announced.

I stood in mute admiration of this master of deductive reasoning.

As we took a hansom cab to Buckingham Palace, Holmes
described how he had gained entry to Moriarty's study—and
thus to the safe—by disguising himself as a Barcalounger. "I
recovered the missing sense of humor but at some personal
sacrifice: On the second day, Moriarty had me reupholstered
and Scotchgarded."

When we were ushered in to the royal presence, Her Majesty
greeted us. As she turned to Holmes with hope in her eyes, she
paused to scratch me between the shoulder blades, causing my
foot to begin thumping on the floor. "You bring me news, Mr.
Holmes?"

"Yes, Your Majesty. I have rescued your missing sense of
humor from the clutches of a fiend. You will find it in here," he
said, bowing and handing her a thin blue envelope.

The queen opened the envelope and peered inside. "If this is
your idea of a joke, Mr. Holmes, we are not amused," she said,
shaking the apparently empty envelope.

To prove his assertion, Holmes then regaled her with many
witticisms of the most sophisticated minds of the time, Oscar
Wilde and Bernard Shaw.

"We are not amused," she said flatly.

Regrouping, Holmes next sang to her the comic operas of
Gilbert and Sullivan.

But her face remained severe. Not so much as a smile. "We
are *still* not amused."

"Hmmm. What have I overlooked?" Upon his keen hawklike
features, frustration was stamped. "Must I admit defeat at last?
What *can* the true solution be, Watson?"

To which I replied "Elementary, Holmes," and bit him on
the ankle.

At this, suddenly Her Majesty smiled. Just a small one at
first. Yet it grew into a snicker, then into a chuckle, and then
into gales upon gales of royal guffaws. She finally grew weak
from laughter and fell to the floor, breaking her hip.

"A simple case, after all, Watson," Holmes said as we left the
palace. "And now, if we hurry, we just have time to dine at
Simpson's, hear Carina sing at the Albert Hall and then get my
rabies shots."

The Sciences

When the future does not compute

Do you have a fear of computers? Do you say the word "computers" the same way that a hemophiliac says the word "guillotine"?

At social gatherings, when the talk turns to spreadsheets or databases or batch files, do you crouch down and whimper? Do you quickly try to change the subject, even to topics that you normally would avoid, such as sex, religion or politics? Or all three: "Say, has anyone here ever French-kissed a Methodist incumbent?"

Many folks are still afraid of computers, you know, especially those of us who have reached an age when we can't remember puberty except under hypnosis. We become set in our ways and dread having to learn to use newfangled inventions in our homes and offices, preferring instead oldfangled inventions such as the steam-driven swizzle stick.

To you, computers are incomprehensible, complex instruments of the devil, aren't they, crammed with mysterious things from Japan called IC chips, which, as smug young computer whizzes are always telling you, are each no bigger than your

Aunt Bernice's ingrown toenail but which have more transistors than Attila had Huns.

And just what are transistors, anyway? Have you ever seen one? Can you describe it? Oh, you can, huh? If it had a scar on one cheek and walked with a limp, that was a diode, you dummy, and don't you feel foolish now?

Anyway, the point is that computers have few moving parts. And I know you: You *trusted* moving parts. At one time you had several yourself.

I have heard it said that if the electronic parts of a home computer last through the warranty period, they probably will last the next 500 years. Which is more than you can say for yourself, with *your* blood pressure.

And like it or not, computers are here to stay. According to the latest pie charts in the latest news magazines, soon most American jobs will be computerized to some extent. White-collar, blue-collar, arts and sciences. Even novelists will be replaced by computers as soon as someone can design a computer that can be temperamental, drink too much, and die tragically at a young age.

So wouldn't you like to become computer literate and land a high-paying, high-tech job where you can cause $9 million in phone bills to be sent to someone you don't like and then blame it on computer error?

OK. Here's what you do. Go down to your favorite department store, find the computer department and hang out with the computer salesguys. Listen to everything that they tell customers, memorize it and then promptly forget it. Because most of those guys were working in the shoe department last week.

In spite of that, computers are revolutionizing our culture. With computers, your old mindless, meaningless job can be done with greatly improved mindless, meaningless efficiency. For instance, using my computer as a word-processor, I can churn out twice as much inane drivel as I could back in the days when I used a wood-burning typewriter.

So I have come to love my home computer. We spend many pleasant hours together. It is a tireless, dependable partner. It helps me to write and edit, can check my spelling, count my words, print perfect copies and do everything that a writer needs except cheat on expense accounts.

I have come to think of my computer as just a typewriter that has been to finishing school.

So to those of you who are afraid of computers, I close with this bit of advice: Check your antifreeze twice a year, don't talk to strangers, and get Aunt Bernice to a good podiatrist.

No, no, wait. That's not it. Here it is: Relax. Go with the flow. This is the '80s. Remember that if your computer could talk to you, it would tell you, "I am your friend."

Of course, that's also what Attila the Hun said to Europe.

Heaven is havin'
an ever-lovin' oven

I think I'm in love.

Is it possible for a man and a machine to have a meaningful relationship?

Perhaps, but no ob-gyn on Earth would guarantee what their children would look like.

The machine that has turned my head, stolen my heart and made a serious assault on my stomach is a microwave oven.

Please forgive my zeal. I realize that I am the last living person to buy a microwave oven. Temple carvings show that the Incas had crude oxen-driven microwave ovens well before I got mine. Hermits have long used them to cook nuts and berries. Natives in the South Seas use them to reheat Missionary Surprise.

As a typical bachelor, I spend as little time as possible in my typical bachelor kitchen. So I finally bought a microwave oven, and I love it, and we're very happy together, and it's all mine, and you can't have it, so there.

I made it a niche between the fridge and the mound of dirty dishes, which scientists have traced back to the Mesozoic era. How I love its sleek, feminine lines, its cute little dials, its gently rounded turntable. I love how its timer bell beckons me with a seductive *ding,* as if saying, "Hey, big fella, if you've got the sour cream, I've got the baked potato."

Sometimes, while a pizza is bubbling in my oven, spinning merrily under the light, I just stand and stare at it through the glass door, with the dials at the side. It's like watching TV, only without the Preparation-H commercials.

As I stare, I marvel at this technology. My oven's manual tells me that these microwave waves are actually similar to radio waves. Did you know that you can cook an omelet in a microwave oven for five minutes, then hold it up to your ear and hear Casey Casem's Top Forty?

Try it sometime.

Such ovens heat food by bombarding the water and fat molecules with microwaves, causing the food molecules to vibrate 2.4 *billion* times a second. (I once knew a coed named Olga who had the same effect on *my* molecules.)

Yet impressed as I am, I still wonder just how safe these ovens are. We all know that if you wear a pacemaker into a 7-Eleven store where a microwave is in use, your pacemaker will begin to tap dance an old Busby Berkeley number. And just how much testing was done to assure that after twenty years of eating microwaved food, we won't watch our body parts begin to fall off in alphabetical order?

Do you remember the moment that you put your hands into your new microwave oven for the first time to pull out your very first Stuffed Eggplant or Veal Elegante? Perhaps you trembled with uncertainty. Would the container be melted? Would the food be cold? Would your fingers be fused together, seriously affecting your bowling average?

A first like that rates right up there with other firsts in my life—first car, first apartment, first date with Olga, all those vibrating molecules ago.

Ever since my oven and I met, we've been preparing more and more meals together, experimenting with cooking times and temperatures, trying all the dishes that microwave ovens do so easily: corn on the cob, macaroni, vegetables, hot fudge sauce, nachos, quiche, rice, noodles, caramel popcorn balls.

I find myself eating five or six meals a day just to have an excuse to be with my oven, to sample the wondrous meals that it renders up unto me with nary a complaint. All it asks from me is some 110-volt current and a 15-amp breaker.

Yes, I think I'm in love. But alas, ours is a doomed romance. My darling microwave oven and I shall never select our silver pattern, never have a church wedding, never honeymoon at Niagara Falls.

Because I seem to have gotten too fat to get out the kitchen door.

By the light of the silvery Mylar

Well, there goes the cosmic neighborhood.

Perhaps you read recently that while we Americans are debating our Strategic Defense Initiative, the French are getting le jump on us with their own form of SDI. Ah, you are thinking, France's SDI will monitor the Earth from outer space and fire huge croissants at enemy missiles.

You're close. But in this case, SDI means Strategic Doughnut Initiative. Yes, those zany French types are going to launch a 4.8-mile-wide orbiting doughnut. Mind you, this is not a *real* 4.8-mile-wide orbiting doughnut (headline: Hundreds Buried by Falling Space Jelly). No, this doughnut will be a ring made of 100 balloons of reflective Mylar.

You know about shiny Mylar balloons, don't you? They are rapidly replacing rubber balloons, the balloons of tradition, of antiquity, the balloons of Abraham and Moses. ("And verily, Moses did let loose a balloon, and lo, it did fly about the tabernacle and make a rude noise.") And that's what these French balloons will be, only much, *much* bigger—each twenty feet in diameter—apparently raised on vast balloon farms in France and given steroids in their wine.

The French are calling this big ring thing "abstract art." It will be hung in the celestial gallery in 1989 to mark the centennial of the Eiffel Tower. Personally I think that a small, earth-bound plaque would have been sufficient.

This ring thing will be self-inflating, like a raft. After it gets 500 miles into space, it will pull its own string, inflate to 4.8 miles in diameter and begin to orbit the earth every 90 minutes. It will be visible in clear skies and will appear *as large as the full moon.*

Don't you wish I were lying to you? Don't we both? I had always thought the French were more romantic than this. Yet they are going to orbit a high-tech Hula Hoop that will compete with your favorite and mine: that old devil moon.

That's a sad prospect to us old-fashioned folks who still feel the tug of the moon on our bloodtide. Ah, the moon! The pearl stickpin in God's necktie, the pie in the sky, a china plate set on the black tablecloth of the night. Muse unto the poet, patron cue ball unto the midnight hustler, organic nightlight unto the insomniac. Pale orb whom lovers call chaperone, whom werewolves call Mama.

This ring thing will be a fitting moon only for technophiles. "Look, darling, there's a full self-inflating Mylar ring out tonight. Isn't it romantic? It makes me want to run my fingers through your CD collection."

And worse, it's going to be hard to miss, up there cluttering our sky, the only area that we haven't paved, painted, chrome-plated or plastered with ads.

Uh oh. Methinks I said the magic word. Prediction: After this ring thing gets into space, Madison Avenue will realize that ads-in-orbit are feasible.

We consumers will suffer a new kind of space race as advertisers rush to orbit billboards: golden arches, giant red-and-white chicken buckets, Pepsi, pizza and Preparation-H in space. The man in the moon will be upstaged by a 4.8-mile-wide face of Bob Uecker, beaming down benevolently and taking the "Tastes great!–Less filling!" debate to the heavens.

Yes, there goes the cosmic neighborhood. I fear that the time is coming when a small child, full of curiosity about his universe, will look to the western sky at day's end, shade his eyes and say to his mother and/or father: "Mother and/or Father, what's that big round orange thing shining so brightly in the sky?"

"That, my son, is a Gulf sign."

The myth of math: In search of algebra

Don't you feel that, in general,

$$\frac{2}{x} + \frac{5}{3(1-x)} + \frac{-1}{3(2+x)} = \frac{x+4}{x(1-x)(2+x)}?$$

Well, *don't you?*

Beats me, too.

I've been looking through my old algebra textbook lately. To think that at one time I understood that thing up there in the first paragraph! At one time, at a gathering of fellow algebra students, I could chat glibly about exponents and coefficients, hold my own in a debate about whether an 8 is just two 3's kissing, and tempt the coeds with my etchings of the binomial theorem.

I knew how to conjugate that thing up there or diagram it or throw cold water on it or whatever it was that it cried out for. But now, for all I know, it is actually just the secret recipe for The Colonel's chicken batter.

In school I took algebra because I had to. Being a journalism student, I was never into numbers, other than picas and points and a particular phone number scrawled on the union building wall that indicated that Babette was a good sport. It was even toll-free: 1-800-WHOOPEE.

When faced with math, I would crouch down and whine, "But I'm a liberal arts major! Get those numbers away from me. You don't know *where* they've been!"

But I toughed it out, and, my transcript swears under oath, even made an A.

Where did all that knowledge go? And did I need it anyway?

Is there algebra in the real world?

In the real world you need to be friendly with the four basic math functions plus proportions and percentages. Not much else. You need to be able to figure, for example, that if Mr. A owes the Mafia $2,000, but he has only $17.34, he will very soon be selling $1,982.66 worth of blood.

You need to be able to figure that if Mr. B is driving a truck that is 12 feet high, and he approaches an underpass with a clearance of 11 feet, 3 inches, he should let 9 inches of air out of the tires or pay someone else to drive the truck through the underpass.

(Aside to Mr. B: Mr. A would probably be willing to do it. Offer him $1,982.66.)

You need to be able to measure cups and spoons for a recipe, to balance a checkbook and to know that if your neighbor makes $80,000 a year and you make $15,000, you are a total failure as a human being and should immediately throw yourself in front of Mr. B's truck.

So I decided to search for algebra in the real world. I began by looking for it my spare bedroom. That's where lots of odds and ends like that wind up.

But it wasn't there. It got away.

I looked in my workshop. Lots of fractions and measurements there. But no sign of old Algy. I looked for it down at the office. Lots of numbers lying about, but no need for algebra.

I realize now that algebra has never been of material aid or emotional comfort to me in any of life's myriad crises. It was no help to me when the roof sprang a leak, when my car wouldn't start or when Babette broke my heart.

Or when I took my draft physical. The doctors wouldn't buy it when I pleaded: "But you don't want *me,* fellas. I have a faulty logarithm."

"Shut up, punk. Take this little bottle, and don't try to tell us you gave at the office."

I now suspect that algebra is great training: It trains you to do algebra.

Of course, if this column offends some math teacher who later accosts me and angrily claims that I am trying to endanger his livelihood, I may have to defend myself and bash him over the head with my old algebra textbook.

Now who says algebra isn't useful in the real world?

A quart low on high tech

Please, no more.

Astound me no more with miracles of our high-tech world. Let me live in the past, when men were men and a dipstick was a dipstick.

The other day a younger friend who understands and accepts such things told me how a network signal reaches my TV set. Let's say that ABC is broadcasting a Texas Rangers game from Arlington Stadium. The signal first is beamed up to a satellite 22,500 miles in space. The signal then bounces down to ABC studios in New York City, where the anti-drug messages and beer commercials are inserted, then back up to another satellite, then back down to my local ABC affiliate, then to the cable station, and then, finally, to my TV. Round trip: 90,000 miles.

(My TV set, mind you, is located about seven miles from the stadium.)

And the TV signal makes this 90,000-mile round trip in a half-second. Which tells me that it avoids all known Fort Worth-Dallas freeways.

Imagine: All this technology just to be able to watch a bunch of guys in knee socks pat each other on the fanny!

And the air is full of such TV signals. Right now. Sports events are penetrating your home. Phil Donahue is creeping under your bed. Daytime programming is getting into your fridge and making the cottage cheese tingle to *All My Children*.

Yes, even as we speak, Dan Rather may be bouncing off your bouffant.

All this so impressed me that I told another friend. He said, "You think *that's* something? If each bit of data contained on just one compact disk (CD) were represented as a matchstick, they would fill the Roman Colosseum."

I tried to picture this. Even if science could make a CD player big enough to spin the Roman Colosseum, wouldn't the tourists get awfully dizzy?

All *this* so impressed me that I told another friend. She said, "You think *that's* something? My car's dipstick has an electronic sensor. If I'm driving when the car needs oil, the dashboard computer actually speaks to me, telling me I'm a quart low and to please move over because the Johnny Carson signal wants to pass."

Well, this time science has gone too far. For most of this century, the dipstick was a constant in a changing world. What the dipstick was, basically, was a stick that you dipped. Simple: Undip it, wipe it, redip it, undip it, read it and drip oil on your new Hush Puppies.

After learning these amazing facts, I'll believe anything. Tell me that they now have a bomb that will kill all the people in an enemy country but leave their hot tubs intact so that the victors can roll in with tanks and Jeeps and have a good hot soak. I'll believe you.

Tell me that in the '50s the first computer filled a whole room and required a technician to be on duty all the time, servicing it, replacing vacuum tubes, but that today the equivalent of that computer can be worn on your wrist, now that science has found a way to miniaturize the technician so he can live comfortably in a furnished pore. I'll believe you.

Satellites, compact disks, high-tech dipsticks. Where will it all end?

Even now science is working on a new, improved way for you to check your engine's oil level. A signal is beamed from the dipstick sensor 22,500 miles up to a satellite, thence down to the Roman Colosseum, where it ignites all those matchsticks, turning Rome into a four-alarm pizza. The signal, now smelling faintly of mushroom and anchovies, is beamed back to your car, whereupon your car clears its throat, tells you that you are a quart low and sings side one of *Mario Lanza's Greatest Hits*.

I jest, of course. Not a word of that is true.

At least it wasn't when I wrote it.

The Call of the Wild

Three cats and one heirdale

Every once in a while we read about this sort of thing:

Some eccentric person dies and leaves $3.5 million to her beloved hamster Elroy, who soon gives himself up to riotous living, spending the entire fortune on imported sunflower seeds, a motorized exercise wheel and a lifetime subscription to *Rodents in Bondage.*

Or we read about someone's will providing for a dog to be boarded in air-conditioned comfort with carpet on the floor and three meals a day.

Well, that's going a bit far. I see no reason for my pets to live better than I do. But after I am dead—found slumped over a sentence fragment—I do want them to continue to live as comfortably as they did while I was among the quick.

And as things now stand, my pets will inherit my vast fortune, which includes this rambling mansion, $62 in savings, several valuable cents-off coupons and some antique veggies in the fridge. So I've been giving some thought to my will. I have one dog and three cats, each of whom I am very fond of and each of whom is merely tolerant of me.

I want each cat to have a warm TV to nap on during the winter and a cool windowsill to nap in during the summer. A qualified caretaker should be on duty with a qualified lap for the cats to leap into and knead with their claws while the petrified caretaker's whole love life passes before his eyes.

Now, individually. Pete, my ex-tom, each day should get a dozen roasted peanuts, which he will eat only most of, leaving the leftovers to attract ants. Pete should also receive a lifetime supply of crickets to eat and throw up. And a new carpet to throw up on.

Jo, the timid one, should get a lifetime supply of her own shadow to be afraid of.

Wink, the scrapper, should be supplied each midnight with a stray cat to go out and get into a howling, spitting fight with. Each day she should get macaroni and cheese, which she will lick the cheese off, leaving little naked macaronis on the floor to make sure that the ants get enough carbohydrates.

Then there is Tiger, who, as a dog, is no longer a pup. His tooth has been carbon-dated at about ninety (dog years), his upholstery is worn in places, and he is getting pretty deaf.

To confirm that Tiger is deaf, I sometimes walk up behind him and say, "Tiger, you're a worthless animal. You old dog-eared, hidebound mongrel, you couldn't even catch a dead cat. Nyah nyah nyah."

He never even turns around and wants to fight.

Ah, but just let me rattle a can-opener anywhere in the Central Time Zone. *That* he hears.

Tiger is not really my pet so much as he is my cats' pet. They aren't quite sure what dogs are for. But they are kind to someone whom they consider to be a dumb beast. They often let Tiger give them all the food in his dish. And many's the time that they have let Tiger hold out his nose while they slashed at it.

Assuming that Tiger and his tooth survive me, I want him to get a hearing aid—the same model that Lassie wore in her declining years, when she was so deaf she couldn't even hear little Timmy when he was caught in the threshing machine.

That completes my will.

(Note to police: It's likely that after my pets find out that they are so well provided for in my will, they'll try to do away with me. So if I am found dead under mysterious circumstances, such as having fallen off a curb into the path of a speeding truck, please investigate. I was probably pushed. Dust my back for pawprints. If you find no pawprints, that's just a dead giveaway that my pets did it: They simply wore gloves.)

The cat is just Edison with a tail

Shhh! Please don't read this column aloud—you might awaken your cat.

In fact, I am typing this as quietly as I can—with my fingers in my ears. My cats are asleep, as usual, and left instructions not to be disturbed until half past Armageddon.

Oh, would that I could write these words as well as my three cats can sleep. Would that I could do *anything* as well as my cats can sleep. Cats are to sleep what Bach is to music, what Rembrandt is to art, what Mongo Q. Keefleboch III is to obscurity.

(Who, you may ask, is Mongo Q. Keefleboch III? See *there!*)

Let us consider the cat. Oh, not as it digs in its hind paws and, with eyes shining, crouches to pounce on some defenseless leaf. Not as it arches its back and sashays sideways— spooked!—on tiptoes. And not as it sharpens its claws on your best nylons—often while they're still on your best legs. No, let us consider the cat in its natural state—asleep.

Necessity is the mother of invention, granted, but the cat surely has played midwife a few times through history.

First, I believe that the cat invented the wheel and let us people take the credit. Consider: As the cat sleeps curled up tightly in a ball, the nose is tucked under a paw, the back is rounded, the tail is touching an ear, completing a circle.

In Egypt, the Caffre cat had been domesticated before Cleopatra was knee-high to an asp. The cat was sacred—if a cat died a natural death, everyone in the household shaved their eyebrows. (Thus was the cat—even in death—also responsible for the first eyebrow pencil.) No doubt some artisan, noticing his cat's circular sleeping posture, measured the sacred diameter of the cat and chiseled a round, flat pedestal of precious stone for the cat to sleep on.

Then the artisan placed his Kitty-Ra on the disk and stood back, full of hope, to watch. And the sacred cat, being a cat, took one look at the disk, put its feet on the ground and its nose in the air and trotted outside to the sacred sandbox. Then the dejected artisan threw the disk out the window and watched it roll (!) down the lane and into the Nile.

And in the summer, we should thank the cat for the invention of short sleeves. It is said that the prophet Muhammad once was sitting with his cat Muezza asleep on the long sleeve of his robe. When the time for a council meeting came, Muhammad hated to disturb the cat (oh, how they train us to feel guilty!). So he cut off the sleeve and stole away, leaving Muezza to sleep.

(One of mine just moved. I think it's *alive!*)

On a winter's day, a cat will lie on the kitchen floor in a patch of light as the sun shines through a window. The cat will move only enough to stay within the warmth of the patch of light as it inches across the floor. Thus our early ancestors may have learned to tell time by the cat's relative position on the floor. ("Ye kittye is a quarter past yon table leg. It must be 12:15. Ye Middle Ages will be starting soon.") Thus was the cat the first sundial.

And the cat may have inspired some inventions in those few hours that it is astir.

Can anyone who has been licked by a cat doubt that its tongue inspired the invention of the emery board?

Ever stroke a cat's fur and then touch a conductor, such as a door knob or another person? Imagine what happened when a cavewoman stroked her pet saber-tooth tiger and then touched her caveman: Ouch! The discovery of static electricity. And the invention of the practical joke.

And when you stroke a cat's back, it rises to the occasion, perhaps once inspiring the invention of the hydraulic jack.

(One of mine just woke up long enough to find out if next week is here yet.)

Many of us have gone outside in the morning and found cat tracks on the hood, windshield and trunk of our car. The paw prints form a chain of spots, as if elves had played dust dominoes on the car. Did such prints long ago inspire the invention of that game?

And finally, the cat surely invented immodesty. Ever notice that your cat doesn't sit on the sofa and nonchalantly clean its most private of cat parts until you have visitors?

And the more modest the visitors, the more immodest the ablutions. "Oh, *look*, Rev. Leviticus!" you blurt suddenly, pointing out the window to distract the Rev. (Why isn't your darned cat asleep *now*?) Then you shoo away the cat, who promptly trots out of the living room and into the bathroom.

Where it drinks out of the toilet.

But cat-lovers overlook such, eh, faux paws in so noble an animal — an animal that invented the wheel.

With both eyes closed.

Grate expectations: Sorry, Charlie

This year is indeed a milestone in the history of underwater advertising: 1986 is the twenty-fifth year that Charlie The Tuna has been trying to convince Star-Kist that he has good taste, only to be told, "Sorry, Charlie."

So what better time to learn a bit about this celebrated spokesfish? Here, then, is the highly unauthorized biography of Charlie The Tuna.

Charlie T. Tuna was not always the rich and famous registered trademark that you see today. Oh, no, Charlie was born in 1959 amid humble surroundings in the Pacific Ocean, his mother an unskilled abalone, his father a mackerel who was just passing through town. From that liaison came Charlie and his 10,000 brothers and sisters. All but Charlie soon grew up to be salads and sandwiches.

This left Charlie and his mother all alone in their modest house on the ocean floor. His earliest memory is of how damp his room always was.

Charlie's mother died when he was young. It was a low-cal burial: She was laid to rest in a tin can of pure spring water. Perhaps it was the trauma of those early years as an orphan that caused Charlie to develop his now-famous compulsion to be accepted at any cost, even death.

Charlie's craving for acceptance got him into trouble with the law early on. In 1960 he was arrested off Catalina for hanging around a school of underage herring and whispering, "Psst. Wanna spawn?"

In 1961, still on probation, Charlie forged Jacques Cousteau's signature on a letter of recommendation and was hired as spokesfish for Star-Kist. (Many people thought that the late actor Herschel Bernardi was the voice of Charlie. This is wrong. Actually, Charlie was the voice of Herschel Bernardi.)

This job brought Charlie fame and fortune, but still he was not happy. Star-Kist, Charlie felt, was just using him. He grew despondent and finally, one night off Monterey, he tried to impale himself on a swordfish.

Charlie then began to undergo therapy. He was diagnosed as suffering from fear of rejection, an inferiority complex and a death wish.

"Charlie," the doctor said, "it's not normal to want to grow up to be a casserole."

Charlie always shunned the star scene, although he used to hang out in a Hollywood bar frequented by other product mascots. Charlie, Kellogg's Tony The Tiger and the Vlasic Pickle stork would party with the Schlitz malt liquor spokes-bull. They would have a few too many and then go over and start picking on the Keebler elves. Charlie always woke up at noon with an awful headache and would go have lunch with Speedy Alka-Seltzer.

In 1975 Charlie married the Chicken of the Sea mermaid. It was a mixed marriage: He was chunk, she was grated. But they were happy for several months, until they found out that they had nothing in common from the waist up (not an uncommon complaint). It ended in divorce in 1976.

Soon it was ten years later.

And that brings us to Charlie's twenty-fifth anniversary. Star-Kist officials recently threw a party for Charlie at his pad, a mile underwater. There were gifts, speeches, Pin the Tail on Lloyd Bridges and even a cake with twenty-five candles that wouldn't stay lit.

But the party was marred by a sad incident. After refreshments were served, a Star-Kist executive found a pair of eyeglasses in his slice of cake. Further investigation showed that Charlie was concealed in his own birthday cake, still hoping to be eaten.

Sorry, Charlie.

Notes from the underground

Looking for a hobby? Let me recommend an ant farm.

But why, you protest, would anyone knowingly bring into their home the very pests that got aboard Noah's ark only because two of them lied on the travel forms and claimed to be bedbugs on their honeymoon?

For the lessons to be learned, that's why. Much knowledge can be gained from observing these fascinating beasties.

As Solomon said in Proverbs: "Go to the ant, thou sluggard; consider her ways, and be wise." As Stephen Vincent Benet said in a poem: "The ant finds kingdoms in a foot of ground." And as Naomi Weemish said in her kitchen: "D—! The little —s (Naomi, *please!*) have gotten into my fondue again!"

Still, a student of the human condition would do well to study the ant.

We all know the story of the grasshopper and the ant—the frivolous grasshopper played all summer while the busy ant gathered food. Then winter came, and the grasshopper had no food. Starving, he came up onto the ant's front porch and begged for a scrap of food. And the generous ant went to the door, mistook the grasshopper for a prowler and shot him.

Ants also have a clear division of labor. Some dig tunnels. These are called tunnel-diggers. Some gather food. These are called food-gatherers. Some pad bills. These are called government contractors.

Because all worker ants are female, the sex life of the colony is dull. Especially when compared to that of other species such as the elephant, whose mating season lasts eleven months, allowing just four weeks to get the furniture repaired.

When you buy an ant farm you also get some special California sand and a certificate. Mail the certificate, and your ants soon will be air-mailed to you—also from California.

Now to be honest, I have found that even after the jet lag wears off, California ants in California sand just lie around and wait for someone to holler, "Surf's up." So you *can* use local ants. After all, if they're good enough for Naomi Weemish's fondue, they're good enough for us.

The first task is to name your ants. Otherwise you can't tell them apart. Someone suggested that I name mine after friends or family. So soon I had 143 ants named Grandpa Bob. I found that this created a feeling of unity among them, but it wreaked havoc at mail call. Until I made a slight revision.

Within minutes of being placed in the enclosure, they began to tunnel in the dirt. Ants live to dig. They have mud in their veins. Go Bob-109! Shovel it, Bob-67! Pitch that fork, Bob-32!

When there is no room to turn around in a narrow tunnel, ants can even back up for several inches (human measure) carrying a grain of sand. This is the equivalent of your driving from here to Seattle. In reverse. With a brick in your mouth.

Sometimes several ants will huddle topside and wave their antennae at each other. They seem to be talking, perhaps planning a new tunnel or revealing the location of food. In fact, by lowering a sensitive microphone into the ant farm, you can hear faint, high-pitched noises like this: "Did you hear the one about the queen termite and the wooden leg?"

At other times, a colony member will go off by itself and stand very still. Recently one of mine, Bob-113, seemed to be sulking. I can always identify him because he limps on his no. 5 leg and has a two-inch (ant measure) scar on his cheek that he will never discuss.

Anyway, Bob-113 stopped tunneling one day. He stopped gathering food. He became more and more despondent, and I began to fear that he might do something rash, such as having an "accident" in no. 7 shaft, which was closed and declared unsafe after a cave-in occurred when I slammed the kitchen door too hard.

So I gained his confidence with a grain of sugar, and he admitted that he had an attitude problem.

"I'm just sick of the stereotype, that's all. We ants are supposed to be tireless workers with no thought of self. Well, once in a while I'd like a day off just to go to the park."

I reminded him that the ant farm had no park.

"And another thing—the ant farm has no park!" Bob-113 said bitterly. His scar was ugly.

"And furthermore, Big Shot, I'm tired of having to carry ten times my own weight just to give your scientists something to take notes on. Have you ever tried to get a truss on over an exoskeleton?"

That explained the limp.

To make a long (human measure) story short, Bob-113 went on to spread dissent and to call a strike among his fellow ants. They refused to tunnel, they refused to gather food. And I never got to hear the punchline about the queen termite and the wooden leg.

Led by Bob-113, they would not be moved. The ant farm went to seed. It became a big bore for all concerned.

At which time I simply loaded the ant farm into the car, drove across town and set the colony free by dumping the whole mess—ants and sand and no park—onto Naomi Weemish's fondue.

Bedroom safari:
Cheap trills

It was man against beast, intellect against instinct. Only one of us would emerge victorious.

All this and more went through my mind the night I stalked the rogue cricket.

Oh, I didn't hunt it for the sport. I didn't want some glassy-eyed cricket head hanging on the wall of my den, mounted behind a magnifying glass. And I didn't hunt it for the meat. No, I wanted only to capture it, to get it out of my bedroom so that I could get some sleep.

A cricket, after all, is an official representative of Nature. And Nature, as we all know, belongs outside the house. With the meter reader.

At times, you too probably have had a cricket loose in your home, chirping unseen in the unmapped recesses of a room. Sometimes its song is sustained, sometimes staccato. But always annoying.

Crickets are nocturnal creatures, seeking dark, cozy corners to feed and to mate. That's why you see them swarming at night on the sidewalk in front of singles bars. Only the male cricket chirps. He does this to attract the female cricket. It's his way of saying, "Buy you a drink?"

Predictably, the female cricket is coy. She makes no sound. It's her way of saying, "Beat it, jerk."

The rogue cricket is one of the most difficult of beasts to track. He is never where he seems to be. He may seem to be in the firewood when he is actually under the sofa; he may seem to be in the wall when he is actually under the fridge. Personally, I suspect that he can throw his voice. Once, on "Wild Kingdom," I saw a rogue cricket drink a glass of water while making Marlin Perkins appear to sing "I Gotta Be Me."

At other times I suspect that a cricket is actually able to enter another dimension, only its song piercing the cosmic veil.

At such times the cricket can't be found, simply because it doesn't exist in the physical world. Or at least not in any floor plan by Fox & Jacobs.

So some hunters rely on a cat. Cats are to crickets what metal detectors are to coins. If there's a cricket in the room, a cat will find it. And, if at all possible, eat it. You then will be blessed with silence. For about twenty minutes. Then the cat will sound the dreaded "earp alert." This tells you that you have just 3.4 seconds to get the cat over a newspaper.

(A *Dallas* newspaper, if you please.)

But when I stalked the rogue cricket, I was armed only with nerves of steel and a broom of straw. The chirping seemed to come from under the bed. I pitched camp on the lush veldt of the carpet. But with the cunning of its species, the cricket always hushes as you approach. If you put your ear to the floor, at most you might hear him far away, quietly snickering.

Sure enough, as I approached the bed, he fell silent. It was quiet. *Too* quiet.

For I knew that as soon as I went back to bed, he'd crank up again.

Hoping to flush him out, I jabbed under the bed with the broom. Again and again I jabbed. Then suddenly there he was! He stood before me — 28 millimeters of solid savagery. (Do not think that just because an insect lacks the speed of the lion or the strength of the rhino that it isn't dangerous. Once, in Africa, Hemingway stalked a wounded mosquito in his tent. Papa almost shot off his own foot with an elephant gun.)

Cornered now, the rogue cricket turned on me and charged, scurrying over my bare foot, along the wall and behind the dresser. In pursuit, I moved the dresser and hacked through the undergrowth of cobwebs and dust. There he was, crouching between a long-lost sock and the remains of a TV dinner, circa 1978.

I went after him with my bare hands, bagged him with the sock and tossed him out the front door. It was all over. Man once again had shown who was master. I went back to bed. But not for long. Suddenly the stillness was broken again. There was more big game to stalk.

A rogue June bug was buzzing against the window screen.

How's a snake to slither hither?

The topic of today's sermon is tolerance.

Some of us — and I name no names — are not being tolerant of one of God's humble creatures.

David Shepherd, a professor at Southeastern Louisiana University, has conducted a study that found that drivers will risk life and fender to run over a snake. For three years, Shepherd and his students watched twenty-two thousand motorists react to a fake snake or a fake turtle placed on the road. Drivers swerved across the center stripe to run over the fake snake. Some backed up and ran over it repeatedly.

And lo, the rubber snake was glad that it was not a real snake, with feelings and a family and lapsed health insurance.

One policeman even swerved off the highway to run over the fake snake, backed up, ran over it again, got out of his car and drew his gun before Shepherd stepped out to tell him it was a fake.

We assume that the officer then let the snake go with a warning.

On the other hand, three times as many drivers went out of their way to avoid making soup out of a mock turtle. One driver got out and moved the fake turtle to safety at the side of the road even *after* finding out it was a fake.

For shame. Every head bowed, every eye closed. Why this prejudice against snakes? I guess it all goes back to the Garden of Eden. The serpent, in his best baritone, promised Eve that if she would eat of the Tree of Knowledge, she would have the wisdom of gods and, "if you act today," a bonus five-piece set of copper-plated kitchenware.

Eve was wary, of course, having been taught never to trust anyone who has scales and narrow shoulders. But she gave in, and both Adam and Eve took a bite. "And the eyes of them both were opened, and they knew that they were naked, and they sewed fig leaves together."

Soon we had fashion.

And verily, ever since, snakes have received a lot of bad press. But let me tell you some good things about snakes.

Most are hopelessly harmless. Many actually benefit humanity: eating bugs, controlling rats, letting eight-year-old boys find out how loudly eight-year-old girls can scream. Also, snakes don't bark all night, claw your sofa, get lice or ask to borrow money.

And let's dispel an ugly myth about snakes: Snakes are *not* slimy. You want slimy? Slimy is your Aunt Sophie greased up with so much face cream, hand lotion and skin moisturizer that when your Uncle Mort tries to take her in his arms, she spurts out of bed and across the room.

Sophie and Mort remain childless.

As a boy I always had my father stop the family car so that I could run back and rescue any turtles that were crossing the road. I made pets of them. These usually were box turtles, which apparently come in only one size—four inches across. Maybe they are born this size, full grown. That would explain why their mothers look so bitter.

And I had pet snakes, too. Garter snakes, mostly. But they didn't make very good pets because they refused to eat. So in the end, the only trick they learned was to lie very still and begin to stink.

As a great big adult, I still stop to pick up turtles. I admit that I don't stop to pick up snakes. But on the other hand, I don't try to reduce their status to ex-snake.

So, brethren and sistren, as you leave today and go your own way in this wondrous world, remember to show tolerance and Christian charity toward the snake. For it, too, after all, is one of God's humble creatures.

Someone say, "Amen!"

Save your wrath for spiders. Now *they* are disgusting!

Making waves in the Oval Office

Are you ready for a change?

Are you tired of presidents whose policies are ruinous, whose credibility is in doubt, whose ship of state is a little dinghy?

You say you want your president to have charisma, intelligence and integrity? Then you, like me, are ready to elect a dolphin.

Wait! Now hear me out. I want you to picture in your mind a dolphin. Now just look at that intelligent face, those sincere eyes, that cute little blowhole. (If your image has an intelligent face, sincere eyes but no blowhole, you've just pictured Oprah Winfrey. Don't let it happen again.)

Let's take a brief look at the dolphin's qualifications.

— *Charisma.* Anyone who saw *The Day of the Dolphin* knows how charming these creatures are. When I saw that film, each time the two star dolphins cried, "phaaa" or "baaaa," the theater was filled with such "oohing" and "ahing" that I could hardly hear the besieged young lady who sat behind me in the balcony hiss at her amorous date, "Please, Wilbur! Not *here.* Not in front of *dolphins!*"

Now I ask you: Could George Bush or Michael Dukakis inspire that kind of reaction?

— *Intelligence.* Even skeptics admit that dolphins are at least as smart as dogs. And some experts think that dolphins are smarter than humans but are just afraid to show it. After all, being supersmart must be a big burden. You'd be expected to know Einstein's theory, the square root of Sartre and how to build a robot using just sheet metal, an electric motor and some lipstick.

No crisis would be too intricate for a dolphin, no social issue too complex. Dolphins can rescue drowning people and solve problems. Another sign of smarts: No dolphin has ever appointed James Watt, Earl Butz or Donald Regan to a Cabinet post. In fact, dolphins could be trained, if Watt, Butz or Regan were drowning, to swim the other way.

And their communication skills are legendary. They squeal to convey emotion. Explains one source: "The squeals denote alarm or sexual excitement." Or both, in the case of the couple sitting behind me in the balcony that night.

—*Integrity.* Compare the record of any dolphin to that of other candidates.

No dolphin has ever broken a campaign promise, sold arms to terrorists, been seen with Donna Rice or been related to Billy Carter.

But whoa, you say. Wouldn't electing a dolphin necessitate drastic changes in Washington as we know it? Not really. True, the White House would have to be filled with 10 feet of sea water, which would spoil the effect of much of Nancy's decorating. And we would need to breed Secret Service agents who have webbed feet and are willing to risk their lives by throwing themselves onto a ticking beach ball.

But think of what we'll save in salaries. Instead of $200,000 plus perks, our new president would be paid like this:

"This is Chris Wallace for NBC News. Here at the White House the president and Mr. Gorbachev are signing a treaty completely banning nuclear weapons. The president takes pen in flipper, signs the historic document, leaps through a hoop and is now being rewarded with a mackerel. Well done, Mr. President! Back to you, Tom Brokaw (glub)."

Give it some thought, folks.

But which dolphin should we nominate? How about Flipper, you say? No. Not Flipper. We've already put one actor into the White House. Besides, Flipper is a little *too* smart. I suspect that Flipper is really just Lassie in a wet-suit.

And, you say, who should be the dolphin's running mate? I think that person should be the dolphin's trainer. Dolphin and trainer would have good rapport and form a well-rounded ticket. And after they take office, America's vice-president would at last have a meaningful duty.

He or she could carry the bucket of mackerel.

A Lone Star
State of Mind

Kin Ah hep yew, little lady?

The first tourist in Texas, of course, was Alonso Alvarez de Pineda of Spain, who landed on the Gulf coast in 1519 looking for a new route to the Orient.

He didn't find the Orient, but he did find a land that would defy dominion for 300 years and definition for even longer. While here, he did some exploring and made some charts. Then, like every tourist to Texas, he returned to his homeland awed by the size, the resources and the roller-coaster at Six Flags.

Ever since, Texas has fascinated foreigners, whether they be from England and France or from that appendage known as the forty-seven contiguous states. About 37 million tourists came here last year, and even more are expected in 1986 for the Sesquicentennial.

They come to marvel at a world that Texans take for granted but wouldn't trade for all the halos in heaven: J.R. and U.T.,

151

Longhorn cattle and shortbed trucks, Big Tex and "Little lady, kin Ah hep yew?"

To help outlanders during their visit this year, here's a decidedly incomplete guide to Texas.

We do curious things to speech. Put words in a Texan's mouth and they may come out such that even their own mother tongue wouldn't recognize them. We can be very economical. San Anton. Forget the *io*. And *thow* is what you do with a ball. Take out that *r*, but hang on to it — we'll use it in the next paragraph. And the suffix *ing:* Who needs that *g* clutterin' thangs up?

But counter to those shortcuts, Texans will ooze their words through a drawl so that a word may be two minutes passing a given point. A one-syllable word such as *more* becomes *mower*. And that *r* that we leave out of *throw* shows up bobbing in the Pe(r)dernales River, where it doesn't belong a-tall.

Check your long *i's* at the border, too, Pard. But pack plenty of short *a's*.

Bob War — not a man and not a battle but something you strang along fence posts.

Tars — what cars roll over armadillos with.

Far — what the Texas sun is hotter'n.

A few other common phrases:

Purt near — almost.

Chunk — thow.

A holt of — what you grab.

What fur? — why?

Whurbouts? — where?

Over yonder — the answer to whurbouts.

Crick — 1: a small stream 2: the sound a Japanese tourist's camera makes 3: a pain in the neck.

Goathead sticker — a pain in the foot.

55 mph — a pain somewhere between the neck and foot.

Which brings us to laws. Perhaps it's a vestige of our Wild West heritage, but Texans hate laws, especially those for speed limits, open containers or seat belts. Why, Texas hasn't even passed the law of gravity yet. That's why we finally had to have the seat-belt law: Folks in convertibles kept floating out of their cars, causing the buzzards to get lazy.

Even the law of averages is still stuck in committee in the Texas Legislature.

Of course, nothing is average about Texas. That's one law we *do* have: Everything in and about Texas must be bigger and better. Both, if possible.

Violators will be prosecuted.

Everything in Texas is 11 on a scale of 10 (13.63 on a scale of 9.78, metric measure). This applies to both our mystique and our mistakes. (An example of both: The last battle of the Civil War was fought at Brownsville—more than a month after peace broke out at Appomattox.)

In Texas, the only things higher than glass banks are tall tales. (Your ears may pop just listening to them.) The only things lower than rattlers are rustlers. The only things richer than oilmen are farmlands and college athletes.

We make a business out of sports and a sport out of business.

Texans have four main modes of ambulation:

Mosey—the slowest speed—two parts saunter, one part shuffle. It's how a Texan gets down to the mail box on a fine spring day.

Sashay—equal to a double mosey. How a Texan gets down to the mail box when he's expecting an oil-well royalty check.

Traipse—implies a value judgment by the speaker. Traipsing is common among hussies.

Skedaddle—what Bubba does when fiancée Jody Sue finds him with a traipser.

Some general don'ts:

Don't, when driving, expect ever to reach that town of Litter Barrel.

Don't refer to a bull as a cow or vice versa before you're sure of your biology. Check for telltale clues, such as a vice or a versa.

Don't bring up the subject of Alaska.

Status quo,
not westward ho

Frankly, Fort Worth is getting just a little too big for my britches.

These days there are just too many cars and too few parking spaces, too many people lined up ahead of me at too few teller windows. Too many folks from other parts of the country moving here to enjoy our nether regions.

Why, you can't stand on a street corner in the Stockyards district anymore without seeing someone from Vermont or Michigan buy a pair of pointy-toed cowboy boots, bite off a chaw of Redman and try to milk a bull.

I am entitled to be a bit reactionary: I was born here and hope to grow up here. Fort Worth is a great place to live, to work and to make a bull real nervous. So I say let's keep Fort Worth our little secret. With emphasis on "little." To keep it that way, I suggest that the Chamber of Commerce send this letter to any corporations or individuals who are considering moving here:

Dear prospective sir or madam: Below are just a few of the many advantages that Fort Worth offers.

— *Religion.* Fort Worth supports all the popular religions. But most of our residents are Druids. As such they are tree-worshippers who believe that the yellow pine came down to earth and died for our 2×4s. To Druids, Pinocchio was holy and could reveal the way to heaven, the meaning of life and how to understand the new tax laws. The Druid communion service involves partaking of a wooden nickel and a cup of Old English.

— *Transportation.* The West Freeway doubles as the runway of our modern airport. Drivers of convertibles are reminded that 747s have the right of way.

— *Weather.* Yes, often. For instance, Fort Worth is famed for its summer rain and humidity, leading the city to promote itself as "Fort Worth: where the mildew begins."

But in the spring Fort Worth skies are always blue. Mainly because the air is polluted by smoke from the local Ty-D-Bol plant. Drive down main street (due to be paved in 1992), and on a clear day you can see your windshield.

— *Recreational areas.* The Nuclear Test Range is a favorite. Take the whole family on a picnic there and let the kids play Mommy, Mommy! The Potato Salad is Glowing!

— *Education.* Grades one through six are offered. But due to budget constraints only forty-nine states are taught in geography class; in English only seven parts of speech are taught; and in ethics (how to tell right from wrong) only wrong is taught.

— *Housing.* We have many affordable single-family homes, some with roofs.

— *Culture.* Fort Worth is proud of its many cultural offerings. The Fort Worth Opera and Snake-Handling Society presents many fine performances during the season. Refreshments and first aid are available at intermission.

And each season, members of our symphony orchestra divide up into two gangs and have a rumble in the parking lot, during which several members of the string section are always critically pizzicatoed.

Then there is the Fort Worth Museum of Modern Skin Diseases, whose curator recently developed a nagging itch after the museum acquired Picasso's abstract *Woman With Eczema*. Docents give tours on Mondays, free samples on Tuesdays.

Also, our annual Human Sacrifice Week is always a crowd-pleaser.

As is our popular I Never Even Heard of Shakespeare in the Park Festival, when the whole family is invited to the park to toss out beer cans, dig up the grass and carve their initials on the trees. The latter activity is sure to catch the attention of members of our fun-loving Druid community, who hold the infidels down and give them Dutch elm disease.

There. That pack of lies should do the trick. Let me close by saying a single word to those folks who are considering moving to Fort Worth:

Dallas.

Heroes and Zeros

Mona Leo?
Golly gee-o!

I feel so . . . so . . . well, so *dirty*. I feel like I just kissed Castro on the mouth.

How else *could* I feel when I find that for years, everytime I gazed with yearning upon the Mona Lisa, I was entertaining thoughts about a man?

Yes, the Mona Lisa is the Mona Leo.

Or at least so says a researcher for Bell Labs, who used a computer to reveal that the Mona Lisa's eyes, hairline, cheeks, nose and *that* smile are actually the mirror image of a self-portrait painted by Leonardo da Vinci.

Naturally, the art world is agog and agag over this revelation. In museums everywhere eyebrows are arching, tongues are clucking, nose hairs are bristling. Just last week in Boston, a distraught museum docent impaled herself on an Alexander Calder mobile.

Personally I will never again be able to hear the song "Mona Lisa" without picturing da Vinci: an old man with a scowl, long white beard and bad breath. Well, OK, I made up that last part. But I'm glad that Nat King Cole, famous dead singer, didn't live to learn the truth.

Just what do we know about this da Vinci guy, anyway? Sure, he was *the* Renaissance man: mathematician-mechanic-engineer-chemist-author-architect-musician-sculptor-painter. He led the entire Renaissance in hyphens three seasons in a row.

But what other pranks was this madcap genius up to? More than 400 years ago, he drew the plans for a flying machine. Were these plans, too, a practical joke on us the public? If aeronautical engineers today built this flying machine, would they get it up to 32,000 feet only to find to their horror that it had no in-flight movie?

Yes, I feel betrayed. I once stood in line two hours at the actual Louvre to see the actual Mona Lisa and contribute my "oohs" and "ahhs." It sounded like mating season for vowels. Well, I want my money back. Plus a personal apology from the nation of France, the film concession at the Eiffel Tower and a vat of Yoplait yogurt with Catherine Deneuve at the bottom.

Any flavor will do. I mean I am *not* an unreasonable man.

A few days later, in Milan, I walked my little tourist legs down to their little tourist bones getting to the church where da Vinci's *Last Supper* is displayed. In light of this recent news, who knows *who* those thirteen men really were. Maybe a girls' softball team.

Just in case, I want a personal apology from the nation of Italy, a red Lamborghini and a Venetian gondolier (to stir the yogurt).

The Mona Leo? What a blow to the idealism of men. To think that this ageless embodiment of feminine pulchritude, with her enigmatic smile, her coy eyes, her winsome, soulful, almost angelic . . . OK. Hold it. Let's be honest.

The Mona Lisa is one ugly broad.

There. I've said it. *Someone* had to. I know I will receive engraved, pastel-tinted death threats from the art world ("the curator and staff of the Metropolitan Museum of Art cordially invite you to join us at 8 P.M. Monday for your gala disemboweling — refreshments will be served"), but it had to be said.

This Mona Lisa dame looks like the girl at the high-school dance who stands in the corner of the gym all night, shooting free throws.

Yes, she is homely. And now we know why. But at least this painting — unlike abstract art — can be understood. It has a definite up and down, realistic proportion, just two eyes, and a nose where a nose goes.

Still, esthetics aside, an ideal has been trod upon. Something dear has been taken from each one of us. The Mona Lisa a man! Now we all must learn to live with this shocking revelation. Until, of course, someone discovers that Leonardo da Vinci was really Queen Isabella wearing a fake beard.

Then everything will be OK again.

Oh, man! 'Tis good to be a guy

Recently I was lying on my back in a field of flowers, staring up at the clouds, when I suddenly remembered that today is Charles Bronson's birthday. (This should tell you that those were pretty manly, two-fisted flowers and pretty manly, two-fisted clouds.)

As I was pondering just what to give Bronson for his birthday, I fell to thinking about this whole business of being a man: the responsibilities, the rewards, the prostate trouble. With manly spontaneity I slapped my manly thigh and decided that a day should be set aside each year to celebrate the institution—nay, the *art*—of manhood. And I think that Bronson's birthday—November 3—is as good day as any for Boy, Do I Enjoy Being a Man Day (or Man, Do I Enjoy Being a Boy Day, for those who can't show proof of age).

After all, Charles "a smile, a handshake and a knee in the groin" Bronson is *the* macho, red-blooded, he-man, scotch-and-soda, strong-and-silent type of our time. Yet he's also a gentle, sensitive man who has recently written a book of verse dedicated to his Luger and whose shy way of saying, "I think you're special," is to pull your pelvis out through your nostrils.

This is probably the best time in history to be a man. There are so many choices in the eighties. Let's stroll along the buffet line of manhood and look at all the dishes behind the glass. A man can hunt, fish, get tattooed, drink, smoke, cuss, chew, spit, whittle, brawl, pass, punt and kick, hunker down, make military-industrial decisions endangering the lives of millions and pick his nose.

Fine. Anything for dessert?

But what if none of those choices appeals to you? Fine again. Me, either. Well, we can get out of here and go try to pick up a couple of chicks.

No, no. Just kidding, of course. No disrespect intended. But I'm sure that Bronson and my other brothers in the great fraternity of man would agree with me that the best thing about being men is women. Well, that and being able to sing bass in the shower.

Women are the people whom I most enjoy being the opposite sex of.

In fact, studies by Masters and Johnson have shown that in every man-woman relationship, the participants should agree early on which of them is going to be the opposite sex.

I remember the first time that I was glad that through an accident of birth I had been born male. It was the first day of first grade, when I saw my teacher. Miss Harris was lovely. She was the Mona Lisa with Play-Doh under her nails.

But like it or not, for ages, it was men who ran the world. Right into the ground, more often than not.

Many of the attitudes and cultural roles ascribed to men can be traced back to our primitive ancestors. A million years ago, man was the hunter-aggressor-protector-fighter. Even today we men prefer to walk around with our hands free (no purses) and our feet ready (no silly high heels) to spring into action in case we suddenly have to arm wrestle a woolly mammoth downtown someday.

Only recently has our culture progressed to the point that a man can be sensitive without being thought a sissy. Previously, if a man was moved by, say, a touching movie, he had to take out a ball-peen hammer and whack his kneecap right there in the theatre to mask the real cause of his tears.

Granted, there have been a few liabilities to man's estate: the draft, baldness, hemophilia, a shorter life expectancy and being expected to know which end of the hammer is the ball and which is the peen.

But gad, it's a great feeling to wake up in the morning and know that you can spend the whole day shaving, splashing on Chaps, popping your knuckles, lighting your pipe, slouching around in boxer shorts and wingtips, driving an old truck, whistling a Waylon Jennings song, carrying the twins piggyback and later, if it happens to be Father's Day, unwrapping a monogrammed truss.

Yes, being a man is a job for a man. It's a dirty job, but someone's gotta do it. After all, without men, who would portray "we three kings of Orient" in the Christmas play? Who would wear all those ugly leisure suits? Who would leave the world's toilet-seats up?

That concludes my modest proposal to celebrate manhood. And I want any man out there who doesn't agree with me that this—Charles Bronson's birthday—henceforth should be Boy, Do I Enjoy Being a Man Day to step up here right now so that I can pull his pelvis out through his nostrils.

Pretty please?

If you can't lie, lie low

Heaven help us, Harry.

Next Friday (Halloween) will be the sixtieth anniversary of the death of Harry Houdini. For ten years after his death, his wife conducted seances to try to contact him beyond the veil. But she finally stopped trying, and by now even his most devoted disciples have given up hoping to hear from him. Harry is either good and dead or else is really sulking.

But in life, Houdini was just a marvel. He could escape from handcuffs, chains, straitjackets, jail cells, vaults and packing cases dropped into rivers. He could get out of any situation.

Well, I wish Harry were still with us. Because there are a lot of situations in life that are just as bad and just as hard to get out of. For instance, I'd like to see Harry get out of:

—Dinner with the boss's boss's boss. This is someone of whom you stand in major awe. To you he is all-powerful, all-knowing and vengeance-seeking. To you he is like God, only with a bigger office.

What will you talk about? You can't ask him what it's like to pull down two mil a year. So you will look around the table, searching for some topic, and end up babbling something like this:

"Say, look at this, sir. This sure is some white bread here. I guess this is just about the whitest bread I ever saw. I suppose that its white color is due, in large part, to some innate quality of whiteness that it possesses."

Boss's boss's boss: "That's your napkin."

—The family reunion. Ah, time for another dollop of Aunt Nellie's potato salad, which, if airlifted to Africa, would be gratefully accepted and used to build schools. Time for the relatives to gather in the park to swat flies, cuss Uncle Joe's bratty kids and listen to Gramps call everyone by the wrong name:

"My, how you've grown, Jane."

"I'm John, Gramps."

"And how old are you now, Jean?"

"*John,* Gramps. Fifty-seven."

"And what do you want to be when you grow up, Jan?"

"J-O-H-N, you old fool. In another family."

Gramps has called so many relatives by the wrong name that it was finally discovered that he is someone else's Gramps who had just wandered into the park to feed the squirrels twenty-two years ago.

Gramps then tells about how he fought with General Patton and how the two of them crawled on elbows and bellies through the mud of France. What he doesn't tell you is that they were outside a bar in peacetime Paris at the time.

But you can't get out of going. After all, blood is thicker than water. Unless the water is in Aunt Nellie's coffee.

—A date (ladies). In a weak moment, you agreed to go out with some guy who looks as if he gets his haircuts by walking beneath a ceiling fan and then standing on tiptoes. At dinner, he loudly abuses the waiter, has a coughing fit and keeps putting his hand on your left knee — the one you were saving for marriage.

If only you could follow in the fading footsteps of Houdini and simply dematerialize, magically reappearing somewhere far away. Maybe in Mark Harmon's hot tub.

— An awards banquet. How you dread them. They're all the same — same food, same speeches. But you can't back out — the caterer has already put your name on a chicken leg. And worse, your colleague, Mort Snibly, will be the speaker. Mort is dull. If Mort were a work of art, he'd be a velvet bullfight.

You know that halfway through the banquet your mind will begin to wander. You'll lean over and whisper to your neighbor, "Say, this sure is some white bread . . ."

Yes, how I wish that Harry were still with us. Even if he couldn't show us how to get out of these situations, maybe he'd go in our place.

White lies: A bogus bio

Vanna White, of course, is the most wildly popular, immortal American since the last most wildly popular, immortal American, whoever *that* was.

What Vanna does, basically, is smile from ear to ear (or from coast to coast, whichever comes first) on TV's "Wheel of Fortune." Yet Vanna has lived a life of such breadth and, yes, butterth, that at age twenty-nine she had already written her autobiography, *Vanna Speaks,* published by Warner Books.

Well, personally, I can't wait to read this important book. So I have been forced to just imagine what Vanna's autobiography reveals. Here, then, in my own words, is her own story.

Chapter 1. I am born. I come into the world with eighty-seven teeth and padded shoulders, wearing a Christian Dior diaper with a slit up the thigh. As a baby, I love to play with blocks, turning them over one letter at a time. Each time I spell out a word or phrase, I clap with glee. But my little hands keep missing each other, and a pediatrician fits me with training mittens. Life is good.

Soon I am eighteen.

Chapter 2. It's hard to believe that I was a homely, unhappy child. But that was before I developed my philosophy of life: "A smile is just a frown turned upside-down." I discover this truth one day when I am standing on my head, frowning, and someone walks up and asks me what's so funny.

Soon I am beautiful.

Chapter 3. In college I major in Vowels with a minor in Applause. As a result of this training, on "Wheel of Fortune" I will hardly ever have to rely on the cue cards that read, "Clap. Clap. Clap."

Soon I am 25.

Chapter 4. In the competition for the job on "Wheel of Fortune," I beat out 200 other young women, mainly on my ability to smile without falling down.

As I become a star, some people think that I am just another pretty face, an airhead who can only turn letters, smile and clap. This is a vicious lie. I can also whistle.

Soon I am still beautiful.

Chapter 5. At age twenty-nine I get by on a salary of just $150,000 a year. My accountant tells me that breaks down to $2,884 a week and $576 a show, or about $41 a word and $11 per clap. Once, during a taping, there was a gnat on the set. I began trying to smush it between my palms, and in no time I had clapped myself into a higher tax bracket.

I still don't understand just why I am so wildly popular and immortal, but I have not let it go to my head. As proof of this, my phone number is still listed. On the stock exchange.

But how I yearn to stretch my horizons, to become a serious actress! I hope to star in a remake of *The African Queen*, reprising Katherine Hepburn's role as the prim missionary in Africa, steaming down the parasite-plagued, treacherous river with Bogie. But I want to re-interpret her role, bringing the word of God to the natives one letter at a time.

Native: "Is there an *o*?"

Me: "Yes! Two!"

Native: "Is there a *t*?"

Me: "Yes! Three!"

Native: "Is it *Thou shalt not kill*?"

Me: "Yes! (Clap clap clap.) Now tell him what he's won, Jack!"

I hope to begin rehearsal soon. In fact, I've already begun to practice smiling while picking off blood-sucking leeches.

Chapter 6. In ceremonies in my home state of South Carolina, my cleavage is given a state historical marker.

Epilogue. What does the future hold for me? Is there life after *Vanna Speaks*? Yes. I have already started writing part two of my autobiography, *Vanna Speaks, Sits Up and Fetches a Stick*.

Small world: Getting an eyeful

To paraphrase Tennyson, in the spring a young man's fancy lightly turns to thoughts of pond scum.

For it was on this date—April 24—in 1676 that Anton van Leeuwenhoek, using his simple microscope, first observed protozoa and bacteria in stagnant water. This discovery, of course, was to radically change our concept of life itself, after Leeuwenhoek read his paper to l'Académie des Sciences: "Gentlemen, never drink from a glass of water if it is looking back at you. I thank you. Good day."

So, in van Leeuwenhoek's honor, recently I scooped up some pond water, dusted off a great grandchild of his microscope and studied the great-grandchildren of his so-called little "animalcules." For two long hours I practically lived among these wee savage beasties. I came to know their ways, even to recognize a few of them on sight by some physical characteristic — size, color, perhaps a limp, a mole or a coy smile.

The first thing that I, as a trained observer, noticed about these creatures is how small they are. The second thing that I noticed is that they are simple, misshapen, grotesque. Looking at them was, in fact, a lot like looking through my old high-school yearbook.

As promised by all the biology books, I found a drop of pond water to be a world teeming with life. I further found that there are advantages and disadvantages to living in a tiny drop of water. If you are inclined to misplace things, they can never be very far away. But once you find them, they are likely to be pretty damp.

What parallels are there between their world and ours? Well, just as humans do, these simplest of animals carry on the nine processes that define life: motion, sensation, nutrition, respiration, circulation, secretion, excretion, reproduction and two weeks' paid vacation.

They just do them less conspicuously.

The one-celled animals are, in fact, self-reproducing. This, too, has advantages and disadvantages. Sex with yourself probably becomes monotonous after a while, but it at least assures you of a date every Friday night.

I found two types of animals dominant amid the dense floating algae. The first were fascinating: translucent green monsters — cylindrical, tapered, with a heart like a steam engine and a mouth like an upright Hoover. They would inch along like a Slinky, blindly groping for food. And from what I could tell, they'll eat anything and with very little sign of table manners.

Singling out one of these creatures under 50-power magnification, I could see its internal structure; under 600-power magnification I could see its heart beating; and under 1,500-power magnification, I could see the gravy stains on its tie.

The second creatures were balloon-shaped, single-celled animals that are built for speed. They dart frantically about, kinetic, frenzied, capable of great speeds and maneuvers. It was almost impossible to keep the lens trained on them. Compared to the aforementioned huge green monsters, these paramecia are tiny, or — to use the microbiologist's technical jargon — "itsy bitsy."

Yes, a drop of water is a microcosm mirroring our larger world, rife with social activity, work and play, success and failure. Its inhabitants are born, they prosper, they give us dysentery, they die.

Life is rich, life is good.

I recommend to all of you out there a spring day devoted to observing this tiny world. Then, as van Leeuwenhoek noted on April 24, 1676, you, too, will see "with great wonder, incredibly many very little animalcules of divers sort."

Be watching especially for a creepy little protozoan who looks a lot like Danny S., a senior in my high-school class who was voted most likely to have to settle for self-reproduction.

Coffee, tea or Buddhism?

A personal remembrance of the Wright Brothers to mark the anniversary of their first powered flights on December 17, 1903.

I was but a barefoot boy with cheek of tan that summer when I became friends with young Wilbur and Orville. Wilbur had been born in Millville, Indiana, in 1867. To make it easier for their mother to tell them apart, Orville was born four years later and in another state.

Who could forget those carefree days of yore, when so much had yet to be invented? Originally, the Wright Brothers woke up one morning in 1886 eager to invent the steamboat. They dressed and ran downstairs, only to learn that Robert Fulton already had invented the steamboat. Orville and Wilbur grew pouty and refused to speak to Fulton, who died in 1815.

Turning instead to the skies, the brothers quickly took up mankind's ageless dream of flight. They used skills mastered in their bicycle shop to begin their first simple experiments in aviation. These consisted mostly of pushing me off a cliff and plotting my trajectory, my time aloft and how many times I bounced.

There followed three years of experiments with kites and gliders. Through trial and error Wilbur and Orville discovered, in a breakthrough in aerodynamic engineering, that you could make something lighter by making it weigh less. This led Wilbur to wonder if a glider—made of wood, wire and fabric—could be made large enough to actually carry a man through the sky. Yes, Orville concluded, but for flights of more than 300 feet, you'd need an in-flight magazine.

I remember that they let me fly their glider once. Lying prone across the bottom wing, I soared thirty feet aloft before I lost control of the glider. As it veered crazily, I noted that there was nothing but air between me and an unyielding planet earth. Air is good for many things: for breathing, for cooling soup and for drying fingernails, but very poor for breaking your fall. As I plummeted, during a period of four harrowing seconds, I converted, in sequence, to Catholicism, Judaism and Buddhism.

Badly injured, I survived and soon after invented flight insurance.

I remember that Orville and Wilbur were very close. They thought almost as one person. It was amazing to witness. One cold night, as we huddled around the wood stove in the shed at Kitty Hawk, Orville sat on the stove, and Wilbur got blisters on his behind.

It was blustery the next morning as I helped them to assemble their craft—dubbed *The Flyer*—and to attach the twelve-horsepower engine and two wooden propellers. Then we laid out the sixty-foot track that *The Flyer* would glide along until it was airborne.

The brothers made four historic flights that day, ranging in time and length from 12 seconds and 120 feet to 59 seconds and 852 feet. After the fourth flight, Wilbur and Orville, normally the most taciturn of men, were ecstatic.

To celebrate, they pushed me off a cliff.

I think it had finally occurred to them that they had changed the course of history. Wilbur said, "I wish that someone would hurry up and invent *Time* magazine." "So that we could be on the cover," Orville chimed in.

Wilbur died in 1912. I was with him at the end. Ever the dreamer, he told me that he foresaw a time when the sky could be filled with huge commercial flying machines, carrying what he liked to call "passengers" to Chicago and their luggage to Jersey.

When Orville died in 1948, he was still at work inventing, this time perfecting the in-flight meal. His room was filled with prototypes of progressively smaller and smaller entrees, tiny desserts, tiny spoons and forks. On his death bed, he called me near and gasped his last words: "Coffee, tea or milk?"

He then pushed me off a cliff.

The Wonderful World of Worry

Give us this day our daily dread

Recently a friend told me about a secret worry that she harbors: meat tenderizer.

After you eat meat tenderizer, she worries, how does it know to stop doing what it does best—tenderizing meat. What keeps it from going to work on our insides—on Filet of You or T-Bone of Me?

Thank you, Arlene Thompson, for bringing this worry to my attention. Just when I thought I was on a first-name basis with every worry in the book—the Misfortune 500, as it were—you come up with a new one.

I mean *all* of us worry about certain clear and present dangers: nuclear war, crime, cancer. But some of us worry about subtler dangers. For instance, it takes some finesse in stress, a case of galloping paranoia and a blackbelt in angst to worry about:

171

— *The Boogie Man.* For many of us, our initiation into the Wonderful World of Worry came in childhood with this vague threat. In my case, the Boogie Man lurked at night behind a big cedar tree next to my parents' house. OK, maybe I never actually saw him, but I saw his shadow lots of times, I heard him rustle. Did so! Thirty years later, I still worry about the Boogie Man. But, more and more, these days he wears a leisure suit and tries to sell me an insurance policy.

— *Department store escalators.* What if you get your feet caught at the end of the escalator so that the row of metal teeth shreds your whole body from the toes up and leaves you on the fifth floor in a pile that resembles a taco ingredient?

— *Spontaneous combustion.* Oh, sure, you may say, how often is there a documented case of a person inexplicably bursting into flames? Well, only about once every hundred years or so. But a world-class worrier is not dissuaded by low odds. Just think of how going up in flames at, say, the office would affect your performance review. And spontaneous combustion *could* happen, too, if you don't say your prayers, respect your elders and wear asbestos underwear.

— *Public restroom mirrors.* How do we know they aren't two-way, with someone on the other side, watching us and snickering? Maybe even eating popcorn and filming us: "Just wait until *this* gets on the Playboy Channel, huh, Al? Look at *that* (munch) woman out there—wearing (munch) asbestos underwear!"

— *Metal fatigue.* Never mind if you are the safest driver ever. How about metal fatigue, huh? Have you ever seen a car's front-end stabilizer link-bolt with iron-poor blood? It's not pretty. If that bolt snaps when you are driving on the freeway some day, your car could suddenly veer out of control, hitting a busload of Shrine Temple conventioneers.

You could be fatally fezed.

Which brings up a related worry: What if you have to go through eternity with those people you die with? Do you want to sit around heaven with a bunch of Shriners? Certainly not if they won't show you the secret handshake.

— *Brain cells.* They're dying by the millions. Sometimes I can feel them in there, going belly-up. And they aren't replaced. Already I need training wheels on my typewriter. I estimate that by next week I won't be able to fall down without a map.

A related worry is that of learning capacity. What if the brain attic gets full, and then, for each thing we learn, we have to forget something else to make room? For instance, what if by learning the capital of Peru, you forget how to button your clothes? At the next party you attend, you could go around saying "Lima" all night and no one would be very impressed if your pants were at your ankles.

Yes, there are many worthy worries. Thanks again, Arlene, for pointing out a new one. I bet that lots of folks will read this and begin to worry about meat tenderizer that doesn't know when to quit. After all, who knows? Some night at dinner you may eat it and it will eat you back, devouring your stomach and causing your belly button to fall to the floor and roll under the table.

When that happens, just don't look under the table for it. The Boogie Man might be under there.

Is your first the worst?

Do you make a lousy first impression?

Welcome to the club.

When meeting strangers, do you shuffle and stammer? Does your handshake have the character and firmness of a rubber glove full of nightcrawlers?

Do you have a shrill little voice that only dogs and bats can hear? Are you too shy to make eye contact, choosing instead to look people squarely in the nostrils? So you just stand around first on one foot and then on the other, saying nothing, until at last the hostess puts a mirror to your lips to see if she should call you a cab or a coroner.

Welcome to the club.

Or sometimes at a large gathering, in desperation, you even try to pass for a famous and dynamic person by writing that person's name on your name tag: Ted Turner, Gloria Steinem, Moses.

But then about one A.M. some drunk pours cranberry juice into the punch bowl and wants to see you part the Red Sea.

Welcome to the club.

In social situations do you tend to go unnoticed, to fade into the background, to become just a piece of furniture? In fact, you sometimes are mistaken for a sofa and would complain bitterly about such treatment, but at a party last week you collected $4.76 in loose change.

Welcome to the club.

Or, on the other hand, maybe you come across as obnoxious. You laugh just a bit too loud, talk just a bit too much, slap people on the back just a bit too hard, causing their dentures to rocket out of their mouths, fly across the room and sink into the onion dip.

Sometimes there may be people—be they male, female or undecided—whom you really want or need to meet but to whom you avoid introducing yourself just because you know you will only make a lousy first impression.

And it's a darned shame, isn't it, because people who know you well would testify under oath that actually you are a very charming, witty, likeable person who talks easily about any subject with depth and sensitivity. You are well-read, cultured and equally at home with the arts or sciences, opera or Opry, a *pas de deux* or a do-si-do.

Ah, but let's say you have just met a group of people, and the conversation has turned to, oh, kidney disease among the fungus-growing ants of Brazil.

Panic! You can't think of a single fact about ants. Or about fungus. Or about Brazil. Although you *do* chime in that its capital is Des Moines. Everyone looks at you, slowly inches away and continues talking about teeny-tiny kidneys.

So you stand there with crumbs on your chin, listening, bobbing your head like one of those toy dogs in the back window of a car, and once in a while contributing a "So true. So true."

Then, after you get home that night you suddenly remember

that you have written three books on kidney disease among the fungus-growing ants of Brazil.

What a simp.

And welcome to the club.

Hey, maybe there really *should* be a club for people who make a lousy first impression. There would be thousands of members. Nah. At the very first meeting, members would stand around for two hours picking their dentures out of the onion dip and fishing change from between your cushions, and then everyone would vote with unanimous disgust to disband and go home.

I guess that all you can do is try to be more confident and keep telling yourself that you are just as good as everyone else you meet and that probably they are just as afraid as you are of making a lousy first impression.

Welcome to the club.

But don't get *too* confident. Because you also make a lousy *second* impression.

Fit and firm?
Fat chance

The other day some of us in the office were bemoaning the various flaws in our figures.

"Just look at these," said a reporter, pointing to her hips.

"You think *that's* bad? Look at *this,*" said an editor, pinching his waist.

"Hah! That's nothing. Just be glad you don't have *these!*" snorted a third, slapping a pair of thighs that looked like they had been floated down the Columbia River by men with plaid jackets and long poles.

How we fret about our flab. It has become a subject of national concern, like inflation, war and crime. Any day I expect to read this headline on the front page.

"Inflation, war, crime increase 17 percent,
jiggly upper arms arrested for questioning"

All of this flab, of course, is kindly old Mother Nature's way of making us feel ugly. It is one of her best tricks, along with rainbows, sunsets and dysentery.

Even those rare people with nothing to feel ugly about feel ugly. Especially women. You often hear beautiful actresses and models lament this or that perceived flaw in their figures. In reality, these women have bodies that would trigger armed combat in the streets of a Quaker village.

But most of us fret with good reason. Face it: Your waist, like the universe, is expanding. But while all the universe has to do is drift through infinity, your waist has to fit into size 34 pants.

The once-firm parts of your body have begun to sag, like a '56 Olds with bad shocks. Your belt buckle has disappeared. Soon you will have to hold a seance just to find your feet.

Overall, there are two main problem areas of the body.

For a man, it is the waist. With age, a man's center of gravity, once located near his chest, begins to settle, like the foundation of a house. Gradually his center of gravity slips toward his waist, then farther and farther south until, at last, it is in Nicaragua, where the Sandinistas capture it and hold it for ransom, demanding 100 U.S. tanks, 1,000 M1 rifles and Jane Fonda's workout video.

Not even an otherwise-skinny man is immune. I know. For twenty years of my life I was skinny. I was the national anorexia poster child three years in a row. One Easter I wore a white suit and was mistaken for a fence picket. I still have "Tom + Becky" carved just below my left knee.

But now, while I remain stringy, Mother Nature has tied a knot in the string. At my waist. After a certain age, this bulge cannot be lost. I believe that a man of 38 years, 74 inches and 185 pounds could lose, say, 170 pounds and *still* have a convex waist.

In fact, he could continue to lose weight until every other part of his body had withered and disappeared. He would then be just a fifteen-pound waist. No arms, no legs.

This would make it hard for the waist to walk to work. And just as hard for it to hail a cab.

For a woman, the hips are the problem area. Fat cells from all over her body take early retirement and move to her hips. These fat cells—seen under a microscope as obnoxious little things with double chins and an unattractive waddle—are there to stay, no matter what. Even as a woman works out at the spa, she can hear the fat cells in there, chuckling softly and eating tiny dishes of ice cream.

So don't kid yourself, folks. And don't waste your time and money on home fitness equipment or spa memberships or diets. After a certain age, nothing will get rid of those sags, bags and bulges. You can exercise and diet until you die. Death is nature's way of telling you to try something else.

Meanwhile, the universe and your waist will continue to expand. And you will continue to tell yourself something like this: "Well, OK, so maybe I *don't* have a perfect figure. But I compensate for that imperfection by having a truly wonderful personality."

Uh, that reminds me: We've been meaning to speak to you about your personality . . .

A lark becomes an albatross

I have a problem.

Now, if I just knew what it is!

Sister Madonna knows what it is. Sister Madonna knows all. It says so right in her ad in the supermarket tabloid *Weekly World News*.

On the same page are stories with these headlines: "Prankster bites blasting cap and blows off face!" and "My rich beau gave me money, a snazzy car and herpes!" And an ad for a "miracle doll with magic wand that grants you three wishes. Doll works. $5.95 plus $1.50 postage and handling. Please use wisely."

I love tabloids. Reading them is the most fun that you can have with the lights on. Besides, tabloids help me keep my mind off my problem.

Whatever it is.

It all began as a lark. Little did I know that I would soon be plunged into paranoia. I sent the day, month and year of my birth, as requested, to reader-adviser Sister Madonna in Florida for a psychic reading. Soon I got a personal reply, direct from her personal Xerox machine.

"My Dearest One: I was so sorry to hear about your problem. All I need is your faith in me and I promise you I will take care of your problem. However, I must talk to you about your problem. I want you to call me. Their *(sic)* is something I must tell you, about your problem."

There: She mentioned my "problem" four times! And I hadn't ever told her I had one. This woman *knows* something.

And here I had thought that my life was going well. I have my health, a job and an IRA that, when I retire in the year 2014, will be worth $184,399, enabling me to buy several loaves of bread.

I sleep well, laugh often and am not heavily in debt to anyone named Scarface.

But still, Sister Madonna insists that I have a problem.

I wonder how these women derive their power to see the future? From astrological charts? Tea leaves? Crystal balls? Or in this day of specialization, instead of a crystal ball, perhaps Sister Madonna gazes into:

—*A meatball.* Maybe she can foresee that I'm going to eat at an Italian restaurant and die of heartburn.

—*A beach ball.* Perhaps she can predict that I'll be attacked at the seashore by a 97-pound weakling. Carrying a 98-pound bazooka.

—*An eight ball.* Maybe she can foresee that I will walk into a billiard parlor to get change and accidentally bump a tough guy, causing him to miss a shot. He will then chalk his cue stick, take aim and sink my tonsils in the side pocket.

—*A mothball.* Maybe she can predict that I'll be rummaging around in the bedroom closet someday and be crushed by a falling box of Christmas ornaments. I'll be fatally tinseled.

Sure, I could call her, as she urged. But I'm not sure I want to know.

What if my problem is inevitable? Does it involve a junkie and a dark alley? Does it have anything to do with the ten plagues of Egypt? I don't look good in locusts.

What if my problem is muscled and mean and has the tattoo of a ship on his chest—full-scale?

What if my problem involves an inferno or something with wheels or an alligator?

God, what if it's all three: I'm going to die in a burning motel room with a Roller Derby queen wearing an Izod shirt!

It has been weeks now since I got that ominous letter from Sister Madonna. For weeks I have jumped every time a car backfired, every time the phone rang. Every time I pass a Ramada Inn, I put on an asbestos body-stocking.

But nothing has happened yet.

In fact, I'm beginning to suspect that Sister Madonna is a fraud and that there *is* no problem looming over me.

But just to be on the safe side, I've sent off for my "miracle doll with magic wand."

Running fitness
into the ground

I know that some fellow joggers are out there in the audience today. I can hear you sweating.

These days millions of folks jog, some more than others. I have otherwise-normal friends who each year run in the local Cowtown Marathon and after completing the race still have the wherewithal to perform complicated tasks such as putting on their street clothes, finding their car and passing out in the parking lot.

I am no such fanatic. I am neither fast nor fancy. I run only a mile a day. But it is a very sincere mile, and I suffer with great conviction.

I run in a fairly isolated, wooded area. So no one ever sees me. This makes me fear that some day while I'm jogging, I will collapse in my tracks from all this good health, and my body won't be found until long after the squirrels have mugged me and taken my wallet.

Another fitness-related death.

Why do people decide to start jogging anyway? Some of us start in midlife, as our bellies begin to cause a total eclipse of our toes. Others of us start the day that our physician looks at our X rays and openly weeps.

Not that jogging is without risk. It can do bad things to our joints. But we decide to make a deal with fate: The risk of bad joints is traded for the hope of one strong heart, two good lungs and an outfielder to be named later.

If we want to suffer, why don't we just stick both arms into a buzz saw? At least that way we wouldn't have to keep up our violin lessons anymore.

Not only is jogging painful, it is dull. If the act of jogging were a person, it would be Mister Rogers. In a coma. When you jog, all you do is feel the various once-firm parts of your body jiggle and sweat. For variety, you can sweat and jiggle. Meanwhile, you no doubt are jarring loose blood clots and tumors and perhaps some internal organ that you might need in your declining years.

Yet I prefer jogging to other forms of exercise. Jogging requires no special equipment, no bats or racquets, no uniforms or courts. Just some rubber-soled shoes, a couple of legs, a couple of feet, and you're off. Then it's just you: you testing your endurance, you stretching your muscles, you feeling the wind in your shin splints.

Life is rich, life is good.

And although jogging seems a recent fad, it is really quite old. Scientists believe that those prehistoric tracks in the creekbed down at Glen Rose were made by jogging dinosaurs who could do a mile in under 6.5. As measured on the Richter scale.

In ancient Rome only male members of the wealthy classes were allowed to jog. Caesar was so wealthy that he kept a slave on staff to run *for* him and another slave to get a charley horse for him, although he sometimes allowed his wife, Calpurnia, to sweat for him. In ancient Rome, if a commoner was caught jogging, he was flogged for thirty minutes; fifteen minutes, if he seemed to be enjoying it.

Later, during the Dark Ages, joggers had many quaint ideas. Because the earth was thought to be flat, a jogger ran the risk of falling off the edge. Falling off the edge of the earth was thought to be a poor way to start the day. Nevertheless, many joggers still tried this because, of course, once you were over the edge, it was all downhill.

Eventually, it was the great thinker-jogger Descartes who based the existence of existence on his now-famous statement, "I ache, therefore I am."

And now millions of us jog, painful and dull though it may be. And speaking for myself, I'll keep on jogging right up until the time that I collapse in my tracks some day in that wooded area.

After I'm dead, local merchants would be wise to watch for squirrels trying to use my credit cards.

To a worrier, the sky is the limit

Do you have a fear of flying?

For sheer enjoyment, do you rate flying only slightly above being strapped to Colonel Qadhafi and dragged slowly down Main Street, USA? Do you dream of the day when an airline offers 747s that taxi all the way to most major airports?

Me, too. And people like us—who fear flying but keep right on getting into airplanes—provide an essential service to everyone else who flies. We are just as important as the flight crew, the air-traffic controllers and the airport security personnel who bombard our luggage with X rays, causing the skies each day to be filled with thousands of pairs of glowing pajamas.

The last time I flew I had a revelation: It's worry that keeps a plane in the air. I realized this when the plane suddenly dipped. Air pocket, a flight attendant assured me. But I knew better. I realized that the plane had dipped exactly at the time that I — lulled by the drone — momentarily had ceased to worry.

Yes, it is worry generated by cowards like me that keeps a plane from falling out of the sky and crashing right into the ten o'clock news.

I worry wonderfully well at high altitudes. In fact, at 32,000 feet, an aura of angst forms around me and is visible for several rows. If the person next to me falls alseep, I can even worry enough for two. And once, when twenty-seven VFW conventioneers canceled, I was able to fill in for them, moving back and forth across the aisle, sitting on both sides, worrying each wing onward through the night sky and singing forty choruses of "It's a Long Way to Tipperary."

Of course, what I and others like me suffer is not technically a fear of flying, but rather a fear of *not* flying. We fear that the plane will be hurtling merrily along and then "something will happen," and the plane will stop hurtling and start plummeting. Ugly word, plummeting.

Some winged worriers, I am told, suffer claustrophobia in an airplane. Claustrophobia, of course, is the fear of being trapped in an enclosed 747 with 100 businessmen who are reading *Fortune* magazine.

Others suffer air sickness. That's indeed one of the great advances of modern transportation: to be able to eat lunch over Omaha and lose it over Denver.

Sometimes, just to delay that inevitable take-off, I will interrupt a flight attendant as she's giving us her little speech about oxygen masks, life jackets and emergency exits.

". . . and if the cabin pressure were to drop, oxygen masks would dr–"

"Excuse me, but didn't you go to North Texas State University."

Then, because she knows her spiel only by rote, she has to start all over.

"Welcome aboard National flight 221. I'm Rhonda, and before we ta–"

"No, you're not. You're *Sheila*. Good ol' Sheila from Psych 101!"

"Ahem. Welcome aboard National flight 101. I mean 221! I'm Sheila. I mean *Rhonda* . . ."

Because I always sit in the tail section, I am aware of all the people who go aft to the tiny restroom. Personally, I would never use a restroom six miles in the sky, because it would mean getting out of my seat. Once we're in the air, I never move. I am afraid I'd jostle the plane. My kidneys average 12,000 miles between major overhauls.

Once I sat next to some sort of engineer. When he saw that I was fingering my complimentary peanuts like worry beads, he tried to reassure me, telling me I'd feel safer if I understood aerodynamics and structural principles. He proceeded to tell me how much the paint on the jet's exterior weighed, how many passengers this equaled, and how much just the dirt on the paint contributed to drag.

I was *not* being reassured.

Then he grabbed the back of the seat in front of him and ripped loose the upholstery. It was fastened with Velcro, but I didn't know that at the time. I thought he was starting to disassemble the plane directly above a fairly deep ocean.

But he was just showing me where the seat frames were perforated, thus rendering the plane even lighter. Lighten the plane wherever possible, he said. That's important.

I began to wish that I had worn socks with holes in them.

Then came the worst part of flying: the descent. On a flight from D-FW to New York, the pilot apparently starts the descent over Arkansas. The engines change pitch constantly. They whine. To whine is fine, down here on earth. Dogs can whine. Kids can whine. Sirens can whine. But nothing should ever whine 32,000 feet in the air. I find that whining at that altitude is contagious.

By the time we landed, I was in an ecstasy of worry. I had attained a transcendental state of perfect, symmetrical worry. As I wobbled off the plane, I overheard one flight attendant (Rhonda) tell another that it had been an unusually smooth flight and landing.

"Shucks, Sheila," I said, turning to her, "it was nothing."

So, fellow winged worriers, remember your responsibility.

Next time you get aboard a plane, furrow those brows! Clench those jaws! Whiten those knuckles!

And let's keep it up.

Flight fright: Dang that ding

Thirty-two thousand feet straight up — *ding!*

How I hate those *ding*s.

I'm a nervous flier, and those *ding*s over an airliner's PA system always seem to herald bad news, such as an announcement that we're about to fly into turbulence. Those *ding*s seldom seem to herald good news, such as that we will have a perfectly smooth flight or that my lab tests were negative.

But to me, the worst time is the few seconds between the *ding* and the actual announcement. That's when I brace myself to hear all sorts of ominous news.

And sure enough, the last time I flew, we weren't in the air ten minutes before it began.

Ding.

I then expected to hear something like: "Ladies and gentlemen, there is no need for alarm, but the pilot's mustache has just caught fire."

But, no, it was only: "Ladies and gentlemen in the coach section, due to some confusion at the airport, we regret that we're short twenty in-flight meals. We're terribly sorry, and we are asking if twenty of you would be gracious enough to volunteer not to have a meal. Volunteers are welcome to free soft drinks or cocktails."

The flight attendant sounded like Colonel Travis asking the men of the Alamo to step across the famous line that he had drawn in the dirt. "Men, if you're willing to die, step across this famous line I've drawn in the dirt. Because the situation is hopeless: We're outnumbered, we're out of ammunition, and there's no entree."

So this is what flying has come to—we're so used to frills that we expect them, and an airline expects us to expect them, and we expect the airline to expect us to expect them, and the airline expects us . . . oh, fly this sentence to Cuba—I want to get off!

Understand that my sole concern while 32,000 feet in the air is that that figure not decrease by more than 31,999 feet. So going without an airborne meal is of microscopic consequence to me.

So I volunteered. But I *did* say I'd take one of those free soft drinks. A Coke. But horrors: They were out of Coke, too. The flight attendant asked me if I'd be gracious enough to settle for Pepsi. Again, she talked as if she were asking me to go outside and sit on the wing. Or read the in-flight magazine. Or both.

Then came another scare.

Ding.

Uh oh. I imagined: "Ladies and gentlemen, there is no need for alarm, but the blaze in the pilot's mustache has gone to three alarms, and firemen have cordoned off his sideburns!"

But, no. We were simply asked to buckle up and expect some turbulence.

The flight indeed got rough, and soon I was drinking Pepsi straight out of the can and getting a little obnoxious. I said to the flight attendant, "You guys obviously aren't afraid to fly. What *are* you afraid of?"

She thought a pretty, poised moment and said, "Snakes."

Good point. But you never read a headline like, "Python crashes, killing all on board."

Meanwhile, we twenty brave volunteers were still being pampered. "Can I fluff your pillow, sir? Read you a story? Burp your first-born?"

I was beginning to enjoy being a martyr. But then:

Ding.

Uh oh. I imagined: "Ladies and gentlemen, there is no need for alarm, but wind-blown sparks from the pilot's mustache have spread to his toupee, which is made of wood shingles!"

But, no. It was just: "We again wish to express our thanks to those of you who graciously gave up your meal. We apologize for the inconvenience."

Aw, it was nothing. A simple marble statue in the airport gift shop will suffice.

Soon it came again.

Ding.

Uh oh. But, no, this time it was good news: "Ladies and gentlemen, thank you for flying with us today and welcome to Dallas-Fort Worth Airport. There is no need for alarm."

Somehow, while I was fretting, we had landed safely. Once again, I had survived a plane flight. And without an entree! Suddenly I felt so silly for having harbored all those fears and morbid fantasies.

But as I got up and we all filed out past the cockpit door, I could have sworn that I saw the arson squad in there, sifting through the smoldering rubble of the pilot's mustache.

I just hope he's insured.

Shear terror: The barber chair

Third chair from the end — the little *c*'s stand for "cringe."

What man has not sat before his barber, looked down and read his fate in the snippets — the dark, wet *c*'s of hair that fall to the floor? Little *c*'s that stand for "chagrin," "calamity," and, yes, "cold ears."

Because no matter how many times I get my hair cut, I never feel comfortable being pinned helplessly in a chair while a strange woman comes at me with a sharp instrument in one hand and a copy of *Cosmopolitan* in the other.

It all goes back to Samson, I guess, who showed so much promise at slaying Philistines with the jawbone of an ass until Delilah cut his career short.

At my barber's — Lawanda's Discount Hair Boutique and Muffler Shop — the agony begins in the waiting area. Twenty-three minutes past the appointment time (this delay is established by the state barber board), my name is called. Then the fantasy unfolds.

Walking slowly, the warden comes for me. Beside him is a kindly priest, played by Pat O'Brien. The warden says, "It's time, Killer."

Then Father Pat asks me if I want him to pray for my cowlick. I laugh scornfully. As I walk past others in the waiting area, their eyes are averted. From somewhere comes a basso profundo voice singing "swing low, sweet char-i-ot, com-in' for to car-ry me hooooome."

I am led to Old Sparky. I sit down stoically, sneer suavely and go to pieces. "No! No!" I scream. "You can't! Not me! I'm too young to have a little off the top!"

It is not pretty.

The barber wraps a sheet around me like a shroud. She pins it behind my head. There is Vitalis on her breath.

I continue to whimper fluently in several languages. Then a phone rings. "It's the governor!" I shout. "My pardon! I'm saved! I'm saved!"

My barber answers the phone, listens intently a moment and then hollers, "Hey, Lawanda! Do we have a tailpipe for a '58 Impala?"

The warden steps back and nods solemnly to my barber. She picks up the clippers and flips the switch.

Bzzzzz-z-z-z-t!

(The little *c*'s also stand for "current.")

The lights dim. Suddenly, in the brief darkness, someone shouts, "Yeeech! Where's the lights? I just stepped in some styling mousse!"

When I regain reality, I see my cowardly face. "Ha ha," I try to joke with the barber as she cuts. My voice is brittle. "At least with a firing squad, you get a blindfold."

She stops clipping a moment, considering this. Then she goes to fetch a blindfold and resumes work.

"No, no! For *me*. Not for *you*," I correct as she gropes wildly, snipping a frond off a Boston fern.

As I fidget, I wonder how others react to a haircut—the great equalizer of men. Somewhere, right now, is Springsteen or Cronkite or Kennedy sitting helpless with his hair slicked back, ears naked to the world?

Shakespeare and Moses had to get haircuts, too, you know. So did the great seer Nostradamus, who once predicted that he would get a haircut but that his sideburns would come out uneven.

Even heads of state get shaggy. Does the Ayatollah Khomeini, too, put off getting a haircut as long as he can? Is his barber's tongue stapled to a camel's hump if he gets hairs down the ayatollah's neck?

Yes, those little c's are disturbing. And yet I have started asking the barber to give me my floor sweepings in a doggy bag. I keep the little c's in a hope chest and will put them to good use some day.

Because eventually nature will have one more c-word that makes us men cringe.

The little c's will stand for "chrome dome."

Mind your P's and IQ's

I felt like Ironside in a drag race.

Like the Venus de Milo in a typing class.

Like a knothole in a sequoia convention.

Recently I crashed a meeting of the local Mensa chapter. Mensa is an organization of people who score in the top two percentile on a standardized IQ test. You remember such tests from school. You answer questions such as "Which of the following does not belong: red blue green 1812 yellow brown," and after the tests are graded a vocational guidance counselor tells you that you are best suited to be a doorstop.

I found Mensa members to be fine, friendly folks. Normal. Just like you or me. They tell jokes, they discuss current events, they build nuclear reactors using only a toaster oven and a pair of pliers.

In the presence of such aggregate intelligence, I naturally wanted to be at my best. When asked how many years I have worked at the *Star-Telegram,* I was careful not to count on my fingers or to answer by tapping my foot on the floor seventeen times.

Then came a *real* challenge. The meeting was held in the hospitality room of a local brewery. The choice of beverage was Coors or Coors. But I wanted a Coke. A member told me of a soft-drink machine in a snack room located somewhere in the interior of the building. I was given directions:

Go out that door and turn right, look for a guard desk, take a left and go straight until you see a potted plant, turn right, then left, then right and look for a stain in the carpet, take the next left and there it is, deposit nickels, dimes or quarters.

Oh, the self-imposed pressure I felt to follow those directions deftly and not get lost! As I took the first left (or was it right?), I wondered: If I don't get back within a certain time, will the Mensa members feel sorry for me and start talking to me very slowly?

"And . . . does . . . being . . . a . . . doorstop . . . pay . . . well, . . . Mike?"

That's when I realized that instead of the standard written IQ tests, there should be real-world IQ tests.

1. Change a typewriter ribbon—the old-fashioned, two-spooled kind, like the one that Moses used to write the book of Exodus. You'd be graded on how much ink got on yourself, how much ink remained on the ribbon and, if you threw the typewriter out a window, how many times it bounced.

2. Refold a road map in such a way that it does not resemble an origami swan.

3. Open a childproof medicine bottle.

4. Arrange these stages of life sequentially: adolescence, infancy, childhood, adulthood, birth, prostate trouble.

5. Fold the four flaps of a box top so that they are interlocked. I realize that this is easy for some folks. Not for me. When my friends hear that I am about to try to interlock a box top, they pack a picnic lunch and come watch. The more-callous among them place bets on how soon I will develop a facial tic.

6. Assemble a toy on Christmas morning: Fit left subflange

to right subflange, which is bent; fasten sprocket 1a to spacer 2b, which was not included; bolt swivel base A to center brace B, which your two-year-old just ate.

7. Which of the following phrases does not belong: "to have and to hold," "for richer, for poorer," "in sickness and in health," "*my* lawyer will call *your* lawyer."

8. Fill out the new W-4 form without bloodshed.

Well, it was just a thought. If you are interested in Mensa and think you might qualify, attend one of their monthly meetings. If you aren't a beer drinker, there are Cokes in the snack room. Just ask for directions.

And take along some bread crumbs.

Can't sleep? Then read this

To misquote Shakespeare, some men are born boring, some achieve boring, and some have boring thrust upon them.

I am three for three.

We all harbor fears that at times we are boring. But I harbor more than mere fears. Each year my hundreds of closest friends select me as four of the ten most boring people in the free world. The other six honorees are notified by letter, which is forwarded to them at Forest Lawn.

And now I find that being boring is finally being recognized as the terrible social affliction that it is. I recently read a news story about the findings of a study that were published in the *Journal of Personality and Social Psychology.* As soon as I read it, I recognized in myself most of the symptoms of halitosis of the personality.

The study found that boring people talk in clichés. "Well, basically . . ." "That's the way the cookie crumbles." They respond noncommittally. "Uh huh." "Really." They show interest in only one topic. They monopolize conversations by complaining about their own problems.

I first sensed that I am boring when a date excused herself from our restaurant table to go to the restroom just as I started telling her how lately I had been memorizing the atomic chart and that calcium has a chemical valence of two. This was in 1969. I am sure she'll return to the table any minute now.

Meanwhile I am keeping her breadsticks warm.

Nowadays, a friend will call me up and say, "Hey, some of us are going out on the town tonight. There'll be good food, good drink and good fellowship aplenty. Whaddaya say, sport?"

Well, no fool I. My reply is, "No, thanks. I'm up to manganese now. Did you know that its density is 7.43 grams per cubic centimeter?"

Or another will say, "Hey, a bunch of us are chartering a Concorde and flying over to Paris to spend the weekend at the Ritz, where we have invitations to a catered orgy. Wanna tag along?"

I will agree to go, but only if I can bring my chemistry book.

Here's a quick quiz to test *your* boring quotient.

As you are talking to your boss, Mr. Snerple, does he gradually tune you out? Does he begin to watch a fly crawl along the desk? Does he offer the fly your job?

In the throes of passion, does your spouse reach for the TV remote control and switch on "Bonanza"?

At your last birthday party, were you not invited?"

It isn't easy to remain boring in this age, you know, when everyone seems to have a wide range of interests and a veritable choke-hold on the social graces. And we boring people provide a valuable public service: We make the marginally boring appear interesting by comparison. We even help the truly interesting to fall asleep.

A friend called me, too keyed up to sleep. He was just back from a weekend of hunting lions in Africa with Robin Williams, Carl Sagan and the Radio City Rockettes.

I told him, "You think *you* had a weekend, fella? Let me tell you about *mine*. Well, basically I spent Friday pulling my dental floss out of its dispenser. See, the label says it contains fifty yards. But I wanted to be sure. Well, basically, it was right. And you think *you* have a headache? You ought to see *mine*. I spent Saturday trying to put fifty yards of floss back into the dispenser. But I guess that's just the way the cookie crumbles."

He began to snore as I was getting to Sunday and the really exciting part: how I had just memorized the atomic symbol of molybdenum.

It's Mo. It is, you know. Uh huh. Really.

Gone fission:
A peace mission

"No column today. Gone to get world peace."

If you ever read that notice in this space, it will mean that I am attending the next summit meeting on nuclear disarmament. I will be attending as a neutral party, having packed a bilateral toothbrush and a change of non-aligned underwear.

Oh, and my homeowner's insurance policy.

Because I am suddenly alarmed after having spent Friday, Saturday and the better parts of Sunday poring over my policy. (This tells you the sort of bachelor debauches that I hold around my place on weekends.)

Of course, having majored in journalism and minored in English, I don't speak fluent insurance. But one clause did catch my eye, and I was able to wrestle it to the ground and subdue a few nouns.

Under "Basic Exclusions" I read: "The company shall not be liable for loss, bodily injury or property damage resulting from hostile or warlike action. . . , it being understood that any discharge, explosion or use of any weapon of war employing nuclear fission or fusion shall be conclusively presumed to be such a hostile or warlike action."

So I called my insurance company — Mutual of Bubba — and asked if this is true. Bubba just giggled. Which, I take it, is insurance jargon for "conclusively."

I just can't believe that Reagan and Gorbachev were aware of this loophole in my policy when they failed to reach disarmament in Iceland. Now there is talk of another summit. Well, I'm going to attend it to make sure that Reagan and Gorbachev know next time. I just know that my disclosure will be the deciding factor in reaching disarmament.

I will call a news conference and ask these two bigshots: "Just who the heck do you think you are, anyway?"

While they are asking their aides for help in drafting a reply to *that* one, I will read to the world press a list of all my personal belongings that, I now know, won't be covered in the event of the Ultimate Disagreement.

I have coin and stamp collections. I have a Sears catalog from the sixties that features an itty-bitty Cybill Shepherd wearing itty-bitty women's underwear. All these belongings are — I now realize — atomically uninsured.

I have a paint-by-numbers version of the *Last Supper* that I hope to finish some day. But I ran out of the flesh tone (number 41) before I got to Matthew, and he still looks like Claude Rains.

I have five clean socks, hundreds of books and two 8-millimeter color films from a Hong Kong mail-order company: *Helga, Bibi and Monique Change a Flat Tire on the Interstate in the Nude* and its sequel *27-Car Pileup*. All these, I now know, lie defenseless, vulnerable.

Then there are many items of great sentimental value: diaries, yearbooks, my old wood-burning typewriter, and several touching letters from women responding to my romantic overtures. These letters are complete, although the enclosed poisonous spiders have gotten loose in the house somewhere.

And it won't necessarily have to be a direct nuclear hit on my roof or anything, either, to cause irreparable damage. I suspect that a 500-megaton device landing, say, in my neighbor's flowerbed still would be sufficient to cause my soufflé to fall.

As for "bodily injury" in the event of war, it could take many forms. For instance, my bathwater could become so contaminated by radiation that I wouldn't be able to freshen up for 500 years without fear of becoming my own night light. And Mutual of Bubba would not owe me a penny for pain and suffering.

Because mine is a standard homeowner's policy, chances are that *your* policy, too, contains this most unfair clause. So you may want to attend the next summit meeting with me and tell these clowns to cool it.

(Bring your own non-aligned underwear.)

We must get peace. Otherwise, after the dust of World War III settles, if you want to buy new drapes to spruce up your crater, the money will have to come out of *your* pocket.

If you still have a pocket.

Rich Man, Poor Man

Tax money?
Fork it over

Picky, picky, picky.

Two recent news stories show how picky people can be. Rep. Jack Brooks is in a snit because the government has spent $2 million to replace the silverware in U.S. embassies. And Sen. William Proxmire is in a separate-but-equal snit because the government has spent $10,000 a year to provide decks of playing cards as souvenirs to passengers who fly on the vice-president's Air Force Two.

It's just that sort of nit-picking that threatens America's position as the silverware and playing-card leader of the free world.

Sure, you say, any registered voter could go down to the mall and pay less than our Uncle Sam pays for most things. But that's beside the point, you incredibly cheap person you. The point is that if our Uncle Sam began to comparison shop, eliminate frills and live within our means, soon he would no longer have a $2 trillion deficit, and then what would *we* do with all our hard-earned money that goes for taxes?

So please, no more nit-picking.

The $2 million was spent to buy 72,000 pieces of silverware to replace any pieces that were missing or worn and any pieces that did not feature the current Embassy Scroll pattern.

That averages $27.77 per knife, fork or spoon. And the cost would be even higher for specialized utensils, such as your caviar prong or your pheasant reamer or your truffle forceps.

But shut yourself into your linen closet and ask yourself this: "Do I, (your name), want *my* ambassadors to sully their lips with silverware that has an obsolete pattern? Do I, (your name), know what would happen if an ambassador's well-bred palate had to taste *pâté de foie gras* from a worn spoon? If I, (your name), had *any* sensitivity at all, I would throw up at the mere suggestion."

Soon, all over the world, ambassadorial taste buds would suffer such shame that they would leave little suicide notes pinned to ambassadorial uvulas and jump to their deaths down ambassadorial throats.

And those playing cards are a bargain, too. Because anyone who flies on Air Force Two naturally wants a souvenir of the great and solemn occasion. Better to give them cards than to have them start taking home parts of the plane.

"Guess what, honey! I just flew on Air Force Two!"

"Aw, go on! I don't believe you."

"Really! Look: I got this wing. I tore it off somewhere over Idaho."

Yes, let's face it: Our Uncle Sam is a Yuppie. And if that means that to support him, we—his beloved nieces and nephews—have to live on Spam and government cheese, well, what of it?

At least we can sleep easy at night knowing that each Air Force Two playing card is made to the most rigid government specifications, able to withstand in-flight champagne spills and sustained shuffling at 32,000 feet.

We'll know that for our embassies, each knife, fork and lobster chisel is certified, balanced, tested under combat conditions at formal dinners and able to withstand pressure from the dentures of even the most voracious envoy to the United Nations.

Because, you know, we can't afford to lose the flatware race with the Russians, who even now are developing a particle-beam ambassadorial silverware pattern. Mark my words: If we let the Russians gain superiority in knives, forks and spoons, the next thing you know they will be on our very borders, rattling their cups and saucers and godless commie napkin rings.

So please, let's hear no more nit-picking. Our Uncle Sam needs our trust and support. I know that right this minute he is up there in Washington trying to put into words his profound gratitude to us. Probably something like what Marie Antoinette said.

"Let them eat cake.

"With plastic forks."

W-4 as simple as 2 plus 2 is 18¼

Have you seen the new IRS W-4 form? Judging by the look on your face, I'd say that you have. That or you just had your appendix removed. Through your ear.

The form itself is just part of the W-4 booklet, which includes two pages of instructions, a worksheet with twenty-one blanks, two tables of numbers and a warning that if you don't file the form by October, two IRS agents named Knute and Knute (here's an easy way to tell Knute and Knute apart: they don't look anything alike) will come to your home some night and put your appendix back in for you.

Essentially, you, as a taxpayer, do all this fretting and figuring so that you can supply the answer to a single question: How many exemptions should you claim?

In view of this attempt at "tax simplification," here's how your government would simplify the process of adding 2 plus 2:

1987 Federal 2 Plus 2 Is 4 Worksheet,
Recipe for Okra Gumbo,
and All-Penguin Rumba Band

In accordance with the Math Reform Act of 1987, the process of adding certain whole numbers vital to national security has been simplified. To bring *your* old math skills into line with this new standard, please practice by adding 2 plus 2 using the following simple process:

A. Add 2 plus 2 in the old, outmoded way. Enter 4 in the blank.

B. From 4, subtract 1 argyle sock. Enter 3 in the blank.

C. Referring to table 1, find your age. Enter 37 in the blank.

D. Add blanks B and C. The sum of 2 and 2 now stands at 40.

E. Multiply by the 5 of spades. Enter 200 in the blank.

F. What if I've already had my appendix removed? Would my tonsils do?

G. Do *what?*

H. Dice 23 okra pods, add and let simmer, entering 223 in the blank.

I. If line D is greater than line H, look under the sofa. Hey, look: There's your other argyle sock!

J. If married but adding single, subtract 73 and put 150 in the blank.

K. If adding single but seeing double, put a cold towel on your forehead.

L. Are you now or have you ever been?

M. If you are, send for Federal Publication 100: *Am Not!* If you are not, send for Federal Publication 101: *Are So!* If you aren't sure, send for Federal Publication 102: *Would You Like to Be?*

N. Subtract 9 penguins and a rhythm guitar. Enter 140 in the blank.

O. If you are a single woman earning $10,000 a year or less, add 6 to the total and see table 2.

P. If you are a single woman earning $20,000 a year or less, add 6 to the total and see table 3.

Q. If you are a single woman earning $100,000 a year or more, add 6 to the total and see me under table 4 after the last rumba.

R. The sum of 2 plus 2 now stands at 146. This could never happen in a godless communist nation, could it?

S. Divide 146 by 8 cups of tomatoes. Enter 18¼ in the blank, stirring often.

T. If allergic to tomatoes, send for Federal Publication 590: *You and Your Hives.*

U. Add ¼.

V. Subtract ¼.

W. Do you do *every* darn-fool thing that some federal form tells you to do?

X. The sum of 2 and 2 now stands at 18¼. And we are quickly running out of letters of the alphabet.

Y. So subtract 14¼.

Z. The sum, then, of 2 and 2 is 4.

There, pretty simple, eh? If, however, you still have any questions, send for Federal Publication 515: *Huh?*

Where there's a will . . .

God bless you, Ben Kamin.

Old Ben, of Chicago, has died and left his entire fortune to Uncle Sam—the black sheep of everyone's family. Ben specified that his $271,956.38 be used to help reduce the national debt.

As a responsible reporter, one who lives and dies by the First Amendment, the Fourth Estate and the fifth race at Pimlico, it is my duty to reveal to you what the national debt was the last time I had the courage to peek. This is going to be kinda scarey, so send any small children and Democrats out of the room.

OK? Here it is: $2,120,568,000,000.

Guess how many Americans would have to die and each leave Uncle Sam $271,956.38 in order to retire that $2 trillion-plus. If you guessed 7,797,467, you were exactly right, according to my admittedly liberal-arts math skills.

That means that if every person in New York City died
tomorrow and each left Uncle Sam $271,956.38, only then
could the national debt be retired. But at least you'd be able to
get a seat on the subway.

(You have now been reading this column about forty-five
seconds. That's how long Ben's $271,956.38 suspended the
growth of the national debt.)

You know, if a man doesn't keep up the payments on his
house and car, lives beyond his means on the brink of insol-
vency, and writes his Visa card number on washroom walls, he
is called a darned fool.

Yet if 535 people in serious suits do all that, they're called a
Congress.

Imagine that Uncle Sam really were just one person. How
would you like to live next door to him? He'd always be coming
over and mooching. He'd borrow your barbecue grill, swearing
that he was going to use it for peacetime purposes, and it
would wind up being airlifted to Central America, where ill-
trained soldiers would use it to hurl pork chops at the com-
munists.

He'd ask you for $5 here and $10 there to subsidize tobacco
farmers and cancer researchers. Or to award federal grants to
study the social life of moss. Or to establish a federal archives
to store Tip O'Neill's chins. Or to develop a $1.2 million,
combat-strength, counter-terrorist, heat-seeking pork chop.

Yes, economic studies have shown that Uncle Sam could be
replaced by a large white duck, and the country would not be
able to tell the difference. Except that the price of eggs would
go down.

But I applaud the efforts of the late Ben Kamin to help his
favorite uncle get out of debt. And I figure that if I continue to
wear last year's jeans, drive last year's truck and eat last year's
TV dinners, I, too, will someday be able to die and go to pro-
bate, leaving Uncle Sam $271,956.38.

Well, the $.38, for sure.

Yet many people *can* match Ben's bequest. Why, there are
now one million millionaires in this country. So I am calling on
7 million Americans who are of sound mind and wallet and
who have nothing planned this weekend to die. Or at least to
close your eyes and lie very still until Uncle Sam can get is
hands on your money.

And even if you are not a high-roller but someday expect to find yourself in the position of being dead, you can leave Uncle Sam your stamp collection, TV, ten-speed bike, bowling ball, lake lots, turquoise jewelry, some combat-strength barbecue sauce — anything of value. Well, *almost* anything.

Whatever you do, don't leave Uncle Sam your credit cards.

I think old Ben would have wanted it that way.

Bears, bulls, bucks and slugs

A recent survey by *Money* magazine concluded that, compared to men, women are only half as likely to understand financial terms.

Compared to *which* men, I'd like to know. Certainly not to *this* man. I can't understand any financial term more complex than "beg," "borrow" and, sometimes, "steal."

But I have a woman friend who understands financial terms perfectly, thank you very much. Cathy has been a bank or brokerage officer for years, ever since she escaped from journalism school by carving her reporter's notebook into the shape of a pistol.

She is on speaking terms with words such as "sub-accounts" and "downside risk" and "portfolio." She knows the difference between "bears" and "bulls," "puts" and "calls," and "Dunn" and "Bradstreet," even with her eyes closed.

She speaks fluent pork belly.

And oh, I love it when she says "collateralize."

Recently, through some oversight by the Internal Revenue, I had some spare money to invest. But I wanted to put it into something more exotic than certificates of deposit. CDs are dull. They are the Mister Rogers of investing. I wanted to try something that would make me unconscionably rich while I slept and yet would not automatically entitle me to a free clock-radio.

"Cathy," I said, "I have some money to invest."

"Fine. Fine. How much money are we talking—a little, say $5,000?"

"No!" I said indignantly, "a *lot,* say $5,000."

Sheesh! Some people.

So she gave me a prospectus on a tax-exempt high-yield fund, whatever *that* is. I had to put on a three-piece suit and turn my Democratic voter-registration card face-down on the table just to understand all the nice charts and graphs. There was no way I could understand the actual words, although I did become friendly with several punctuation marks.

Finally, I got a headache. I crouched down and whimpered, "Get all those numbers away from me, Cathy. I was a liberal arts major!"

Cathy tried to explain it all to me. Soon *she* had a headache.

But I did understand enough to realize that my money could end up invested over in Tennessee in Jackson Sewer Revenue bonds or up in Oregon in Port of St. Helens Pollution Control Revenue Variable Rate Demand Note bonds.

Think of it: I could make money off bodily functions and volcanic ash! It makes you proud to be an American.

The prospectus also included a letter of intent. This form concerned "right of accumulation" and "escrow" and something called—I swear—"telephone redemption," which, I take it, reveals to you God's own 800 number.

The form also had boxes for you to check according to how much money you wanted to invest. There was even a box for "$5 million or more." Think of that! No one who has "$5 million or more" to invest ever came by it morally.

In fact, I'm not so sure that there really *is* that much money in the whole world. I suspect that any sum larger than $9,999.99 is done with mirrors.

I suspect that if you gathered all the real money in the whole world into a room, there would be maybe two million dollars in bills, a little more than a dollar in change, two bus tokens, one slug and a bushel of pocket lint.

Predictably, Cathy never could get me to understand that prospectus. So I guess I'll just continue to keep my money in a sock under the mattress. Granted, that system doesn't earn me much interest, but at least I understand how it works.

Looking over the overlooked

I know that I'll just sound bitter.

But really I'm not. It's just that I don't understand America's value system. To this scribe, it just ain't fair. Those who get the gold and glamour are always the most expendable: athletes and entertainers. Meanwhile, our culture takes for granted its most-valuable members: teachers, social workers, nurses, police and fire fighters, philosophers, scientists, the clergy and my VCR repairman.

Take your Don Mattingly. He makes about a zillion bucks a year plus a bonus clause that pays him $2,500 every time he cleans up his room and $500 for each state capital he can name.

Granted, Don Mattingly is a great athlete. But just an athlete. You wouldn't call on him to fix your fridge or teach your kids.

Or take your Ozzy Osbourne. He makes a fortune and has thousands of screaming fans.

Granted, Ozzy Osbourne is a great . . . a great . . . I have just been informed that Ozzy Osbourne is a great rock musician. And he is the first person you'd call on to bite the head off your bat and urinate on your Alamo. But you wouldn't call him up and say, "Oh, Oz! Come quick and fix my fridge and teach my kids! Don Mattingly refuses to do it until he remembers the capital of Minneapolis!"

Now before all you Ozzy fans write me nasty letters with tubes of Clearasil, let me say that I love rock and roll. I can name all the members of Hall and Oates. I know all the words to Cyndi Lauper.

This scribe is just saying that there should be more appreciation of those who make our culture work: those who hammer and saw, type, cook, deliver the mail, pump gas, trim your dog's toenails, make sure your car runs but your nose doesn't and so on.

Why do *these* people never achieve stardom?

How about you, Miss Superior Waitress? Do adoring fans sneak off with your pencil or order pad as souvenirs?

And how about you, Mr. Great English Teacher? When you go to the blackboard and diagram a sentence, do a dozen giddy girls faint and have to be carried out moaning, "Oh, I just know he was looking at *me* when he did the noun clauses"?

And *you*, Mr. or Mrs. Very Good Doctor? You save the actual lives of actual people. Why don't *you* have hangers-on hovering around the operating-room door waiting to make a plaster cast of your stethoscope?

And *you*, Mrs. Superb School Crossing Guard? Why don't people wait in line ten hours in the rain to buy tickets to watch you motion, "Come on across, kids"?

Why do reporters never ask you if you sleep in the nude, Mr. Excellent Banker?

How about you, Mrs. Top-Notch Receptionist? Anyone ever want to bronze your pantyhose?

And *you*, Mr. A-1 Lathe Operator. When was the last time fans tore off your clothing as mementos? Of course, you may not want that. Especially if you happen to be wearing Mrs. Top-Notch Receptionist's pantyhose at the time.

Sign many autographs, Mr. Excellent Pothole Patcher?

Make a million this year, did you, Mrs. Really Fine Cafeteria Cook?

And *you*, Mrs. America's Best Secretary? Ever been asked to appear on the Phil Donahue show to discuss your philosophy of filing?

Theoretically, you know, we *could* determine the best secretary in America. But the no. 1 secretary remains a complete unknown, while the no. 101 rock singer is a hero with hot and cold running groupies.

And yet where would the world be without secretaries?

Ten minutes late for something, probably.

See? I just sound bitter, don't I?

But really I'm not. However, if, when I get to work in the morning, 500 screaming strangers are at my desk, chipping off chunks of my adjectives as souvenirs, it would make this scribe feel *so* much better.

Tempus Indeed Fugits

Has-Ben: Time Thoreaus a curve

Franklin said, "Time is money." Thoreau said, "Time is but the stream I go a-fishing in."

The two men never met, and it's just as well, because there might have been a terrible argument when Franklin, off wenching and fomenting revolution, showed up for lunch fifteen dollars late, only to have Thoreau sentence him to ninety trout in jail.

But this at least gets us into the subject at hand: time. Ah, time! How it governs life. It and space. Time and space are the infinite craftsmen, shaping our happiness, sanding and smoothing the edges of the sharpest pain. Remember that time a creature from another planet hovered over your sister's home, beamed her aboard his craft, got her in the mood with a Don Ho album and then had his way with her?

Time and space helped your sister to get over that traumatic experience, didn't they, even though her child-support payments later would take 4.3 light-years to reach Earth.

But which came first: time or space? Time, I think. And being older, time is the journeyman. Space is the apprentice. They work well together. Time tells space how long it takes to get from point A to point B, but space gives time a place to keep its watch.

A watch is like a time compass — showing us where we are in time just as a compass shows us where we are in space. For instance, if you have car trouble in the bad part of town, and you look at your watch, which reads 1:16 A.M., you know exactly where you are: just north-northeast of Big Trouble. Because those young men sauntering up to you with tattoos, brass knuckles and poor marks in Citizenship are going to take your Rolex time compass and in turn leave you with some space: between your teeth.

The most-maddening aspect of time, of course, is how it passes — sneaky fast — moment into moment into millennium, each day a dollop of eternity until, finally, one morning you wake up dead. When that happens, not even a brisk shower and a balanced breakfast are going to cheer you up.

Franklin might say that time nickels and dimes you to death. Thoreau might say that time trickles past as you stand on the bank a-casting. You reel in a minute here and a minute there, only to find when you get home that your wife refuses to clean anything that small.

I spend a lot of time worrying about time: how much time is left for this wobbly world, how to use what little time is allotted to me to best benefit humanity, how to find time to collect all the albums that Don Ho ever made.

On the other hand, I spend very little space worrying about space. I find that I have much more space than time. In fact, I wish I could trade some of my spare space for some spare time. I have an empty drawer in my desk that I would gladly trade for five more minutes of sleep in the morning. I have a spare bedroom that I'd trade for a couple of good days. And I have ten acres of pine trees and deer droppings in East Texas that I'd trade for a year. Especially if it were a clean, low-mileage year once owned by, say, Imelda Marcos and used only on Sundays to drive across her shoe closet.

Life is just too time-consuming. There is too much to get done. You play a chukker of polo in the morning, have lunch with Jackie O. (*love* her new ensemble!), take the Lear over to Paris for a *fabu*lous party, and soon you ask yourself, where *did* the day go?

All this, of course, is assuming that you have traded the state of Montana for a Saturday that Truman Capote was not using.

In conclusion, looking at my watch, I see that we all have four minutes less time than when we started this essay back there with Hank and Ben. I urge you, when next you look at *your* watch, to contemplate the deeper meaning of time, of what each tick, each tock is really saying to you:

"It's $1.98 past two trout."

Get "u" and "i" out of "routine"

Just in case no one has caused you to weep into your coffee yet this morning, let me be the first. Did you know that during your lifetime, you will spend a total of thirty-five days just washing your hands?

Yes, I've been calculating how much time we devote to dull routine. We spend most of our existence engaged in repetitive, engaged in repetitive, engaged in repetitive activities. They may be necessary, they may be the means toward truly exciting ends, but nonetheless they are the cereal filler in the weiner of life.

Of course, even jet-setters, centerfolds and secret agents are slaves to routine. We mere mortals just don't hear about it. Ever read a James Bond novel? Notice that while he is saving the world and getting the girl he never takes time out for bodily functions? Realistically, 2.3 pages of each book should be devoted to such. But then who wants to read about this?

Well, maybe urologists.

Yet Bond *must* go to the bathroom sometime. Maybe between chapters. Otherwise somewhere out there would be a secret agent with cruel good looks, nerves of steel and a bladder the size of a weather balloon.

Let's say that you will live seventy-five years. Of course, you sleep away a third of your life. So kiss off twenty-five years right there. You're down to fifty years already. Then there's your job. Granted, a few jobs are interesting—organized crime boss, snake charmer, pope—but most of our jobs could be performed by a clump of moss wearing a necktie. So, if you work eight hours a day, five days a week for fifty years, dock yourself a solid eleven years. Down to thirty-nine years.

If each day you spend just one hour watching the same old programs on TV, one hour dressing and grooming for your job, one hour getting to and from that job, and two hours performing home and car maintenance and/or cleaning house, subtract fifteen more years. Twenty-four years and ticking.

What good does it do, for instance, to dust everything in the house, anyway? Even as we speak, hot-blooded little dust particles are reproducing, spawning in the rays of sunlight that stream in through your windows. Which you just cleaned. Which already are getting dirty again.

If you spend just ten minutes a week standing in line, in a lifetime that will total twenty-seven days. You easily may spend more time standing in line than you will spend on more-gratifying activities such as hugging your loved ones, watching beautiful sunsets or cheating on your taxes.

You'll spend twenty-one days per lifetime just sneezing, coughing and blowing your nose. Too bad you can't set aside three weeks and get all that nonsense over with: Do nothing but sneeze, cough and blow your nose. Of course, you soon would disappear beneath a pastel mountain of Kleenex, and your friends would spend, oh, up to three minutes searching for you before giving up and having the whole mountain of Kleenex recycled into a tree.

You'll spend six days trimming your toenails. And even longer trying to reach them.

You'll spend 162 days shopping for groceries, four days looking for things that you've lost and eleven nights worrying that your teenager is out breaking Commandments one through ten inclusive.

And finally, if, against the advice of your physician,

congressman and clergyman, you regularly read this column, you would fritter away another twelve days of your life.

So, overall, you have a total of maybe twenty-three years of free time in your life. And many of those are already behind you. So come on! Spend what precious time that remains doing something spontaneous and daring, something you have never, *ever* done before. Break free of the fetters of routine! Why not leave it all behind today and devote your life to searching for the Loch Ness Monster?

But when you're finished, for goodness sake come in and wash your hands.

The test of time: A longevity quiz

How many years can you expect to live?

In life's golden moments, do you ever stop to wonder just how much time is left for you? When the world is your oyster, when life is a lark, when the lion's share of happiness is yours, do you ask yourself this question: Am I spending too much time in the company of animals?

Don't change the subject! We were talking about how many years you can expect to live. So quick—while you're still with us—take this longevity quiz.

Domestic Atmosphere

Your home life most resembles an episode of:

10 points—*Father Knows Best*

0 points—*Divorce Court*.

A common sound in your home is that of:

10—someone kissing

5—a gun

0—someone kissing a gun.

Your household consists of:

10—you, your wonderful mate, your 2.3 children and your faithful dog Rags.

0—you, your neighbor's wonderful mate, 2.3 children you never saw before, your faithful cobra Rags, and your cousin Fenton, who is loud, loathsome and lazy and has this awful disease that only yesterday caused him to cough so violently that his ears fell off.

Vices

Use of tobacco:

10—you don't smoke

5—you smoke but don't inhale

0—you smoke but don't exhale.

To you, a seven-course meal should consist of:

10—moderate servings from all the major food groups

0—a six-pack and one fatburger.

Occupation

Your job is:

10—fulfilling, pleasant and neither too sedentary nor too strenuous

5—Mafia stool pigeon

0—what is this with you and animals, anyway, huh?

Exercise

Every morning you:

10—work out for twenty minutes

5—watch a friend work out for twenty minutes

0—stretch, jog and run (the truth, your memory and off at the mouth).

Physical condition

You can touch your toes with:

10—ease

5—effort

0—a yardstick.

The lettering on your underwear is:

10—BVD

0—Goodyear.

Heredity

Your grandfather:

10—lived a long and healthy life

0—was hanged.

Your grandmother:

10—lived a long and healthy life

5—was hanged

0—hanged your grandfather.

Environment

You live:

10—in a small town

5—in a large metropolitan area

0—in a mine field.

Attitude

You last laughed:

10—within the hour

5—when your cousin Fenton's ears fell into his soup

0—during the War of 1812.

To you, life is:

10—a bowl of cherries

5—a cup of prunes

0—a constant nightmare of tedium and disappointment. And over much too soon.

OK. Now total your points:

140 points—a perfect score. You will live to be 126 years old, unless someone strangles you to wipe that smug smile off your face.

140 to 80 points—you'll outlive your contemporaries but not your mortgage.

80 to 40 points—got any last words?

40 points or less—you are probably already dead, and this quiz is being completed by your heirs at the reading of your will. I do hope you left your record collection to cousin Fenton.

When life gets in the way of living

First thing tomorrow.

More than anything else that we put off doing, life is the one thing that we put off doing most.

As we get older, we fall victim to the most powerful force on earth: the force of no force at all—inertia. Inertia sets in, and the next thing we know, we can't even get up off the sofa to take out the trash unless electrodes are inserted in our neck and connected to a kite during a thunderstorm.

Oh, how we dig ourselves a rut. We settle in, settle down and settle for.

Well, I intend to get *un*settled. After all, here I am already well into the last half of this week, this month, this year, this decade and this century. Where did it all go? Why, on a clear day, I can remember June.

Each night, usually about 11:23, I realize that life is passing me by. And worse, as life is passing me by, it slows down only long enough to moon me.

There's so much I have yet to do. Overachievers realize this at age four when they learn that by that age, Mozart was already composing music. I realized it only recently, when I learned that by the time Mozart was thirty-six, he was already dead. Yet here I sit at thirty-eight, not even sick yet.

So each night, usually about 11:24, I tell myself that I am going to chuck my lifestyle (which is a penny short on "life" and a pound short on "style").

I'll put my typewriter up for adoption and kiss my Thesaurus goodbye, farewell, so long, adieu, adios, ta-ta and bye-bye.

Then I'll go for the gusto.

First thing tomorrow.

Because when I am old and my verbs are feeble, I don't want to open the morning paper some day and read:

"Mike Nichols, retired columnist, died today after a long and exceedingly dull life.

"Friends gathered to remember him for the many things that he never did.

"Said one: 'I recall the time he didn't learn to sky dive. Oh, he could not-learn to sky dive better than anyone I ever knew. He also was a whiz at not-learning to speak French and at not-learning to play the guitar.'

"Said another: 'I remember all the times he never went back to school to become a veterinarian. And all those times he never took off a year to bum around the world, living by his wits. He did try once, but got only as far as the county line before he ran out of wits. Seems like it was just yesterday. In fact, it *was* just yesterday. He was an inspiration to us all.'"

So, while I still can . . .

I want to visit Thoreau's Walden Pond, cross Europe by motorcycle and stroll through Casablanca wearing a white linen suit. A 42 long, cuffed pants.

I want to live in New York City, among 7 million mumbling people. Ah, to be in Central Park in the spring, when the muggers are in bloom.

Then I want to live on a deserted tropical island, where the only traffic jams are six-crab collisions on the beach, where phone solicitors can reach me only by a note in a bottle.

I want to see a rainbow and a sunset on every continent.

I want to sail out off the coast of Baja to see a real, live whale. A 948 long, no pants.

I want to be taken hostage by the Simpkins twins, Molly and Golly, who live up the street.

I want to find a parking space downtown.

I want to meet Jacques Cousteau and tell him how I admire him. He will respond by telling me that I left the price tag on my white linen suit.

Yes, I'm going to stop wasting time and live life to the fullest. I swear I will. This time I really mean it.

First thing tomorrow.

Or, at the very latest, the day after.

In the News,
of the News

Double standard wearing thin?

Brassiere alert! Double standard at four o'clock.

The subject for today is ladies' underwear. Please, no snickering. Anyone caught snickering will be taken out and lashed with a pair of control-top pantyhose.

This is the day that the three major networks begin broadcasting lingerie commercials that reflect relaxed standards on how lingerie can be shown on TV.

Until now, of course, a bra always was shown worn by a headless mannequin or, if worn by a real woman, over her leotards, which were certainly never flesh-toned. But as of today, a commercial for Playtex Cross Your Heart bras shows two young women preparing to leave town on a trip. As each woman heads separately for the train, brief shots of them wearing a bra against their own personal skin are intercut with shots of them fully clothed.

That's it. No big deal, right? Or is it? What can we conclude from this commercial, other than that these two women will have little trouble getting a seat on the train?

"Here, take my seat!"

"No, take *my* seat!"

"No, no, take my *wife*'s seat!" (pushes wife out window of moving train).

Can we conclude that television's double standard is falling? Isn't it about time that lingerie commercials had the same standards as those of soap operas, print ads and other commercials that peddle everything from Coors to cars? After all, those commercials gratuitously feature topless men or women in bikinis or jeans that are so tight that you can tell not only if that's a quarter in their pocket but if George Washington is smiling.

He is. And boy, is Martha sore. But she's just bitter because she wore a wooden bra.

Ah, but then there is the larger double standard, which is alive and well and living on psychiatrists' couches everywhere. Do you know how many emotional hang-ups and sexual offenses probably are caused by our ambivalent attitude toward the human body? It is an attitude of love and hate, fear and fascination, and yes, lifts and separates.

What reasons do we have to fear the human body and its coverings? Sure, you say, there's your Aunt Sophie, who head-on in a bra looks like a '56 Cadillac in low gear. But think about it: Guns are much more fearsome than underwear. No one was ever killed while cleaning a brassiere that they thought wasn't loaded.

Or take the subject of condoms. Once in a while, on a newspaper's real estate pages, a typographical error in a headline about condominiums (called "condos" for short, and I can see that you know where this is headed) will result in something like this: "45-story condom planned downtown."

This always triggers laughter. In light of AIDS and the population explosion, why does the subject still draw nervous giggles? And what's so darned funny about a 45-story condom?

Not a thing, if it falls on you.

The networks defend the new lingerie commercials as "restrained and inoffensive." And truly, who could be offended by the TV image of a woman wearing a bra? Not men (the animals!). And not women, rationally, because they purchase and wear the product. Why be offended about something that is a part of life? That takes care of men and women. So who is left to object? Sure, your Uncle Sally, but he's just bitter because a 45-story condom fell on him.

If I could, I'd ask the two young ladies who wear the brassieres in the new Playtex commercials these questions, in my best interviewer's voice: How do you feel about being pioneers in television advertising standards, what are your views on the social-sexual implications of the cultural double standard, and would you both have lunch with me tomorrow?

Maybe in the dining car.

I have always loved trains.

Cross my heart.

Happy UFO Day!
Pass the thrib

I hereby declare this to be National UFO Day. Take someone green to lunch.

Yes, it was on June 24, 1947, that pilot Kenneth Arnold reported seeing nine saucer-shaped objects cross the path of his plane as he flew over Mount Rainier. Thus did the UFO phenomenon enter the public eye. Forty years and some fifty thousand reported sightings later, we are still asking ourselves, Who is out there? How did they get here? Couldn't they have phoned ahead first?

Many UFO sightings can be explained, of course — conventional aircraft, swamp gas, weather balloons. But some remain baffling. Here are some UFO cases that you probably haven't heard about. They have been suppressed by the federal government until this very minute, when I made them up.

— Philo Feemster revealed that in 1982 he was contacted by scouts from an advanced civilization that had conquered war, disease, poverty and most child-proof medicine bottles. He described the encounter: "This space craft landed, see, and out came creatures that resembled parking meters wearing too much makeup. I stood gaping, my heart pounding, my emotions swinging wildly between cringing fear and abject terror."

Feemster is, in fact, a card-carrying coward and is licensed to faint. Which he did. When he came to, the space ship was gone. So were both of his legs. Ever since, he has walked with a noticeable limp.

—In 1973, a starship landed in rural New Mexico. This sophisticated craft was piloted by a crew of moss. Very intelligent moss, granted, but ugly, soggy clumps of moss all the same. But then it's all relative, isn't it? In other solar systems, being a clump of moss may well be considered quite sexy. Especially if the moss has a nice smile and is a good dancer.

—Earth is visited regularly by beings from Jupiter. Their space craft travel at 20 million mph (the trip is mostly downhill). Thus they can make the 400-million-mile trip to Earth in ten days: one day to get here and nine days to circle the earth looking for a place to park.

—One popular theory has suggested that aliens from space gave the ancient Egyptians the technology to build the pyramids. But a new theory by Professor Emil Ganza of the Leipzig University of Astrophysics and Needlepoint contends that the aliens simply stood by and shouted encouragement to the Egyptians: "Come on, guys, you can do it! Heave! Gosh, those big stone blocks sure look heavy, don't they?"

—Located between the constellation Aquarius (the water bearer) and Sagittarius (the archer) is Curious (the Peeping Tom). From this constellation in 1957 came a night visitor who stared into the bedroom window of Ms. Lawanda Minx of San Diego, a working girl who lists her hobbies as "reading, gardening and the Seventh Fleet." This glowing alien stood in a flowerbed and observed activity in the room for more than an hour, took notes and left. To this day, tulips in that flowerbed grow to be thirty-seven feet tall.

Back in the constellation Curious, the alien was met with skepticism. "Sure, sure, Zurk-23. On this 'Earth' you saw creatures that have just two eyes and a 'nose' where we have a glimik? On which head? And they reproduced *how?* Quaint.

Zurk-23, are you sure you were not absorbing thrib straight out of the bottle at the time?"

"I *swear* to you, Creeb-19, they were hideous. They made my larzbot crawl."

"You've had a traumatic huulmiq, poor thing. Come to bed now, Zurkipoo, and show me this thing called a 'French kiss.'"

Yes, the UFO craze is forty years old today. Are visitors from other planets fact or fiction? Who knows? But just to be safe, next time you go out to feed the parking meter, if it looks sad and thin and its mascara is running, be a sport—give it an extra quarter.

You're no dope?
Then get rich

I have decided to get in on *the* hot new growth industry of the eighties: selling drug-free urine.

After all, the ACLU predicts a flourishing black market in drug-free urine as drug testing becomes more common. And already Jeffrey Nightbyrd of Austin is selling drug-free urine for $49.95 per eight-ounce bag. He has sold more than a hundred bags, mostly to "Yuppies and students going out into the job market."

His ad in an Austin newspaper claims that the urine is "100 percent pure" and "suitable for unanticipated urine demand."

I want in on this. I can guarantee my urine to be of the finest quality and 100 percent drug-free. My kidneys are open to public inspection (after 9 P.M. and on weekends, please call for an appointment).

And I recommend this new career field to the rest of the drug-free community, which, according to the weekly news magazines, now numbers upwards of eleven or twelve persons. Just think of the hundreds of thousands of dollars' worth of a valuable commodity that you, too, have let slip away. Why, you've probably passed up $150 today alone.

And the beauty of it is that you can start making money the very first day. It requires no special training or tools. It is low overhead: All you need are some kidneys, which are commonly found in most homes. Then you just add water.

Now I realize that I can't match Nightbyrd's volume. (He buys his urine wholesale from elderly Bible students at a church. Honest.) Mine will be just a cottage industry, a one-jar operation. And besides, I don't want my business to get *too* big. Because then it would catch the attention of wealthy investors and be vulnerable to a corporate takeover by T. Boone Pickens' bladder.

But how can I get the competitive edge in this lucrative new industry? After all, drug-free urine is drug-free urine. Well, first I'll undersell Nightbyrd. I'll advertise specials.

"Yes, we here at Urine R Us will sell you eight ounces of drug-free urine for only $39.95. And if you order now, you'll get free 8 × 10 color photos of Len Byas, John Belushi and Jimi Hendrix.

"Folks, what a perfect Christmas gift for the person who has everything, including a habit. Just hold this urine up to the light. Note the full body, the fruity color. Subtle yet vile. Yes, four P.M. was a very good year."

And I'll have endorsements from famous athletes.

"Uh . . . yes, I always drive a Ford Thund- . . . huh? Wrong product? Oh, yeah, man. Sorry. I'm hip. Uh . . . like . . . uh, what was the question again?"

I'll subcontract for specialty items: designer urine (Pierre Cardin's), Kung Fu urine (Chuck Norris's), nostalgia urine (Pat Boone's, mailed to you in a white-buck shoe).

Yes, I can see it all now. I'll be known as Mr. Bladder. King Kidney. The Sultan of Slosh.

But, you ask, wouldn't all this bother my conscience? Wouldn't a drug opponent's selling his urine to further the subterfuge of sleazy, slime-ball dopers be a bit like a Hindu's selling barbecue, like a pacifist's selling ICBMs?

Well, yes, perhaps you're right. But I must defend people's right to self-destruct in any darn-fool way they choose. Especially if it profits the drug-free community. In this case, me.

And if they don't get drug-free urine from me, they'll just get it from someone else, perhaps on the street, from low-life urine pushers. And then who knows *where* it's been?

Oh, OK. I'll reconsider. But in the meantime I'll just go drink another sixteen glasses of water.

Clan of the cave wimp

Anthropologists have been climbing around in our family tree again.

While they were up there they found—along with several bird nests, two kites and a case of leaf blight—another new theory.

Yes, at a seminar last week, anthropologist Lewis Binford of the University of New Mexico disputed the traditional belief that our earliest ancestors were macho types who carried clubs, hunted big game and crushed beer cans with their bare hands.

Rather, he said, they were timid souls who "regularly scavenged the carcasses of animals killed by other predators" and who used their stone tools merely to crack the bones of dead animals. He said it was much later that humans turned to hunting for food.

Behold the very first underachiever: *Homo wimpus.*

Get your desk calendar and flip back 2 million years. Now let's take a peek at the life and hard times of the cave wimp.

Homo wimpus suffered the same handicap suffered by any pioneer: He had no role models. There were no Clint Eastwoods, no Rambos, no Schwarzeneggers to pattern himself after. To make matters worse, he also lacked the killer instinct.

So when his wife, Mrs. *Homo wimpus,* would urge him to get out of the cave and go kill something for dinner, he would look away and mutter, "I don't want to." He said this so many times that through the eons it has been contracted to "Idawanna" and can still be heard in today's three-bedroom brick caves when it comes time to rake the leaves or clean out the garage.

Thus *Homo wimpus* devised indirect ways of getting his food. He would stand atop a cliff and drop water balloons onto passing mastodons and wait for them to catch cold and sneeze to death. He would patiently follow saber-toothed tigers, waiting for them to die of gum disease. He would stalk prehistoric armadillos, waiting for them to be run over by prehistoric tractor-trailer rigs.

His attitude toward other animals was fatalistic: "Live and let live. And if you can't live, try to die near a large bottle of steak sauce."

And when the wife reminded him that *she* had spent the day constructively, gathering nuts, fruits and roots, he would get defensive. "You think it's easy, waiting all the time for something to die? Well, it's hard work, I tell ya. Sometimes there is an epidemic of good health and then I have to wait twice as hard.

"And these prehistoric animals are huge and ill-tempered. Today in the park I was chased by an eight-foot squirrel. I escaped, but later I walked under a tree, and he bounced a fifty-pound acorn off my head."

"I know," she said. "That's gonna be your lunch all this week."

Binford also said the large size of *Homo wimpus's* brain is misleading. *Wimpus* wasn't really all that bright. The first time he saw fire, he got excited and wanted to surprise his wife with it. He tried to gift-wrap it.

Further, Binford said the language skills of *Homo wimpus* were more limited than we traditionally have thought. Apparently, *wimpus* would grunt "well" and "uh" a lot and often leave prehistoric participles dangling.

Too, Binford said, our early underachievers didn't have much social organization. They did not cooperate well in gathering food, they did not work together to make their simple tools, and they seldom could get up a fourth for bridge.

All in all, our hero was a sensitive, eighties kind of guy. He would sit around the cave at night—his eyes shut tightly, his teeth clenched—trying to evolve. "Aw, what's the use anyway?"

he would ask in his self-effacing way. "Millions of years from now, creationists won't even believe I existed."

He would sometimes stare at his reflection in the swamp and brood. "You are a disgrace," he would say to himself. "You have neither slain nor wounded nor rent asunder all day. And watch your posture, bub — you're supposed to be walking semi-erect by now."

Yes, Binford's theory is fascinating. And all this reflection on our early ancestors, aggression and hunting makes me wonder if I shouldn't dust off the ol' club, go out into the woods and atone for the shortcomings of *Homo wimpus*.

Aw, on second thought, Idawanna.

I think I'll just stay inside, right here on my Naugahyde sofa, made from the hides of savage man-eating Naugas. Then, for dinner, I'll creep stealthily into the kitchen, pounce and — with my own bare hands — subdue a TV dinner.

Tradition is foiled again

An obituary to mark the passing of an old friend.

The original aluminum TV-dinner tray — a pioneer in the field of convenience foods — died last month after a long illness. It was thirty-four years old.

The tray's family physician, Dr Pepper, was at its bedside when the end came. "The old tray coughed weakly and wheezed, 'After I'm gone, Doc, make 'em keep my peas and carrots cold.'"

Dr Pepper said the cause of death was progress.

But in Camden, N.J., a spokesman for Campbell Soup Company's Swanson TV dinners, makers of the tray since 1952, defended its switch to plastic trays: "We hate to have to change the trays, because they are, well . . . a classic in eating. But with the popularity of microwave ovens, there was no way we could continue with the aluminum tray."

Thus in May, another faithful friend of the single person and the harried homemaker went to that great Hefty Bag in the sky.

A memorial service for the tray was attended by hundreds in the food-container industry, including some who themselves have become obsolete. Honorary pallbearers included a glass milk-bottle, hobbling on a cane, and a waxed-paper bread wrapper, now quite wrinkled and deaf in one flap.

Present were the tray's next of kin: some Campbell's soup cans.

The eulogy was delivered by a — ahem — Billy Graham cracker: "I didn't know the dearly departed well. I was always in a kitchen cabinet, and it was in the freezer. Oh, once in a while, we'd meet in front of the TV in the den when someone ate a snack. How the old tray loved 'Perry Mason.'

"And sometimes, do you know, as the person ate, my crumbs would fall into the tray's whipped potatoes. Did it mind? No. It was selfless. A good and humble servant. Every head bowed, every lid closed."

The soup cans openly wept into their chicken noodles.

After the service, refreshments were served by Betty Crocker, the symbol of General Mills. At sixty-five, Crocker has just had her sixth face-lift and now looks thirty years younger. In fact, she attended the service with a much younger man — the sailor boy from a box of Cracker Jacks.

While some at the service tsk-tsked behind her back, Crocker explained: "You gotta stay young, gotta keep up with the times. The old aluminum tray wouldn't. Now (sob) it's gone . . . Now where did my Cracker Jackie go? Oh, I *love* a man in a uniform!"

Many of those in attendance lamented the changing times. Said a tarnished bottle-and-can opener, "I'll be the next to go. I'm being made obsolete by twist-top bottles and pull-tab cans. Mark my words: The next funeral will be for us church keys. Uh, beggin' yer pardon, Rev. Graham Cracker."

Also attending were many single persons. Said one bachelor, "That old tray kept me from starving. I've had more hot TV dinners than hot dates. I never owned a pot or a pan. And just one fork. I wash it every leap year.

"I remember the first time I met the old tray. It looked so cute with its four compartments. The little hunk of cornbread, the apple sauce, the fried chicken. It was a good friend and a great American. I'm going back home to my kitchen and fly my No Pest Strips at half-mast."

But the memorial service was marred by tragedy. Witnesses described what happened: "Betty Crocker was talking with a box of French's pepper, y'know? Suddenly she sneezed, and all six of her face-lifts fell, causing her ears to slip down around her heels!"

"Someone go fetch the doctor," a cardboard egg-carton shouted in panic.

"You mean Dr Pepper?" a roll of white butcher paper asked.

"No. Dr. *Scholl's!*"

Not-seeing is believing

Here's your *Guide to Missing the Celestial Show of the Century.* I am well qualified to offer it, having personally not-seen Halley's Comet on eight separate attempts so far.

—*How?* The optimum times for seeing the great comet are gone. But take heart: You can still not-see it. In fact, conditions for not-seeing it are improving each night. Between April 25 and May 14, you must (1) get far away from town; (2) go at an inconvenient hour; (3) squint through binoculars; and (4) if under 5-foot-2, stand on a stepladder.

—*Who?* Studies show that people who *don't* see the comet find the experience more memorable than people who *do*-see it. That's because those who do-see it simply say, "Yup, that's it, all right. Now let's go eat Mexican food." But those who

don't-see it wander the forbidding countryside all night, getting
sleepy, grumpy, sneezy and doc.

So members of my comet party have asked that I not identify
them. Thus, when I say they were Kevin and Whitney Gibbens,
210 Wooddale, Euless, TX 76038, rest assured that I, as a
responsible journalist, have falsified their ZIP code.

Each comet party should have one skeptic. Ours was Kevin,
a level-headed banker who understands that wife Whitney was
a liberal arts major and thus is not responsible for her actions,
such as recruiting comet commandos at two A.M. Kevin was the
only one of us who was confident that we would succeed in
not-seeing the comet. (I suspect that he was the only one of us
who actually *did*-see it but was just too embarrassed to admit
it.)

There also should be one dog. Ours was Brooklyn. His first
duty was to prowl the roadside, marking his territory. By five
A.M. Brooklyn was showing signs of dehydration. By six A.M. he
had marked more property than Century 21 Realtors.

—*Where?* Astronomers tell us to find a place that has no
lights, has no trees or other obstructions and faces the southern
horizon. They don't mention the fact that there *is* no such
place. So you keep wandering south, thinking, "Just a bit
further and we'll find a perfect place . . . just a bit
further . . ." By dawn you're in Mexico, where you are arrested
for not having any drugs in your possession.

It seems that Halley's is very shy. Clouds, fog and even humidity can obscure it. That's why you're supposed to drive out
into the country, where—as every schoolchild knows—there *are*
no clouds, fog and humidity. Just hundreds of farmers, each of
whom sleeps with a shotgun and a copy of *In Cold Blood* at the
bedside.

This brings us to your dog's second duty. When your comet
party parks near a rural farmhouse at four A.M., gets out and
begins the celestial search, your dog barks one time. Just once.
This triggers the Great All-County Farm Dog Oral Relays.
Soon 400 farm dogs are sounding the Comet-Watchers Alert.
This alert is a cross between a bark and a snicker. It goes on all
night. Farm dogs have to bark all night. It's in their contract.

This awakens the farmers, who are comet-watcher watchers.

"Jim Bob, they's some more of them comet-watchers out

there. You get the binoculars, dear, and I'll make some pop-corn."

"OK, Loretta Bob. And wake the twins, too—Joe Bob and Bob Bob. I sure hope these comet-watchers are as much fun as the last ones. I thought I'd die when one of 'em was out there stumbling around in our pasture trying to see a ball of gas 50 million miles away and didn't see our old bull two feet behind him."

"Hooo-eeee! Talk about your unidentified flying objects!"

"I think I'll do like last time: sneak outside, climb a tree and light a sparkler."

"That always works good. But say, how many comets are there, anyway?"

"Just one, I think. Why?"

"Well, I see three comet-watchers out there, and they're all looking in different directions."

(Note to Loretta Bob: That's because citified comet-watchers lose all sense of direction in the alien countryside. And apparently, it takes at least four college graduates to remember to bring a compass. We were one graduate short.)

— *What?* As best I can tell, we were looking for a fuzzy thing with a tail. I know that Brooklyn sure was. Actually, it's easy to see a bright, fuzzy thing in the sky: turn the focusing ring on your binoculars all the way left or right. Then *everything* looks like a comet. Especially when your arms begin to tremble after holding up binoculars for two hours while you stare at a sparkler in a tree.

Here are some other objects that have been mistaken for Halley's: planets and stars, airplanes, fireflies and Gulf signs, yard lights, flashlights and Bud Lights, and the spotlight of the approaching county sheriff's car.

Which brings us, finally, to

— *Why?* Why seek out the comet in the first place? Because, dear heart, the search for Halley's is, after all, a metaphor for life itself. You search, you strive, you lift your eyes to the heavens and then, at last, just when things seem hopeless, you get arrested for trespassing in Jim Bob's pasture and inciting a bull to riot.

Yes, those millions of us who seized the moment, who strove mightily and who still managed to not-see Halley's Comet will get over our disappointment. But I'm kinda worried about all those farmers and their dogs. The next seventy-five years are going to mean some mighty dull nights for *them*.

Veritas bewaritas: The press secretary

A curious animal stalks the land these days: the press secretary.

The duty of press secretaries is to communicate. They do this by taking a simple yet exalted thought from an exalted yet simple personage, converting it to gibberish and delivering it unto the rabble press, who convert it back to a simple thought that is continued on pages 2, 5 and 6.

Aspiring press secretaries attend special schools. In Mealy Mouth Math 101, for instance, they learn the arithmetic of evasion. "Students, use your four '-ates' and you're halfway home. Heh heh." These four "-ates" are equivocate, vacillate, obfuscate and understate. The students then have all their active verbs surgically removed and are recruited by Washington.

Let's look at how some press conferences of the past might have gone.

—Monsieur Croissant, press secretary for the French Revolution, is fielding questions from reporters in Paris in 1793.

The Rabble Press: "No one has seen Marie Antoinette in days. Rumor has it that she is dead. Would you comment on this?"

"She does not feel well. That's all I can say at this point in time."

The Daily Parisian: "Is the queen resting quietly?"

"I can say with confidence that she has never rested more quietly."

The Herald: "Then you deny that the queen was beheaded?"

Women's Wear Daily: "And was she wearing a hat when it happened?"

"To answer you both: No, the queen was not beheaded, and yes, she was wearing a hat when it happened."

—Captain Twaddle, U.S. Army press officer, is conducting a news briefing after the battle of Little Big Horn in 1876. Beside him is a horse.

"General Custer and his men have just engaged in heated debate with a minority group that has been trespassing on U.S. soil for at least 800 years. The outcome has resulted in 226 sudden job openings in the Seventh Cavalry. The lone Army survivor was this horse named Comanche. Your questions will be answered thus: one tap on the ground for yes, two taps for no."

The Examiner: "Could General Custer's death be considered a setback to his military career?"

Captain Twaddle taps the ground one time.

The Daily Racing Form: "Who's good in the fifth at Aqueduct?"

Captain Twaddle looks at the horse and then taps the ground four times.

Racing Form: "Hmm. Two *no*'s. Ah! Double Negative to win! Thanks!"

—The press secretary to Lady Godiva.

"Today, at oh-twelve-hundred hours, Lady Godiva rode through the streets of Coventry to carry out the terms of an agreement made with her husband, whereby our lordship will reduce the crippling tax on the citizenry."

The Post: "We hear that Lady Godiva was ye olde buck nekkid."

"I am at liberty to say that she was underdressed for the time of year."

The Globe: "How did she travel?"

"Her mode of transportation was a large fur-bearing quadruped."

Daily Racing Form: "Was it Double Negative?"

"Yes. She put 120 pounds on him to show."

—The press spokesman for an English shipping line in 1912.

"Early reports indicate that the *Titanic,* on her maiden voyage, has been negatively impacted by an unidentified mass of solidified water. Fifteen hundred and thirteen passengers have since failed to attend the captain's tea."

Refrigeration Weekly: "Was that crushed or block ice?"

"Block. Then crushed."

The Chronicle: "Can you describe conditions aboard the ship?"

"Damp."

—From Napoleon's press secretary in 1814.

"At the urging of England, Russia and their allies, the Emperor Napoleon has consented to take a well deserved vacation."

The Telegraph: "We understand that he is going into exile on a giant piece of toast. Is that why he has been overheard working on a palindrome: 'Able was I ere I saw melba'?"

"Elba, you Fourth Estate twit! *Elba!* And it's an island!"

Tribune: "Isn't it true that Napoleon is a raving egomaniac in love with himself?"

"There is no truth to that at all! Napoleon and himself are just very close friends."

—But the very first press secretary, of course, was a smooth-talking serpent.

"Adam, head gardener of Eden, today underwent surgery to have a rib removed. As a result, the world's population has doubled. Her name is Eve. I'd love to tell you more, but I gotta rush. I have time for just one question."

The Ledger: "Is it OK for Adam and Eve to eat the fruit of the Tree of Knowledge?"

"Sure. Why not? Hey, would a press secretary mislead anyone?"

Go to the head of the class

Take a few "attaboys!" or "attagirls!" out of petty cash, dear reader. For you are smarter than you think: You know a second language.

No, your second language is not Chinese or Portuguese, but the shorthand of newspapers—Headlinese. Headlinese is the breath of English with the wind knocked out of it. It is the meat of communication with the fat fried away. It is the skeleton of syntax with the soft, supple, yielding flesh torn . . . oh, you get the idea.

You grew up with "heads." Deciphering their telescoped message is second nature to you now. You've come to accept the present tense for past events. You've learned to do without modifiers. You can survive for days without an auxiliary verb.

(Children of the fifties got a head start by listening to Hollywood Indians talk in westerns. "Braves ride far, take many scalps." "Senate cuts tax bill, hikes aid plan." Paleface reader see heap big similarity?)

Here is a little-known fact: The people who write the stories usually are not the people who write the heads for those stories. No, heads are usually written by copy editors. Copy editors are an unsung, disciplined, intense subspecies. They can reduce any human thought, emotion or action to five words or less.

Their minds are a precision instrument—a shoehorn.

They think in monosyllables. Two copy editors passing in the hall: "Hi." "'Lo." "How do?" "Good. You?" "Fine." "Bye." "S'long."

In Headlinese, space is at a premium. So smaller is better. Thus "compete" becomes "vie." "Consider" becomes "eye." "Connection" becomes "tie." And should Princess Diana compete for the chance to consider a connection: "Di to vie to eye a tie."

Sigh.

Yes, dear reader, you can read headlines. But how would you like to learn to *write* headlines? Amaze your pals! Amuse your colleagues! Abuse your ulcer! Neat-o, eh? All right. First, shut yourself into a phone booth. Then put your head in a lunch box. Then put the lunch box in a vise. *Now* you are in the proper frame of mind.

So let's try one. Remember Hamlet's soliloquy? Eloquent, to say the least. No, to say the *least,* we'll reduce those 276 words to a headline. A three-word headline. Find your old copy of *Hamlet* (it's under that short table leg in your dining room) and review that time-honored passage:

". . . that is the question . . . slings and arrows . . . there's the rub . . . mumblemumble . . . mortal coil . . . mumblemumble . . ."

What is Shakespeare saying? Well, Hamlet is considering killing himself to escape the torments of life. But he then wonders if the unknown torments *after* life might not be even worse. And he realizes that he has thought too much about it to be able to take his own life. Besides, he wouldn't want to miss the annual office Christmas party, when his uncle—the evil Claudius—always drinks too much mead and wants Hamlet to help him sing "My Buddy."

Now squeeze those several thoughts into one basic thought. Think short.

"Prince
rejects
suicide."

Not bad. Squeeze still more. Think stubby.

"Dane
picks
life."

Better. Come on—squeeze just once more. Think *stump* (kids, do not attempt this headline at home without adult supervision).

"He
to
be."

There! You did it! Just like ol' Will woulda. For a first effort, that was satisfactory. Make that "acceptable." No, make that "decent." No, better make that "good." Better yet, make that "OK."

Say, has anybody out there got a shorter word for "OK"?

Remember: You read it here last

Have you been reading the newspapers lately?

Well, I have. And it's not pretty.

They're full of stories about Whig fighting Tory, and Tory fighting Whig, a couple of sheriffs being thrown into the Tower of London, and the poor lord mayor being jostled by some hooligans.

Oh, did I mention? These are London newspapers.

One edition has a report on a public meeting: "It is yet Notioufly Known, that the Whiggs Affronted my Lord-Mayor to his Face; Juftled, and Ruffled his Perfon, infomuch that if his Officers had not upheld him, he had been tumbl'd down in the crowd. And with the fame Rudeneff and Intolence, they treated his friends about him, till they were forced to Clear his Paffage out of the Hall with Cudgels."

Oh, did I mention? These are 305-year-old London newspapers. Those seemingly misplaced *f*s are serif *s*'s, in case you were thinking that the story was phoned in by a police reporter with a lisp. ("Hello? Gimme the city defk . . . Chief, we've got a fix-oh-feven here. Yeah—that's right: juftling a lord mayor and caufing his paffage to be cleared with cudgels. Holy Mofes!")

Yes, recently I chanced upon some 1682 London *Observators*. Now I guess that most folks might regard these newspapers as just antique fish wrappers, suitable for wrapping antique fish. But to us newspaper folks, these are our heritage.

It's like a teacher finding a 305-year-old textbook, a farmer finding a 305-year-old plow, or a restaurateur finding a 305-year-old "No shoes, no shirt, no service" sign.

To put these papers into historical perspective, folks still among the quick in 1682 included Stradivari, Newton, Milton and Edmund Halley. Halley was but twenty-six years old in 1682. In fact, his famous comet appeared in that very year, and his rivals suspected that he timed the comet's passage thus just to impress a woman he was dating at the time.

In 1682 the Great Plague of London was just seventeen years past. Cromwell had been dead but twenty-four years. The world's last dodo bird had been dead just one year; sympathetic passenger pigeons were still wearing black arm bands.

It had been but sixty-six years since Shakespeare had died, ceasing at last "to bear the whips and scorns of time." And that was a shame, too, because Anne Hathaway had just gotten a new batch of whips and scorns from a mail-order place in California.

In America, none of the revolutionary heroes had been born yet. In Russia, Peter was not yet the Great. In Germany, Bach was just a glissando in his father's eye.

These old papers were for sale, so some of us in the office eagerly bought them. We can't fully understand their stories, but we understand their history. They speak to us of hand-set type and ragstock paper and a fledgling freedom of the press.

They are single sheets, political in nature, containing no real headlines, no photos, comics, sports or stocks and no personal classifieds pleading, "Dearest Will, come home! I love you, and I promise no more whips and scorns. Anne."

Much would change in three centuries. During the next 305 years, newspapers would evolve into comprehensive, sophisticated mirrors of the world. In the next 305 years, journalism would produce some immortal names — Ambrose Bierce, H.L. Mencken and A Reliable Source.

In the next 305 years, Ann Landers would update her mugshot twice.

Newspapers are among the most disposable products of a culture. Yet somehow these fragile *Observators* survived. They are simply fascinating. I wish that there were a way for all of you to read a 305-year-old newspaper.

Hmmm. But how could we distribute them to you?

I guess we'll just have to wait until we can find a 305-year-old paperboy.

Those Special Occasions

Take your liver to lunch today

October will be National Liver Awareness Month, as you already know if you are the least bit organ-conscious.

Even as we speak, the selection of a National Liver Poster Child is being narrowed down to Ed McMahon or a lush in East Millinocket, Maine.

But I'd like to take this opportunity to say that I am a bit weary of seeing organs such as the liver, lungs, heart and eyes get all the recognition. These are your glamour organs. They get their own months and have their own associations to solicit contributions. These organs are invited to the best parties, earn big bucks doing product endorsements, get gossiped about in *People* magazine.

Don't get me wrong—I am pro-liver. I take mine everywhere. But it's time we recognized some of the unsung organs or, better yet, some of the unsung glands—those that toil in the shadow of the liver and lungs, forced to live as second-class citizens. Day after day they do their jobs without a word of praise, faithfully glanding away.

But where should we start? I'm glad you asked. Of course, some of the southern glands lead very adult life-styles. Anyone who reads this essay hoping to hear about the sordid, tawdry lives of the reproductive glands can just put this paper down right now and go watch Dr. Ruth.

Instead I nominate the Brunner's glands, which are found in the duodenum, which is a tubular organ located practically next door, abdominally speaking, to that big shot, your liver. (Who says this column isn't educational? Betcha you won't learn about Brunner's glands in Art Buchwald's column.)

As you may have guessed, the Brunner's glands are so-named for the scientist who discovered them — Dr. Robert Glands. And what do your Brunner's glands do? Oh, they secrete or something like that. Who cares? The point is that they do it well and never get any recognition for it.

In fact, in a recent survey of our nation's schools, 62 percent of students could not pick their Brunner's glands out of a crowded room, 17 percent could not find the room, and 21 percent said they think Ronald Reagan is doing a good job.

The Brunner's glands secrete their juices — called, one assumes, Brunner's juices — into some other digestive glands called the crypts of Lieberkuhn. Honest. Check any anatomy book. Doesn't that sound grand? The crypts of Lieberkuhn. It sounds like the title of a movie about World War II. *The Guns of Navarone. The Heroes of Telemark. The Crypts of Lieberkuhn.* Starring Kirk Douglas as the small intestine, James Mason as a peptic ulcer, and Sophia Loren as a Tums tablet who swore she would not be taken alive!

But back to the Brunner's glands. I admit that these are not photogenic glands. They are very, very small and don't have good posture or nice smiles. But they were put there for a reason. They have their vital duties, just as your liver and lungs do. If they just up and walked out one day, you'd know about it and fast, I'll bet.

Thus the Brunner's glands have played an important role in history down through the years, which is where history most often is found.

When Michelangelo was painting the Sistine Chapel, his Brunner's glands kept right on working, leaving him free to give the ceiling a second coat.

And Charles Goodyear's Brunner's glands never once failed him during his research on rubber. Thanks to them, we have elastic. So now, when you are staring up at the Sistine Chapel, your underwear won't fall down.

Yes, in conclusion I say let's do what we can to bring recognition to our hard-working Brunner's glands. A National Brunner's Glands Awareness Month would be nice. Then we can get to work on publicizing those overlooked crypts of Lieberkuhn.

In the meantime, be thinking about whom you want to play the part of the pancreas.

United we stand,
divided we hum

Nations of the world, please rise.

Tomorrow is the forty-second anniversary of the founding of the United Nations. In keeping with the spirit of the day, I've spent the better part of a TV dinner listening to an album entitled *National Anthems of the World.* Now who out there can tell me what is on this album? Yes, Paraguay, you're correct: national anthems of the world. And a very fine bunch of anthems they are, too, each one just chock full of notes and other musical stuff.

You're all here on this album: from Japan, the land that gave us sushi, kabuki and Godzilla, to Denmark, the land that gave us Hans Christian Andersen, Victor Borge and my aunt Frank, to Germany, the land that gave us Elke Sommer and that was enough.

Let us now listen to some of these anthems and analyze their musical message.

—Spain's majestic "Marcha Real" evokes visions of the running of the bulls, of Don Quixote and El Greco. General Franco, when still alive, said of it, "Like, it has a good beat, man. I like to dictate to it." Indeed, Spain's "Marcha Real" is symbolic of the nation itself—proud, bold, full of Spaniards.

— Likewise, England's "God Save the Queen" is symbolic of the nation itself—proud, bold, full of American tourists. You will notice that this tune is very familiar. In fact, it is identical to America's "My Country 'Tis of Thee." For years the two nations argued bitterly over which country really 'tis of thee. Finally, the two nations fought the War of 1812 over jukebox rights to the tune.

— France's rousing "La Marseillaise" has been in the national anthem Top Ten for generations. Just *try* to stand still while it is played. (Sartre tried it once and strained something.) "La Marseillaise" is perhaps best known to us from that tear-jerker ending of the film *Casablanca,* in which Rick and Louie walk off arm-in-arm to open a chain of tanning salons in the Sahara.

— The first seven notes of Norway's "Ja Vi Elsker Dette Landet" are the same as those of "Deck the Halls." Honest. "Ja Vi Elsker Dette Landet" in English means "those darned reindeer made jellybeans in the bedroom again, Lars."

— Then there is "O Canada" from the country of the same name. Its stately first four notes—who listens beyond that?— are familiar to major league baseball fans. Notice the use of the high tinny brass notes to call to mind the country's frigid climes. And then, amid it all, we detect the sad cry of a clarinet, which seems to be pleading, "Fly this orchestra to Miami. It's *c-c-c-cold* here!"

(Russia, please stop fidgeting, stand up straight and stop picking on Afghanistan.)

— Italy's "Inno Di Mameli" at first sounds a bit like Western shoot-em-up theme music. But this gives way to a more stately, Old World lilt. In keeping with the emotional nature of its people, midway through, the brasses and strings get into a fight over a lady bassoonist. During a pianissimo, much cursing and breaking of chairs can be heard.

— In Australia's stirring anthem, the woodwinds yield to the brass, the brass yield to the strings, and the xylophone is asked to leave the room. The song builds slowly to full orchestra and to that tune that we all learned as kids and still know so well, "Waltzing Matilda, waltzing Matilda, something something, waltzing Matilda."

—Sweden's "Du Gamia, Du Fria" is the only national anthem performed entirely on Volvo exhaust pipes.

—Switzerland's "Rufst Du Mein, Vaterland" rises and falls like the topography of the land itself. This anthem is the Alps set to music. Listen carefully for a trombone player to fall off a high note during the refrain and plunge to his death among the kettle drums.

Well, that's it. Happy United Nations Day to everyone. OK, all you countries, you may sit down now and continue your fighting.

The name of the game is blame

Don't blame me. It wasn't my idea.

Nevertheless, today is Blame Someone Else Day, as proclaimed and perpetuated by one A.C. Moeller, who lives way up in Michigan, where the major export is hypothermia. That's enough to make *any*one a bit quick to criticize.

The purpose of an annual Blame Someone Else Day, A.C. explains, is "to share the responsibility and the guilt for the mess we're in." And in case you died recently and haven't read the papers, it definitely *is* a mess we're in: Irangate, drugs, crime in the streets. Why, on Groundhog Day, Punxsutawney Phil came out of his hole, saw a mugger's shadow and forecast six weeks of hospitalization.

Of course, blaming someone else is something at which most of us excel. Personally, I majored in Blame with a minor in Fault Finding at dear old Scapegoat U. and would have earned a letter in Casting the First Stone if not for my varsity coach, who failed to recognize real talent when he saw it.

I hold him directly responsible for all of my shortcomings since then.

So on this special day, get on your mark, get set, go blame someone else.

Men can blame women; women can blame men. Parents can blame kids; kids can blame parents.

And all of them can take a few minutes out to blame Lt. Col. Oliver North.

Students, you can blame your teachers if you attended exactly 4.2 days of class during twelve years of public school and graduated thinking that the three leaders of the Axis powers were proteins, fats and carbohydrates. Teachers, you can blame your graduates for being dumb if for twelve years you taught them that the three basic classes of nutrients are Hitler, Tojo and Mussolini.

Husbands, you can blame your wife if she gets a headache each time that you come home from deer-hunting covered with stubble and unidentified bits of Bambi and want to get romantic. Wives, you can blame your husband if he pretends to be asleep when you climb into bed with love on your mind and enough cream on your face to lube a '51 Chevy.

And, of course, the weekend handyman who hits his thumb so often that it looks like Lights Out At Carlsbad Cavern has no one to blame but his hammer.

The Lone Ranger can blame Tonto when he rides into camp after work and finds that his dinner is cold. Tonto can blame the Lone Ranger for going off to the office to right wrongs and then coming home two hours late. ("Me guess it too much trouble to phone, eh, white man?")

Americans can blame Soviets; Soviets can blame Americans. Mickey can blame Minnie; Minnie can blame Mickey.

And both can blame Oliver North.

Young, you can blame the old for not letting you make a statement by wearing orange spiked hair, earrings the size of a chandelier and clothing that looks like an abstract painting that lost its lunch. Old, you can blame the young for having the spunk that *you* lost along with your hair, teeth and waist.

Readers, if you think that this column has been a waste of time, you can blame me. If my career crashes and burns, I can blame you.

Gee, isn't this fun?

But if you think that the idea of celebrating a Blame Someone Else Day is stupid, you can blame A.C. Moeller. Write him a nasty letter. He lives at (or possibly *in*) P.O. Box 71, Clio, Michigan 48420.

If he never receives your letter, you can blame the Postal Service. The Postal Service can blame you, claiming that you failed to put a stamp on the envelope.

I'll bet that Oliver North steamed it off.

Give boss TLC (Or is that TNT?)

Right now, while we're thinking about it, I want you to remember to set aside your lunch money each day so that you can buy some flowers next Thursday.

Because that will be National Bosses Day.

Now I know what you're saying: "Yeah, a nice bouquet of flowers for the ol' boss. With a lighted stick of dynamite hidden inside."

But you say that only because our popular lore has caricatured bosses as bogeymen with briefcases: aloof, mean, cold, omnipotent, intimidating personages who lurk in their cave-like offices, plotting ways to keep us miserable and downtrodden.

And who am I to contradict our popular lore?

No, no. Just kidding. It's time to show our bosses some kindness. After all, bosses are people, too. It says so in the employee handbook. They are a put-upon, misunderstood breed who must shoulder a lot of responsibility to do what must be done, keeping American business safe for staff meetings.

One boss who certainly merits some recognition is my boss. She is a lovely, charming, talented and fair-minded woman who has never once beat me when I didn't deserve it.

As I said to her just the other day, "Linda, you are a lovely, charming, talented and fair-minded woman who has never once beat me when I didn't deserve it. But I, for one, certainly am *not* some sycophantic, favor-seeking, groveling toady."

And she said to me, "Yes, Mike. You, for one, certainly are *not* some sycophantic, favor-seeking, groveling toady . . . Now, lick the *other* boot."

Think about it: Would you want to be *your* boss, always having to wake you up, having to keep count of how many times you've taken a day off to attend your granny's funeral, having to keep you from sneaking pencils, paper clips and the office Xerox machine home in your lunch pail?

And at their best, bosses inspire us workers to reach new heights of pride and productivity. For example, if Michelangelo's supervisor on the Sistine Chapel job had not kept after him, Michelangelo would have painted the ceiling avocado green—one coat—and been done with it.

If Noah Webster's publisher had not kept after him, Webster would have submitted a dictionary that ended after the letter *k*.

If the pharoahs hadn't kept after the slaves who built the pyramids, the slaves would have built just a rock garden and knocked off at two P.M.

Likewise, Tchaikovsky might have composed the *1811 Overture,* Ken Kesey might have written *None Flew Over the Cuckoo's Nest,* and Charlton Heston might have come down from Mount Sinai with only the Nine Commandments, leaving us all free to covet our neighbor's Jacuzzi.

Some bosses inspire such awe that they are rumored to have supernatural powers. They become the stuff of myths. This tale is typical.

The boss had called Osborn, of the Purchasing Department, into his office to explain a small typing error. Instead of "rubber stamps," Osborn had typed "rubber stumps," which resulted in the company purchasing 2,500 resilient artificial legs.

Later, after Osborn returned to his desk, someone saw the boss take the fire extinguisher off his office wall and then sit down, close his eyes and press his fingers to his temples, as if concentrating. At that moment, Osborn—who was muttering, "Stamp, stump, what's the difference?"—mysteriously burst into flames and burned to a crisp.

The boss ran out and extinguished what was left of Osborn — his shoes — and then docked him a day's pay for going up in flames in a no-smoking area.

Nonsense. It's time to put these myths and unfair stereotypes behind us. Be kind to your boss. And you can start next Thursday. Give your boss some flowers. Roses would be perfect. I suggest a dozen of the long-stemmed variety.

They hide the fuse better.

Trees plentiful (knock on wood)

By an act of Congress, this is National Forest Products Week. Take a toothpick to lunch.

After that, find a good, upstanding tree and sit down in one of the nicest things that trees ever gave us.

Shade.

It's also one of the few forest products that we have not exploited. Maybe that's because you can't saw shade or burn it or mill it. You can just be in it. Shade just *is*.

Watch the sunlight filter through the leaves, dappling the ground around you. And consider the humble tree — surely *the* Renaissance plant.

It is safe to say that we are where we are today because of the tree. Wood gave us the first wheel of industry, the first plow of agriculture, the first salad of roots, bark and nuts. Hold the sap.

Today, wood is the very backbone of Popsicles, kites and corny dogs.

Just try to imagine a world without wood.

Without wood, Columbus would have had no ships. Instead, he would have had to seek an overland route to the New World. And it just isn't the same — painting "Nina," "Pinta" and "Santa Maria" on the fender of three Winnebagos.

Without wood, Pete Rose might have hit no. 4,192 with a crowbar. Stradivari might have crafted tubas. Billions of termites would be on welfare.

Without wood, these very words would fall to the floor and get hopelessly jumbled because there would be no paper to hold them up. You're reading this column on a slice of tree that was pureed in an industrial-strength Cuisinart.

But don't bother to pick up the words. They, too, would not exist: Wood by-products are an important part of printer's ink.

Who can say which has had more impact—the timber with which we have built our environment or the paper with which we have built our culture?

Wood gives us temples, and it gives us taverns. Paper gives us letters that begin "John, Dear:" and letters that begin "Dear John:." Trees are comfort stations to the dog on the go and discomfort stations to the man in the noose.

Some highlights in the history of the tree.

—1,000,000 B.C. In a tree much like the one you are sitting under, our earliest ancestors slide down from their tree houses and so discover the first wood by-product—the splinter.

—999,999 B.C. That same tree gives lightning its first target, letting our earliest ancestors discover the two things that their backyard barbecues had lacked—fire and charcoal briquettes.

—1184 B.C. Odysseus fools the Trojan army with his wooden horse. After the victory, he is decorated and then ordered to go back and sweep up the wooden droppings.

—A.D. 105 The Chinese emperor commissions a man named Ts' ai Lun to create a new writing medium. Ts' uses beaten fibers of the mulberry tree to make paper. On this world's first paper, he presents the emperor with the world's first bill. It is padded. The emperor pays with the world's first check. It bounces.

—1790. George Washington is fitted with wooden false teeth and no longer has to be content to gum the first lady's earlobes.

—1791. Martha Washington is treated for splinters.

—1892. The knothole is invented by Elmer "Squint" Dibble when he is hired to erect a wooden fence around an Ohio nudist camp.

—1985. A consumer group claims that eight brands of bread contain wood pulp. Soon home-builders are experimenting with bread as a building material and hope to offer a low-maintenance house that never needs painting. Every three years, you just butter it.

So much for the past. But what of the future of trees? Oh, sure, the woods are full of 'em now. America still has 488 million acres of commercial forest. The Southern forest supplies from a third to a half of our pulp, plywood and lumber.

Thus some folks act as if wood grows on trees. The U.S. Forest Service says that demand for wood products will double by the year 2000. But the American Forest Institute says that at the present rate of use, supply won't be able to keep up with that demand.

Turn your imagination to the future. The world continues to reap more than it sows. Reforestation falls behind. More lumber and more paper products. Fewer and fewer trees, until there is only one tree left in all the world.

Just one.

Its stark oneness shocks the people, and they begin to honor this last great provider. A chain-link fence is erected to protect it. Guards stand watch. A famous artist is commissioned to capture the tree's image on canvas. The painting will be hung in the Great Hall of the People.

At last the day arrives, and the painting is unveiled in a ceremony in the shade of this last remaining tree. The painting is wondrous in its beauty. The people cheer. Then someone in the back of the throng shouts that such a great painting of such a great tree surely should be set off by an equally great frame.

"Yes! A frame! A beautiful frame!" the people shout.

So they chop down the tree to make a frame.

Life at Large

And a partridge in a penitentiary

Our Christmas songs reflect a simpler time, when sleigh bells rang and children sang and Santa didn't have to squeeze past the burglar bars on the chimney.

But just imagine the complications that would arise today if someone with a traditional nature decided to take "The Twelve Days of Christmas" literally. You know the song—each round adds a gift and repeats the previous gifts. Here are the thank-you notes that might result from those gifts.

"On the first day of Christmas my true love sent to me a partridge in a pear tree."

My dearest darling Daphne: What a wonderful gift! I love it, and everyone says I have just about the neatest fiancée a guy could have. True, now my landlord is demanding that I put up a $50 partridge deposit, and pears give me hives. But, hey, it's the thought that counts.

"On the second day of Christmas my true love sent to me two turtle doves."

My dearest Daphne: Oh, joy. Two doves *and* another partridge in a pear tree. They make the sweetest music, keeping me awake all night. Thus lately I've been pretty groggy at work. And it's not good for a surgeon to get groggy, you know. Yesterday I separated a pair of Siamese twins and joined two interns together with Velcro.

"On the third day of Christmas my true love sent to me three French hens."

Dearest Daphne: Save the giblets, OK? Ha Ha. Three hens, more doves, another partridge. The apartment is starting to smell like Big Bird's laundry hamper.

"On the fourth day of Christmas my true love sent to me four calling birds."

Dearest: Just what *is* it with you and birds? Yep, these birds sure are calling, and so are the neighbors — to the police. To say nothing of all the adorable lice! Everytime I itch, I think of you.

"On the fifth day of Christmas my true love sent to me five golden rings."

Daphne: Thank goodness. At last something that isn't molting or cackling. But just what am I supposed to do with five yellow Hula Hoops?

"On the sixth day of Christmas my true love sent to me six geese a-laying."

Daph: Again with the birds? And, oh, are the geese a-laying. On the book shelves, in my sock drawer, behind the sofa. And they're mean. Last night about three A.M. when I got out of bed and bent over for my slippers, I found out where we get the verb "goose."

"On the seventh day of Christmas my true love sent to me seven swans a-swimming."

Daft: The bird population now totals sixty-nine. My apartment has been quarantined for fowl cholera. I am turning this matter over to my attorney, Philo Feemus of the law firm of Ampersand, Ampersand, Ampersand and &.

"On the eighth day of Christmas my true love sent to me eight maids a-milking."

My dearest darling Daphne: Now *this* is more like it. All is forgiven. How very liberated and open-minded of you to give me these lovely, nubile maidens. I will make them all feel welcome in my bedroom, even if the birds have to sleep in the hall. The cows can stay on the patio and try out the Hula Hoops. Who knows, maybe then they'll give butter. Ha ha.

"On the ninth day of Christmas my true et cetera et cetera."

Dimwit: Listen, these nine ladies dancing had better be friendlier than those eight cold-fish maids a-milking. Boy, have those dames got strong grips! I hope that some of my casts can come off in a few weeks.

"On the tenth day of Christmas and so on and so on."

Ex-fiancée: What do I need with ten lords a-leaping? As soon as I unpacked them, they all a-leaped over to the nine ladies dancing and tried to go cheek to cheek. I had to get the maids a-milking to hose them down. And at best, with 10-9 odds, there is bound to be one very left-out lord. Maybe he can help me a-sweep up all these feathers.

"On the eleventh day of Christmas my true love blah blah blah."

Defendant: Enclosed is the lawsuit I have filed against you for criminal harassment. I have lost my lease, my job and the better part of my sanity. If I can get them to hush, these eleven pipers piping who just arrived will be called as material witnesses.

"On the twelfth day of Christmas I think we'll hum the rest."

No. 4096302: How did you manage to send me twelve drummers drumming from your prison cell? You are a sick woman. My new apartment now contains—let's see—carry the 7 . . . bring down the swan . . . a total of 40 cows, 12 trees, 40 rings, 184 unruly birds and 140 people of assorted sexes. *Playboy* wants to throw its next party here. So does *Field & Stream*.

P.S. But at least I finally found a use for the eggs and pails of milk that have been piling up to the rafters—I used them to bake you a nice cake. And I have hidden in it something that every prisoner wants more than anything.

Yes, to show that there are no hard feelings, on the thirteenth day of Christmas I am sending you a cake containing thirteen saws a-hacking.

Apply them just under your chin.

I'll see to it that you are buried directly beneath (big finish now!) . . .

". . . a partridge in a pear tree."

Grads, life gets harder by degrees

Good news, seniors: I had planned to give each of you a new sports car for graduation, but just in time I realized that you'd probably much rather receive some worthless advice.

As you prepare to take your rightful place in the world, think of life as a theme park, much like Disneyland or Six Flags. After all, in both life and a theme park there is so much to see and do, the time goes much too quickly and in the end there you are: dead, with something pink and yucky stuck to the bottom of your shoe.

Here are just a few of the areas you'll enjoy as you visit the great theme park Adultland.

— *Careerland*. This is the first area of the park. The class of '87 has so many job choices. Remember that appearances are important. Those of you who look good in robes might want to become pope. Those of you who look good in concrete might want to become an organized-crime stool pigeon. Those of you who look good in court might want to become a stock-market inside trader.

Also here you can play Interpret the Help Wanted Ads. For instance, if a job ad says, "Firm offers good pay, great benefits to hard worker; must have own toilet brush," don't expect to get a chauffeur and an expense account.

Next try to climb the Greased Pole of Promotion. You'll need a firm grip and tenacity, but if you keep at it, it will pay off. Yes, sure enough, some day the boss will call you in and say, "Perkins, you'll never get ahead wearing those greasy clothes."

— *Loveland*. The most popular area of Adultland. Ride the Roller-Coaster of Romance: ups, downs, and yes, a certain amount of nausea. Float through the Tunnel of Love, where young lovers thrill to the sweet nothings, the first kiss, the locked braces!

Later, many of you will want to test your skills in the Divorce Mill: Fill your pockets with your life savings and try to run the gauntlet past 500 lawyers with their hands held out. At the finish, you can keep any money still in your pockets and the clothes on your back. If you have no clothes left on your back, quick—take a trip to Barrelland!

Then try the Singles Bar, where you can play that popular game, What's My Line?: "I'll bet you're a Pisces, right?" or "Nice barrel. Come here often?" or "See this robe, baby? I'm the pope."

If you later discover that you have a souvenir rash, congratulations: You've just won a free trip to Sexually Transmitted Diseaseland.

—*Dollars and Centsland.* Because you had the foresight to attend college, in your career you will earn $1,200,931.34. Of that amount, you will spend $1,000,000 on Masters of the Universe and Barbie dolls for your kids and $200,930 on your mortgage. The remaining $1.34 you will apply toward repaying your college loan.

—*Midlife Crisisland.* Here you'll play Who Am I, Anyway? This popular game questions everything that you valued in Careerland, Loveland and Dollars and Centsland.

Here men develop an intense interest in Grecian Formula, motorcycles and Dallas Cowboy cheerleaders. Women begin to have fantasies involving Mark Harmon, some Cool Whip and a hot tub at the Hilton and to dream of the day when having thighs like the Pillsbury Doughboy is considered fashionable.

—*Golden Yearsland.* This is the last area of the park. Here you'll have time to enjoy your hobbies, your grandchildren and your well-deserved retirement. Just be sure to take good care of your health.

Otherwise, uh oh, it's time to play—yes!—Chest Pains! If you don't get to a hospital soon, the next area you visit will be Lying-in-Stateland. But the paramedics arrive and, with skill and speed, place you onto a stretcher and rush you out the theme park gates. Then, as the precious seconds pass and your life hangs in the balance, just in time these alert angels of mercy reach the vast Adultland parking lot.

Where they can't remember where they parked the ambulance.

Scars taken at face value

Scars.

Few of us get through this sharp-edged world without collection at least one or two. Scars are among the most interesting of our physical features. Especially facial scars, because faces are the focus of social interaction, the mirror of humanity's deepest emotions and the first place we go when we want to scratch somebody's eyes out.

I have two terribly rugged scars on my terribly rugged face: one over the bridge of my nose and one on my cheek, just above the timberline.

Scars give a man's face character, don't you think? And character is something that my face had always lacked. In fact, before I came by my scars naturally in the course of my terribly rugged life, I had considered renting a pair of scars, at least to use on weekends and at class reunions.

Before I got my scars, no one noticed me. I was like a piece of furniture. I was often mistaken for a floor lamp. I still am. But a terribly rugged floor lamp, I'll have you know. I like to think that my scars mark me as a man of mystery, as one dangerous hombre in this dark, deadly world of big-city humor.

No one has ever asked me how I got my scars. But if they ever do, I'll be ready. Because terribly rugged scars should have a terribly rugged story to go with them.

One night my gruff-yet-kindly city editor said to me, "Scoop (he always called me "Scoop"), Mad Dog Dobbs had just broken out of prison, and I want you on the story."

"Sure, you old —— [I always called him "you old ——"]. You want me to get on the phone and check out some facts, eh?"

"No. I want you to be his hostage."

"But don't we have a regular hostage writer for that?"

"Yeah, but he's tied up right now."

I never forgave my editor for that line.

Mad Dog Dobbs had holed up in a cabin in the Rockies, which are about ten miles west of Fort Worth. (I know they're really much farther away, but I'm trying to keep this short.) Mad Dog had been convicted of bank robbery, killing two guards and cutting in line at the teller's window. As a result, he was given two life sentences but no free clock-radio.

When I reached his cabin and walked in, Mad Dog broke my arm, poured molten lead into my ears, pleated my spleen and told me to make myself at home. Touched by his hospitality, I slit his nostrils, shattered his kneecaps, broke his back and asked him how the wife and kids were.

With that he grew nostalgic and surrendered. I called the state police. When they arrived, the captain walked up to me and gave my necktie several tugs before he realized that I was not a floor lamp.

I phoned in my story to the city desk just before deadline and then stepped outside the cabin for a breath of fresh air.

There it was, crouched on a boulder — a panther, 800 pounds of snarling savagery. Suddenly I felt like I was in a "Wild Kingdom" rerun. I could almost hear Marlin Perkins reading my eulogy. I braced myself as the panther pounced on me, knocking me to the ground and raking its hellish claws across my face. I passed out from loss of blood and hours later woke up in this paragraph.

What? You don't believe that?

OK, OK. Here's the truth. I got my scars at a friend's house one night when I walked into and through her extremely clean sliding glass door while taking her cat's litter box to the patio. I led with my nose and then threw a quick left jab with my cheek. It was over in seconds. No contest. That poor patio door had to be swept up off the floor in a thousand pieces.

So, yes, if you insist on the truth, I guess I got my two terribly rugged scars while changing a litter box for a pussycat.

Now aren't you glad you didn't ask?

I came, I sawed, I tinkered

Sometimes a man's gotta do what a man's gotta do.

And sometimes that means retreating into his home workshop and making something with his own two hands. Ah, how he looks forward at last to finishing that beautiful bookcase and showing his handiwork to his friends, who will gush with admiration, "Wow, Ed! What a great coat rack."

Traditionally, the workshop has been to men what the kitchen has been to women: a place of creativity. A man who in the kitchen breaks into a cold sweat while trying to read a simple recipe for a soufflé ("Gosh, how many dabs in a dollop? And is that a metric dollop?") will go into his workshop and not flinch at a set of plans for building a nuclear grandfather clock (step 1: get a nuclear grandfather) using just hammer, chisel and a pair of lead-lined underwear.

To relax, some men drink, some chase women. But the smart ones work in their shop. It's better for your liver, and no man was ever shot by a jealous 2 × 4.

Someone once said that the best rest is a change of work. These days so many of us work with intangibles on the job. At the end of the day, we men who make a living using our heads (I use mine as a doorstop, it hopes someday to be promoted to a paperweight) feel the need to produce something tangible, something that can be seen and touched, perhaps even sat on.

Ah, to feel that solid heft of a drill in your hand, the firm flex of a saw! The satisfaction after a nail well driven, the hemorrhaging after a nail not so well driven!

Because, you know, men, you don't need the deftness of Stradivari to enjoy working with your hands. The joy is in the doing. And if you fear power tools such as jigsaws and drills and routers, working with hand tools is a good way to master this fear gradually. After all, what is a screwdriver but a drill that hasn't reached puberty?

People who visit my home are always impressed with my workshop. "Gee, this is a great workshop. The rest of your house looks like Armageddon With Wallpaper, but your shop is great."

And it is. Because my workshop is full of good, useful stuff. That's the operative word here—"stuff."

Men love stuff. Men are like crows—they love to collect shiny, intricate things. It's all so potent: power tools and hand tools, sandpaper and paint, vises and varnishes, the containers abristle with bits and bolts, nails and nuts. Perhaps even some genuine case-hardened no. 6 Scandinavian thingamabobs, made in Sweden by Bob, who is a genuine case-hardened no. 6 Scandinavian thingama.

Sometimes when I'm in my workshop, I don't even build or repair anything. I just stare at all the stuff, knowing that I *could* if I was a mind to. Yessiree. Sometimes I go into a trance of well-being, and a neighbor finds me the next morning, pawing through some shiny brass screws and smiling serenely.

Stuff instills confidence.

And so do the words of the workshop. This is where strong, active verbs hang out—"chisel," "grind," "mortise," and, yes, "countersink." None of your namby-pamby office verbs: "was impacted," "was nonrenewed," "was effectuated."

Why, if a passive office sentence such as "The profits, when annualized, will be maximized for maximum maxibility" were to wander into a *real* man's workshop, it would come limping back out in a hurry, with several bruised parts of speech.

But, as in the kitchen, projects in the workshop don't always go as planned. A mismeasurement here, a crooked cut there, and then, once again, a man's gotta do what a man's gotta do: If that solid-oak dining table comes out a bit wobbly, he can always turn it upside-down, tack netting around the legs and call it a playpen.

Just try doing *that* with a burned soufflé.

Hear, hear! Long live adulthood

At some point during life's journey from the rubber sheet to the winding sheet, we suddenly look up and say, "Gad, but I do enjoy being an adult!"

And a good thing we do enjoy it, too, because adulthood is where we have to spend the rest of our lives. Unless we move to southern California.

But just what are the benefits of adulthood that make it worthwhile? What is the payoff for surviving pop tests, mumps and puberty, sometimes all on the same day?

Most of us would say, in twenty-five words or less: "Gad, but I do enjoy being an adult because I can do what I wanna do. And *not* do what I do *not* wanna do."

Once, as a tyke, I had an ear infection. But medicine was one of the first things that I did "*not* wanna do." So my poor parents drew straws. The winner would get a choice: (a) try to "doctor" me or (b) take the rectal temperature of a wounded rogue elephant. Well, naturally the relieved winner chose the elephant, packed a bag of peanuts, a thermometer and a ladder and hastily left for Africa.

The loser (I couldn't tell which parent it was because both were about fifty feet tall) then offered a prayer to Dr. Spock and crept up behind me bearing Some Vile Liquid (a registered trademark), which was to be poured into my ears.

Now my ears happen to be two of the several orifices that I (in common with rogue elephants) guard jealously. So I balked. I balked loudly and longly. I backed away into a corner of the room, keeping out of range of the eye-dropper, which was by now the size of a fire hose. There was a piano in the corner. I climbed to the top of it, my back to the wall, to make my stand.

I struggled mightily, but in vain. My last sensation before I blacked out was Some Vile Liquid melting through from one ear to the other, so that to this day I not only hear perfectly, but when the wind blows, I hear flutes.

(I admit that after all these years, my memories may be distorted. My parents may have been only thirty feet tall.)

There atop that piano I began to look forward to adulthood.

After all, adults get to drive red sports cars and stay up late, even on a school night. They can cross the street by themselves and carry a pocketknife and talk on the phone all day without anyone hollering at them. They can cuss and spit. They can afford baseball cards without having to sneak change out of their mother's coin purse. And no one can barge into their ears without a court order.

And adults do not have to read *Moby Dick* or wear galoshes or be polite to Aunt Bernice. And isn't that what the good life is all about?

As children, we envied this freedom. Many of us vowed that when we were grown, we would (1) eat all the Twinkies we want, (2) sleep late every day, and (3) never take a bath. So as soon as we reached adulthood, we tried all three. And what did it get us, besides fat, fired and friendless?

No fair. By the time we have the freedom to do all the things we've yearned to do, we've lost interest in them.

And, of course, such freedom is not free. For instance, as a child, if you pitch a fit and sling your food up onto the ceiling, it's just called juvenile behavior and is overlooked. But everything that an adult does must have a good reason. So, as an adult, if you sling your food up onto the ceiling, it had jolly well better help to make a car payment or mow the lawn or bring peace to the Middle East.

Yet in spite of its responsibilities, adulthood remains the best place to be most of the time. So I'm sure that people will continue to look up from time to time and say, "Gad, but I do enjoy being an adult!"

Until, that is, they have a small child with an ear infection.

Lost: Idealism; reward offered

Of all the things that we lose as we grow older—including our teeth, our hair and our way home from the bowling alley— perhaps the saddest is the loss of our idealism.

When we were young—eighteen to twenty-two—we were eager to take on this imperfect world single-handed, to right wrongs, to give harsh reality six points and still emerge the victor. We had lofty principles then. We were idealists, perfectionists, especially those of us who came of age during the '60s. We envisioned the United States of Utopia and knew exactly how to establish it.

We couldn't sleep at night, worrying because there was oppression, hunger and poverty in the world, worrying because somewhere people were being denied liberty, dignity and Donovan albums.

Now we worry only if our Cuisinart is making a funny noise.

As we age, we settle for style over substance, form over function, "what is" over "what should be." We compromise, pragmatize, raise our blood pressure and lower our expectations, toiling at a job that will give us this day our daily bread.

As we age, we swing from liberal to conservative. At some point, on our desk, that photo of Eugene McCarthy or George McGovern is replaced by an autographed picture of the Republican National Committee sitting on a Shetland pony.

As Shakespeare said: "O infinite virtue! Comest thou smiling from the world's great snare uncaught?"

Alas the answer is no.

I remember that when I was twenty—just a cub reporter with stars in my eyes and peach fuzz on my verbs—a grizzled old editor warned me, in a fatherly way, that with time my ideals would go the way of the Linotype machine and the flash bulb.

I didn't believe him. Now, eighteen years later, I'm not so sure.

I remember that when I was twenty I regarded my body as a temple. Well, I still do, but lately I am considering putting a Jacuzzi in the baptismal font.

At twenty I was the director of this epic movie that we call *Life*. I vowed to make mine an intelligent, sensitive film with an insightful message. Eighteen years later I've lost creative control. *Life* has been retitled *Beach Blanket Kung Fu O.D.*, and I'm now just an extra in a crowd scene, a panicky bystander trampled underfoot while Annette Funicello (as Inflation), Chuck Norris (as Violence) and Cheech (as Chong) and Chong (as Cheech) run rampant. The insightful message has become: "Surf's up, yellow-dog scum. Far out!"

Yes, when we were young, we had all the answers. Now we have forgotten the questions.

Yet I'd like to think that I have held to at least some of my youthful idealism, that I have not made the complete transition from "one of us" to "one of them."

But if today on a street corner downtown I happened to step off the curb into a time warp and encountered me-at-twenty, how would I assess that kid, with his shaggy idealism? Would I recognize myself? Today would I even like me-at-twenty?

Probably not until he moved his Volkswagen bus off my foot.

And more important, would *he* like me? Or would he call me a square caught up in getting by? Would he call me a sell-out? Would he call me an old fogey? Would he call the police if I punched him in his smart little mouth?

What would I say about his wide-eyed faith, hope and charity? Probably something like, "Kid, faith, hope and charity married Larry, Curly and Moe and left town, leaving no forwarding address."

Nothing, not even (or especially) our idealism, escapes the erosion of time.

What a shame.

Or, as Shakespeare said: " . . . 'tis true; 'tis true 'tis pity; and pity 'tis 'tis true."

To which Anne Hathaway replied: "Huh?"

Getting a read
on real life

What this world needs is subtitles for real life.

Foreign movies and even some opera performances already have subtitles. But those of us who live right here in downtown Real Life have even more need of them so that we can know what people are really saying to us. Granted, developing built-in subtitles for people would be tricky. Perhaps some sort of LCD read-out strapped to the forehead and wired directly to the brain, bypassing the mouth.

But I just know that any country that can conquer space, perform organ transplants and cure the heartbreak of water spots on your fine crystal can meet *this* challenge too.

Here are a few examples of how subtitles for real life could help.

— Suppose a politician's press secretary says:

"Senator Drivel prefers not to take a stand at this time on this crucial issue of naming a state parasite. In fact, even now he's weighing the merits of the issue far from the distractions of the capital."

The press secretary's subtitle for real life would read: "The senator is off skiing in Aspen."

— A lover says (in sequence):

1. "Of *course* I still love you. But I need my own space right now. Try to understand."

The subtitle for real life reads: "I just realized what a loser you are."

2. "Don't you think a man and a woman can be just friends?"

Subtitle: "So long, jerk. I just met the hunkiest senator while skiing in Aspen."

3. "Oh, Honey, I see now I was wrong. Can't things be like they used to be?"

Subtitle: "The senator was married."

—A teacher, to a child's parents:

"This is quite common in boys of his age, I assure you, but I'm beginning to detect in your little Timmy some slight signs of potential discipline problems."

Subtitle: "Timmy is operating a 'protection' racket, forcing people at school to give him their lunch money. We've tried to overlook this, but several of the teachers are getting quite thin. He also has organized the hall monitors into a neo-Nazi terror squad, and in the reading circle he substituted 'Babes in Bondage' for 'Uncle Tee-Hee Counts to 5.'"

—Timmy's mother, twenty years later:

"Timmy went on to spend six years at a state-supported institution, where he was equally adept with numbers and as a man of letters and later held a chair in criminal jurisprudence."

Subtitle: "Timmy went to prison, where he made license plates until he was electrocuted."

—An auto mechanic:

"Your differential's hypoid ring gear is stripped, the piston rod wrist pins have seized, and it looks negative for your positive terminal, although I'm positive about your negative terminal."

Subtitle: "How soon can you get a loan?"

—A doctor:

"After a complete blood-chemistry series and thorough physical examination, with X rays of your hypoid ring gear, I recommend that you consult my colleague a specialist—for further tests."

Subtitle: "I have no idea what's wrong with you. But I have a golf buddy who is two payments behind on his Mercedes."

—A social rival at a party: "My, doesn't your décolletage show off your *lovely* figure!"

Subtitle: "Hmmm. I see that inflation is rampant in Silicon Valley."

—A personnel director interviewing a job applicant:

"You'll like working here at BilgeCo. It's challenging, you'll soon get to know everyone, and there's no place to go but up."

Subtitle: "You'll get an electric typewriter after one year and an electric outlet after five years; we're shamefully understaffed, and the only restroom is on the fifty-third floor."

There now. I think I've made my point with these sample

subtitles. Further examples would be merely redundant.

Subtitle for real life: "I'm too lazy to come up with any more."

It's the heyday
of the theysay

"They say that the United States now has enough nuclear weapons to reduce the Soviet Union to the consistency of tomato aspic."

The above sentence contains the two most powerful words in the English language. Can you spot them? No, they're not "United States," not "nuclear weapons," not "Soviet Union," not even "tomato aspic."

They're "they say."

Faster than a speeding grapevine! More powerful than a rumor! Able to leap tall tales in a single bound!

"They say." Spoken almost as one word: "Theysay."

These two tiny words are the real powers-that-be in this world.

Powerful because they are intangible, untraceable.

Theysay is so much a part of language and life that we no longer notice it when we speak it or hear it. But just pin a theysay like a tail onto most any old jackass of a statement or conjecture and watch it assume the blood and bone of a thoroughbred fact.

Therein lies the power of theysay.

And just who are these they who say anyway?

Are you one of they? Am I one of they? And how about them over there across the street — are they they?

(There will now be a minute of silence for those English teachers who just impaled themselves on sharpened sticks of chalk.)

No, we *all* are they. And we all say. We *all* theysay.

I theysay, you theysay. All God's children theysay.

I remember the first theysay that I ever heard—"Theysay that if a turtle bites you, it won't let go until it hears thunder."

Well, I believed that bit of nonsense, and to this day I have never encouraged a turtle to bite me on a clear day.

Another theysay, circa 1958, was that thirty years into the future we would all be flying to work on personal jetpacks.

Well, it's now the future, but you're still stuck down here in earth traffic—angry, hot, resisting the temptation to bite the steering wheel. (If you do, theysay you won't let go until you hear thunder.)

Other theysays that we all have heard: Theysay there are alligators in the New York City sewers, theysay the energy crisis was a hoax contrived by the major oil companies, theysay you can catch VD from a toilet seat, and theysay the Air Force is hiding a captured UFO in a secret hangar.

How do these half-truths and outright lies get started? Is there a National Unsubstantiated Rumor Clearinghouse out there somewhere with a toll-free number (1-800-THEYSAY)?

The whole truth (and nothing but the truth, so help me, Judge Wapner), of course, is that there are UFOs in the New York City sewers, you can catch VD from alligators, the Air Force has captured an alien toilet seat, and the energy crisis was real, but the major oil companies are a hoax.

Let's conduct a little sociological experiment. Let's just make up some theysays. Then, as a farmer might, let's sow them like seeds among the plowed populace and see if our little theysays sprout and grow into corn, cucumbers and tomato aspic.

Tell the following theysays to two friends. Have *them* tell two friends. And so on. Do not break this chain.

—Theysay that north of the equator, vines twine around a pole clockwise. South of the equator, vines twine around a pole counter-clockwise. Precisely *at* the equator, they just sorta lie there.

—Theysay that President Taft could not say the word "fondue" without giggling.

—Theysay that Elvis was cryogenically preserved when he died and will be brought back to life when a cure is found for Elvis impersonators.

—Theysay that wallpaper paste cures baldness.

—Theysay that wallpaper paste *causes* baldness.

(The last two theysays should be circulated as a matched set. If you later see middle-aged men walking around with only *half* of their head plastered with wallpaper paste, you'll know that we're succeeding.)

Maybe theysays can even be self-fulfilling prophecies. Try this one: Theysay that (your name) is the best darned (your job) in the business and that old (your boss) should give (your name) a bonus of (a figure equal to your Visa balance).

Well, this theysay eventually will get back to your boss, and he might just swallow it and decide that you have been over-looked and underpaid all these years.

But don't send all of that big bonus to Visa. Use part of it to pay for a bomb shelter. Because the Soviet Union now has enough nuclear weapons to reduce the United States to the consistency of tomato aspic.

Or so theysay.

Miles of isles: A crackpot idea

I have a vision.

Well, actually, it isn't exactly a vision. It's more like a crackpot idea.

In my crackpot idea, I see us living on a planet that is made up of hundreds of islands in one big sea. Each island is inhabited solely by folks who share one trait, whether good or bad. Maybe you, too, feel this way at times. "Why don't all those (a social group of your choice) go live together somewhere and just (a verb of your choice) to their hearts' content and not bother me?"

For instance, in my crackpot idea, there is the Island of Smokers. This island is permanently shrouded in Camel fog. From offshore, through the Camel fog you can hear people bumming cigarettes and coughing loose their various internal organs.

Far away, on the other side of the world, is the Island of Nonsmokers, where everyone has lungs like a Hoover and taste buds so sharp that they can detect white bread at fifty paces.

Of course, in this crackpot world of mine, each of us has a rowboat and a paddle. That way we can be selective: We can visit those islands where right-thinking people like ourselves live but avoid those islands where the godless, pinko banana-brains lurk.

Some more islands that would exist in such a world:

Island of Loud, Obnoxious People. Hear car-lot TV advertisers, kids with boom boxes and glass-packed mufflers, and next-door neighbors all living life at a decibel level capable of shattering kidney stones in another time zone.

Its opposite is the Island of Quiet, Shy People. See 80 million people standing on the beach staring at their fingernails. Not a word has been exchanged here in fifty-seven years because no one has been introduced to each other. Although one man did try to break the ice by clearing his throat: He wrote *"ahem!"* in the sand with his toe.

There is an Island of Folks Who Are Deathly Afraid of Computers and Would Rather Kiss a Snake on the Lips Than Be Around Them.

There is an Island of Beautiful, Brilliant and Truly Wonderful Human Beings. It's a tiny island, but I like to visit it once in a while, even though after a while I have to leave and paddle straight over to the Island of People With Inferiority Complexes.

Island of Damn-Fool Drivers. The whole island is paved — 500 miles long and six lanes wide. On any given day here you can see 50 million motorists cutting across three lanes of traffic to exit at a 45-degree angle without a turn signal. The island's chief import is fenders. The chief export is next of kin.

Island of Nudists. At last these nature-lovers have a place to play Show and Tell free of condemnation.

Not far away is the Island of Bluenoses With Powerful Moral

Standards and Even-More-Powerful Telescopes.

Island of Controlled Substances. This is where glassy-eyed folks sit around having insights until they get so mellow that they try to walk across to the Island of Munchies.

Other far-flung islands are the islands of Litterbugs, Religious Bigots, Gun Nuts, Phone Solicitors, People Who Take Two Parking Spaces, People Who Don't Get Their Pets Fixed and the Island of Whoever Borrowed My Copy of *Fanny Hill* and Returned It With Pizza Stains on the Good Parts.

My last port of call for the evening is the Island of Lonely Women in Search of a Deeply Meaningful Relationship Based on Mutual Respect, Common Interests and Certain Druid Fertility Rites.

That is, unless I discover that someone from the Island of Pardoned Criminals has rowed ashore in the night and stolen everything that I own. Then here I'll be, stranded on the Island of Lonely Columnists Who Have Lots of Crackpot Ideas but No Paddle.

Hmmm. I think that in my next vision, I'll see peninsulas.

Is your bod worth a wad?

One of the questions that people ask me most often (besides "How would you like a fat lip, fella?") is: "How much money could I get for my body?"

Naturally, when people start talking about selling their bodies, I always tell them, "Whoa! Try a good loan company first. Don't do anything that will break your poor mother's heart."

But then I realize that they mean how much would their body be worth to a chemical supply house, *not* to a lonely sailor.

In other words, how much are the raw materials that make up the human body worth right here in downtown 1987?

Do you really want to know? Haven't you had enough bad news lately, what with the Christmas bills coming in and the television set going out and your husband eloping with a women's Roller Derby team. (Funny, he had never seemed interested in sports before.)

Tell you what. Instead, let's talk about some positive aspects of your body. After all, the two of you go everywhere together. And you depend on your body for so much: to give you something to scratch when you itch, to keep your place in line at the bank, to fill out your clothes.

Taking inventory, we find that your body contains maybe three pounds of calcium. That is worth pocket change at best to a chemist. But it's worth a fortune to you in the form of bones. And very nice bones they are, I have been told by your closest friends. Without bones, at the high-school prom, all you could do is just sorta lie there and quiver.

Your body contains less than a drop of iodine. Now a chemist wouldn't sully his eyedropper for that piddling amount. But without that dash of iodine, your thyroid gland would file for bankruptcy, and you might begin to babble a lot, to bump into things and to drool more than is fashionable.

Moving right along, we find that your body contains three pounds of sulphur. That's enough to kill the fleas on an average-sized dog. Or to make the fleas on a very *big* dog just feel real bad.

And if we look down your throat, we'll see twenty-seven pounds of carbon. That's like having 900 lead pencils inside you. And if you're like me, every one of them has a broken point.

On a good day, your own personal body also contains:

—.5 pound of potassium—enough to make gunpowder to fire a toy cannon.

—Enough iron to make a marble-sized cannon ball.

—1.5 pounds of phosphorus—enough to make 2,200 match heads. Swallow a 2 × 4, and you could supply more than enough matches to light the fuse on that toy cannon.

—Enough fat to make seven bars of soap.

—100 pounds of water—enough to fill a 10-gallon tub.

Thus the quick among you will realize that you have within

your body the materials necessary to load, light and fire that toy cannon. Right at your husband, the unfaithful jerk!

And enough soap and water to get cleaned up with afterward.

You also contain traces of cobalt, manganese, vanadium, pocket lint, monosodium glutamate, artificial colorings and a baby rattle that you swallowed in 1949.

Yes, your body is a mobile miracle, a walking warehouse of elements. These elements are composed of oodles of molecules, which are just crawling with atoms, which are up to their very ears in electrons, protons and croutons.

Oh, but you say that you still want to know how much your body is worth as a collection of chemicals? Very well. In 1940, it was 39 cents. In 1970, $3.50. In the late seventies, $5.60. In 1980, $7.28. And in 1987 the latest quote on the big board is about $12.

Having seen your X rays, I would give you this advice:

When the value hits $20, sell.

Readin', writin', and repentin'

Each year about this time, colleges mail out their schedules of fall classes.

And each year about this time, I scan these schedules and find them sadly lacking. The courses are just too academic, of little value to us adults living in what we loosely call the real world. It's too late for most of us to go back to school to learn the niceties. Such as English. I, for one, never overcame my fear of diagramming and once had to undergo two years of therapy before I could enter any room that contained a prepositional phrase.

So here are some more practical courses that colleges might consider.

—Everyday Debate. How to use persuasion to get your way. (Prerequisites are Pouting 101 and Advanced Whining.) Learn how to argue with small children, including how to say, "Because I said so!" in thirteen languages.

For the final exam, a student must call the appliance store and persuade the service manager to send out a repairman right away because your new range was not properly installed and you think you smell gas. If the student fails the exam, the grade report will be mailed to the next of kin.

—Religion for Yahoos. This course addresses issues such as "Is there a hereafter? And if so, can I bunk with Elvis?" The course instructor, noted evangelist Isaiah Leviticus, will lay on hands and heal an affliction of your choice: one major illness or two minor illnesses and a fever blister. Rev. Leviticus grades on the curve, with an A starting at a $1,000 pledge.

—Philosophy for Airheads. This course answers the three most perplexing questions of the ages: (1) Why are we here? (2) How can we reconcile our ontological preconceptions with empirical and *a priori* arguments for determinism? and (3) Huh?

Other topics include "Happy hour and its place in the cosmos," "Jean-Paul Sartre's bowling tips" and "Metaphysics and how to dress for it" (course taught by Charro, associate professor of philosophy at Hootchy Cootchy U.).

—Business Skills. Course includes coping with the office copy machine: when to call in a service technician, when to call in an exorcist. Also, the memo as an art form. How to send death threats through interoffice mail.

Course puts special emphasis on meetings: How to survive a long staff meeting—did you know that a person can live for four days on coffee and boiled time cards? Lab focuses on how to shorten a dull staff meeting (students must supply their own coral snakes).

Also discussed is corporate communication: how to use words such as "maximize," "annualize" and "prioritize." Also "input" and what to put it in.

—Domestic Finance. What to do when your Visa balance is larger than your Social Security number. What to do when your bank balance is lower than your IQ. Special emphasis is placed on skipping town as a means of debt management.

—Everyday Ethics. Focuses on right and wrong and how to tell them apart in the dark. Examines the issue of universal values. For instance: America considers it wrong to paint your brother-in-law with linseed oil, while many East European nations figure he had it coming, the jerk, and give him a second coat.

—Sociology. This course deals largely with people. Students take field trips to learn where to find people, how to recognize people, why some people are nice and quiet but others become next-door neighbors. Learn the role played in our culture by the nuclear family, organized religion and the Tupperware Party.

—Home Repair for Fools (And We Know Who We Are) 101. Students learn to refer to tools as more than just "that dohickey there." How to rewire a lamp cord without plunging a major city into darkness. First-year students will learn to hammer a nail without smashing a finger. Second-year students will learn to hammer a nail without smashing *two* fingers.

Yes, when colleges offer courses such as these, I'll go back to school. In the meantime, I'd better call the appliance store again. I think I smell gas.

A nation held smellbound

My Sin. Poison. Opium. Decadence.

Good Lord, what is this, a perfume counter or a confessional booth?

It's a perfume counter. At least it smells like one, and there's not a priest in sight. But it's hard to tell from the words being bandied about, eh?

My Sin, Poison, Opium and Decadence are all perfumes. (And yes, there is even one called Confess.) Such names fascinate me. With perfume, as with most goods in America, we are being sold not so much the product as the product's image.

Thus the way to our wallet is through our nose via our eye and ear, with perhaps a side trip to pull our leg. 'Tis a crooked trail indeed.

Commercials for such la-ti-da fragrances always just reek with chic. Have you seen those for Obsession? They are especially, eh, unusual. They appear to have been designed by Dalí (drunkenly), directed by Fellini (blindfoldedly) and written by Joyce (posthumously).

In the nose industry, I suspect, more money is spent to merchandise the product than to produce the merchandise. For fragrance names, Madison Avenue has to walk a fine line between naughty and nice. Think about it: Not many women would buy a perfume called Nun. On the other hand, not many would buy one called Cheap Little Peroxide Slut.

Likewise, perhaps no one would be persuaded to buy the most alluring scent on earth if it were called simply Good-Smellin' Stuff No. 5 and bottled in a Mason jar.

Imagine that a Madison Avenue ad agency is about to have a product-naming session for a perfume. The project chief is walking down the hall to the conference room when he passes two junior members of the project. He overhears them talking and catches just snatches of the conversation:

"Beautiful . . . Sex Appeal . . . Tabu . . . Whisper . . . Nocturne . . . Obsession . . . Ruffles . . . Scoundrel."

The project chief interrupts: "Great, Perkins! Keep going, son! You're really on a roll. Let's hear some more fragrance names!"

"What fragrance names, sir? I was just telling Ted about my date last night."

But each word is, indeed, the name of a fragrance.

There is another perfume called White Linen. The name implies an ultimate destination, so seductive is its scent.

There is also one called White Shoulders. Very sexy imagery, right?

Taking a cue from that, the perfumes that are missing, in my humble opinion, are these:

— For women who are a bit afraid: White Knuckles.
— For women who intend to give in easily: White Flag.

—And for women who don't intend to give in at all: White Wedding.

Men are not immune from the name game, either: Stetson, Brut, English Leather, Gray Flannel, Gambler, Chaps.

There is even a cologne called Adidas.

I suppose that these names are meant to conjure up rugged images of rugged men with broad shoulders and narrow hips who get together around the campfire, punch each other on the arm and then compare tennis shoes.

If Madison Avenue wants unquestionably masculine images, there are a few good ones still left. I make a gift of them: Why not name colognes something like My Truss by Lanvin, Hairy Tattoo by Jovan or Old Boxer Shorts by Estée Lauder?

Pretty darned masculine, eh?

And if more unquestionably feminine images are needed, how about a perfume called Stretch Marks by Chanel? Or Eau de Leg Stubble by Coty?

Yes, these days, only a few fragrances still have fairly descriptive, down-to-earth names: Old Spice, Jungle Gardenia, Tea Rose.

So what's in a name, anyway? A Tea Rose by any other name would sell as sweet.

Or would it?

The light side
of night side

I'd like to say a few words to my fellow Americans who work nights:

Sunrise, Jane Pauley and the end of the world.

Now you night-siders may not be familiar with the first two items. They are, I am told, things that happen very early in the morning. The third you may have heard some talk about, and it, too, I suspect, will happen early some morning.

As a late riser, I am so weary of day-siders asking me if I saw the great sunrise or heard so-and-so say such-and-such on "The Today Show."

The sunrise and Jane Pauley, I am told, are very pretty. The difference is that the sun has to roll around heaven all day, but Jane gets a limo and chauffeur.

I'll admit that my work schedule denies me the sunrise. But, hey, I often go outside at the end of the day, face east, look into a mirror and watch the sun*set*. Same effect, better hours. And I suspect that I would wake up early for Jane Pauley only if I were Garry Trudeau.

Millions of folks work the night shift: hospital employees, police officers, newspaper staffs, vampires. And day-siders have some funny ideas about us.

Day-siders are apt to think of us as lazy just because we get up at the crack of noon. But it's not that night-siders sleep more than day-siders. They just sleep different hours and often awaken at their leisure and have some slack time. I believe that this slack time is crucial to the well-being of the person, and, ultimately, of the planet.

And I think I know where we went wrong. Back in prehistoric times, some overachieving early ancestor of ours woke one day at six A.M., grumbled at his wife, Mrs. Early Ancestor of Ours, and stumbled out of bed.

"Get a move on," he said to himself, dragging his knuckles. "I have to be down at the office and walking semi-erect by eight. Got a full day: Gotta leave my bones strewn about for the anthropologists to find a million years from now."

This, of course, was the dawn of time. And aren't you sorry?

Because ever since, people have been getting up too early. Of course, it's the getting up — not the being up — that's difficult. (Most day-siders get up at seven, wake up at eight, cheer up at nine and give up at ten.) At the moment of waking, people are the most creaky and crotchety that they will be all day. Scientists tell us that during that moment, mentally and physically a person is actually about nine hundred years old and in fact may even have vivid memories of fighting William the Conqueror at the Battle of Hastings.

Thus we actually get younger as the day gets older, until, finally, about two P.M., we are at our peak, except for some crossbow wounds.

But during that moment of waking, all you can think of is sleep. You would betray your family to the Spanish Inquisition to be able to sleep another twenty minutes. You'd even betray yourself, if they'd just let you have a pillow when they strap you onto the rack.

Obviously there should be an hour or so of civilized scratching and belching before you dash off to work, where you will be expected to be productive and polite, and sometimes both.

No one should have to wake up and rush off to work in a mental fog. Especially those people who have access to The Button. That's The Button as in The Bomb as in The End.

Mark my words: When the Ultimate Misunderstanding occurs, it will be because someone in high places had to wake up at six and be at work at eight. He then pushed The Button, thinking it was the "brew" button on the Pentagon's $1.2 million Mr. Coffee.

This is sure to put a damper on the rest of the day for those of you who sleep nights and work days, what with the fallout and flash fires and all.

But we who sleep days and work nights will be luckier.

We'll get to wake up dead.

Speak softly and carry a big putter

The other day fellow staff writer Michelle Stein played her very first nine holes of golf. Our editor, Linda Gandy, was her instructor. I was her caddy.

Only after the round was over did I notice this proviso on the score card: "USGA rules will govern all play." Uh oh. We're in big trouble now. We're going to get threatening letters from the USGA. The USGA may even come to our homes some dark night and drive their golf carts through our flower beds.

Because we were definitely *not* governed by United States Golf Association rules. We were governed by Hey, This Is Michelle's First Time, Right? So Let's Lighten Up, Like If Her First Six Tee Shots Soar Out of Bounds, Raining Down on the Family Who Is Having a Picnic Across the Street, We Won't Count Those, But Michelle Probably Won't Get Invited Over for Potato Salad, Either rules.

On the other hand, USGA rules are stuffy old things. They require you to add a penalty stroke when you lose a ball, miss a shot or improve your lie.

Imagine!

Our rules were a bit more flexible. You can dynamite your ball out of the rough at no penalty as long as you replace your divot. You can pick up your ball and throw it as long as you don't look too smug about it. A "gimme" shall be any putt that stops as close to the hole as Akron is to Guadalajara. And no penalty stroke shall be added for sawing down a tree that wanders between your ball and the green as long as you don't later sell the firewood for personal gain.

As I watched Michelle play, I realized that golf has rather ambivalent goals. What you do basically is get a ball so you can get rid of it as far as you can and then chase after it so you can get it again so you can get rid of it as far as you can again. This is repeated until it's too dark to play. Imagine what a psychiatrist would say about the emotional conflicts manifest in this alternating attitude of attraction and rejection.

But what does *he* know? He probably plays croquet.

Further, the golf swing is an unnatural act. Nothing in life prepares you to swing a golf club. Poor Michelle. If she swung too high, she missed the ball completely. Apparently her clubs were short. If she swung too low, she hit the wrong ball—the big one called planet earth. If she swung in between, she hit the golf ball. But it landed across the street. In the potato salad.

Obviously *that's* where the hole was supposed to be located all along.

It was my job, as Michelle's caddy, to advise her on the

correct club for each shot. For nine holes I carefully factored in wind, distance and terrain and then just handed her the irons in such an order that they formed my Social Security number: 465-88-9637.

But it didn't matter anyway. Michelle soon came to feel most comfortable with her trusty putter, which she used for any shot of seventy-five yards or less. She'd send balls scorching over the grass, hugging the topography and causing squirrels and robins on the fairway to get religion and seek higher ground.

Sadly, journalism schools simply are not preparing graduates to execute the chip shot.

Yes, golf clearly is a difficult game. That's why ideally your very first round should be played in private. After all, there are times when you don't want the whole world to know of your mistakes. That's why the Catholic Church invented confession.

Likewise, maybe your first round of golf should be played in a nine-hole confessional booth. ("The next hole is a 287-yard par 4 with a sharp dogleg at Monsignor Brown. Hazards on the left include bearing false witness in the rough and, on the right, committing adultery in the sand trap.")

But despite all the usual first-time difficulties, Michelle did quite well. So well, in fact, that Linda and I are encouraging her to take up bowling.

After all, the course is shorter. The ball is easier to see. And not nearly as likely to land in the potato salad.

5-story grape
a tall order

So this is what they mean by "purple prose."

In my life, I've caught a lot of things, including cold, up on my sleep and the dickens from my boss.

And, now, a five-story grape.

Granted, this is nothing compared to what Paul Tavilla will attempt to catch on Saturday:

a 72-story grape
falling right
into his
waiting
mouth

from atop the new InterFirst Plaza Bank building in downtown Dallas.

But Fort Worth is less ostentatious than Dallas, so I was content to catch a grape dropped from just five stories. Oh, maybe I could have equaled Tavilla's feat by catching the same grape dropped five stories 14.4 times, but I wasn't competing with him. I just wanted to know what he faces.

Well, now I know. He faces bruised lips. And stained clothing. And odd stares.

Because if it took me nine attempts to catch a grape dropped from atop the five-story *Star-Telegram* building, even a professional grape-catcher is going to need several misses and near-misses from a 72-story, 921-foot bank building.

But practice makes perfect. And a lot of jelly.

As part owner of a produce company, Tavilla, fifty-one, has grown up around fruit. "I've been catching grapes in my mouth since I was a teenager," he says. So it would be safe to assume that before he caught grapes off a bank, he worked up to it. Perhaps catching raisins off a savings and loan.

After my own modest catch, I have a new respect for Tavilla, who already holds the world record with a 52-story grape. A five-story grape can be seen as it falls. But a 72-story grape is probably not visible until it has fallen 60 stories or so. By then it is speeding mouthward at almost 100 mph. Brave Tavilla doesn't even wear goggles. I did. But more to shield my identity than my eyes.

Just how fast is a five-story grape? I asked Professor Bruce Miller of the TCU Physics Department, Falling Fruit Division. Using a complex formula involving square roots and feet per second and terms such as "air friction" and "terminal velocity," he calculated that a grape falling five stories is probably traveling at about 43 mph.

All I know is that it packs a wallop. When it hits you, it

stings. And when it hits the asphalt, it splatters. Ground zero was left littered with ex-grapes, providing a graphic lesson in gravity.

This is where Galileo meets Gallo.

And what is the grape of choice for our small fraternity? Tavilla says he prefers black grapes to green or white ones because black ones are easier to see. Their color didn't concern *me* as long as they were soft, seedless grapes, grown by soft, seedless Alps villagers. Nerf grapes, if in season.

And what thoughts go through a reporter's mind as he peers up at an editor who is bent on pelting him with grapes? One false move and I may never split another infinitive. What if a grape, indeed, goes in my mouth but keeps on going? What size is the exit wound? Does St. Peter turn away anyone done in by a kamikaze concord?

Regardless, come 2:30 P.M. Saturday, Tavilla faces all this and more. As I'm washing the purple stains out of my shirt, I'll wish him well. I've been there. Well, partly there. I want no more of it.

But after my experiment was over and we all went back inside, I thought I overheard one editor saying he'd just had a great idea for my encore.

Something about a casaba melon and a Piper Cub.

News, nyah-nyahs and nathemas

Is there any creature more pitiable than a collector?

Well, yes. There's my poor Uncle Ed, who is convinced that he's an oak tree. But he's really quite harmless, until his roots get into your sewer line.

But we were talking about collectors, weren't we? Most of us collect things. When there is more than one of a certain thing, you can be sure that someone somewhere collects it.

There is just one big risk in collecting. It easily can become an obsession. You fret and fidget, knowing that someone out there owns a better or bigger collection or that you lack the one item that will make your collection (and your bliss) complete. To the obsessed, an incomplete collection is anathema (and I even know a guy who collects nathemas).

I once read of a devoted bird-watcher who needed just two more sightings to complete her lifetime checklist. She needed to sight the Greater Rude Snipe and the Lesser Rude Snipe. These birds, she said, are identified by their cry ("ter-wit ter-wit *nyah-nyah-nyah!*") and are very similar except that the Greater Rude Snipe cries "ter-wit ter-wit *nyah-nyah-nyah!*" and then spits at you.

Since 1954, this determined woman has been camped in a remote swamp in Louisiana — the nesting area of the Rude Snipes. She refuses food and water; she curses and throws rocks when approached by well-meaning people.

This situation has reached the point now that other bird-watchers go to the swamp in order to watch *her*. And none of them has had the heart to tell her that Rude Snipes have been extinct since 1953.

As a kid I collected Mickey Mantle baseball cards. I'd save my lunch money to buy them every day after school at Collup's corner grocery. But it seemed that for each Mickey Mantle card I unwrapped, I unwrapped twelve of Biff Fergle, a utility infielder who in 1961 led the majors in errors, strikeouts and arrests on moral charges.

I'd even chew that baseball bubble-gum, which was made of bumper-car rubber and sugar and was so flat and hard that you could scrape ice off your windshield with it. But it paid off. Soon my Mickey Mantle collection was known the length and breadth of Miss Pool's sixth-grade class. My collection of cards was indeed impressive. And exceeded only by my collection of cavities.

Next I collected tropical fish. All over my room I had aquariums with gravel, plants and filters. I was always down at the pet shop, waiting for the next shipment of the latest tropical fish. Yes, I admit it: I was addicted. I had a guppy on my back.

Later I collected old tombstones (honestly come by, I assure you). But they were very heavy, and I soon gave them up to collect abdominal supports.

And now, at an age when I should know better, I have begun to collect antique newspapers. Already I know what will happen. Some day my collection will be complete except for a single rare newspaper — perhaps a May 1910 *New York Times.* You know — the one with all those ominous headlines about Halley's Comet ("Comet sought for questioning in bar shooting").

I'll offer the proud owner of this treasure my life savings if he will sell this paper to me. He will refuse. I'll up the ante — I'll get married so that I can offer him my firstborn. I'll trade him two Mickey Mantle cards and an angel fish to be named later. I'll throw in Uncle Ed as a cord of firewood.

I just know that if I never obtain that one antique newspaper, I'll be consumed by rage and remorse. I'll tear my entire collection into a million tiny pieces, throw it all into the trash can and swear that I will never collect anything again.

And the next morning I'll probably jump out of bed, dump the trash can out onto the table and begin cataloging my collection of antique confetti.

Ad-jectives: Whatta crock!

OK, Madison Avenue, you scoundrel, unhand that modifier!

As an occasional guardian of the language, I am appalled at how you force adjectives into white slavery just to help you sell an image. Adjectives such as "fun," "romantic," "glamorous," and "exciting" are used, shall we say, loosely. Shall we say promiscuously? Aw, what the heck, shall we say that these adjectives have become little tramps who will bed down with any advertisement who offers them a warm smile, a pair of nylons and no awkward goodbyes in the morning?

Just look at how you misuse adjectives.

—"Fun" cars. What a crock. Cars can be big or small, fast or slow, practical or impractical, overpriced or overpriced. But they are *not* intrinsically "fun," even though their commercials show them speeding merrily along some picturesque road, hugging the curves and scattering colorful autumn leaves in Utah or New England. But folks, Utah and New England don't really exist. The AAA conducted a search for them in 1978 and found only a movie set.

On the other hand, what we have here in metropolitan Reality are traffic jams, road construction, speed limits, radar traps, one traffic light for every registered voter, and, just in front of every "fun" car, a little old lady driving an arthritic Ford Fairlane whose speedometer is marked off in miles per geologic era.

Thus the adjective that best describes cars in America is "inert."

—"Romantic" wines. Nope. Wines can be described by vintage: "1968," "June" or "3:34 P.M." And, I am told, they can further be described as bitter, sweet, fruity or "reminds me of toad spit." They are not, per se, romantic. Although I guess that if you fell into a vat of Chateau de Cirrhosis '53, drank your way to shore, passed out and woke up three days later in a honeymoon suite with the string section of Col. Dixie's Traveling All-Girl Orchestra, *that* might be described as "romantic." Or "bigamy."

Except in Utah.

Which doesn't exist.

—"Glamorous" clothing and cosmetics. *Au contraire.* Clothes can be described as colorful or drab, designer or Blue Light Special, cotton or polyester, stylish or two months out of fashion and thus "suitable only for mopping up after the poodle." But not glamorous.

Likewise, cosmetics can be waterproof, nonallergenic, light or dark, subtle or "applied with a trowel." But not glamorous. *People* are glamorous. I just can't think of any examples right now.

—"Exciting" restaurants. I'm sorry, Madison Avenue, but restaurants are not, in and of themselves, exciting. Unless their restrooms are stocked with wild animals. Restaurants can be described as expensive or inexpensive, snooty or friendly, dark or well-lighted, spotless or walled with slime. The service can be prompt, slow or semi-annual. The food can be bad, bland or delicious. Not exciting. Unless it is still moving. (If it is, have your waiter count the wildebeests in the restroom.)

People and what they do are exciting. Napoleon was exciting. But even his best baked potato just sorta laid there. Persons A and B could go to the most "exciting" restaurant ever, and Person A would have a dull time if Person B's idea of conversation is coughing. On the other hand, I had the most exciting time of my life at a three-booth greasy-spoon diner with an anatomy major from Bryn Mawr who knew all 206 bones of the body by Braille and 207 ways to get taken out of her daddy's will.

Yes, Madison Avenue, you are a scoundrel. And you think that you can get away with such adjective abuse because the average consumer has the intelligence of asphalt.

What a crock!

Or, as you would say: What a fun, romantic, glamorous, exciting crock!

Magazines from A to zucchini

How many of you have noticed how specialized magazines are becoming?

I see by a show of hands that (1) some of you have noticed; (2) some of you have not noticed; and (3) some of you need a good manicure. Here are some real titles of real magazines: *American Drycleaner, Gleanings in Bee Culture, Chain Saw Age, Dairy Goat Journal, Soybean Digest, Ostomy Quarterly, Fertilizer Progress, The Celibate Woman, Expecting, Pulp & Paper, Brake & Front End* and the ever-popular *American Paint and Coatings Journal.*

If this trend toward specialization continues, soon we'll be seeing magazines such as:

—*Field & Scream*. The magazine for the victims of hunting accidents. Each issue includes helpful articles such as: "Fifty things to do with a hole in your chest," "Creative bleeding" and "The perfect weekend: A six pack, a 12-gauge and 'Looky there, Roy: It's a deer in a plaid jacket!'"

—*Yeeech!* For people who hate certain foods. Read profiles of famous people and the food they hated. Did you know that Attila the Hun had planned to become a librarian until his mother made him eat liver? Or that the Spanish-American War was really fought over a bowl of cottage cheese, with the winner to get Cuba and the loser to get the cottage cheese? Also: "Fifty rude things to do with broccoli" and "Twenty-nine states where zucchini is illegal." Price: $1.95.

—*Wimp World*. The magazine that helps the meek to cope with their crippling affliction. Inspirational essays: "Whining as an art form," "Cringing can be sexy," "How to give a definite 'maybe.'" Price: $1.75. Or $1.50. OK, 95 cents. Oh, whatever you feel it's worth. It's really not a very good magazine and you'd probably rather spend your money on something better.

—*Gnusweek*. For breeders and fanciers of gnus. These cuddly half-ton beasties are becoming popular as house pets because they never (1) eat your goldfish or (2) have puppies. Each issue offers revealing first-person stories: "Our gnu had the house broken before he was."

—*Shoplifter's Monthly*. Includes helpful tips such as how to conceal a dinette set under your coat. Interviews with veteran shoplifters, such as Hymie T., who once hid a frozen turkey under his hat and got frostbite in the express line. Price: Are you kidding?

—*Angst Digest*. The magazine for worriers. Each issue features some new threat of modern life. "How to increase your fear of war, cancer, acid rain, crime and AIDS by 200 percent in your spare time." Also, in a companion article, see what the stylish worrier is wearing this year—air-raid helmet, gauze mask, umbrella, bullet-proof vest, and matching condom. Price: $1, check only. No cash please. I mean, do you *know* how many germs there are on money?

—*Squint*. For people who just could not find Halley's Comet in 1986. Read how to scan the skies and locate objects that appear even smaller: planets, stars, nervous passengers bailing out of airliners. Read about "Blue moons, black holes, and how to dress for each." Plus a bonus how-to feature for you guys: build a telescope powerful enough to see through the window of one Ms. Peaches la Cream, exotic dancer and runner-up in the 1987 Miss Construed pageant.

— *Better Homes and Pardons.* The magazine for those readers of *Squint* who indeed sighted Ms. la Cream and were in turn sighted by a passing policeman. Wives, you'll love the recipes (Hacksaw Surprise cake) and tips on what to do during conjugal visits ("1. Don't suggest Scrabble"). Inmates, learn how to carve a gun from a bar of soap and vice versa. Learn six ways to say, "Sorry, I don't know you well enough" without hurting your cell-mate's feelings. Price: 10 to 15 cents, with three cents off for good behavior.

— *Splash.* The magazine for readers of *Squint* who, while sighting Ms. la Cream, were in turn sighted by her husband, Mr. la Cream, who had just finished building a project featured in the latest issue of *Concrete Overshoes Illustrated.* Price: $1.50, billed to your estate.

Split personality: Crumbs or croutons

A metaphor offering a choice of floor plans, all bills paid and no pet deposit.

Most of the time I consider myself to be a man who is well integrated, consistent of disposition and predictable of behavior, with just enough tragedy around the eyes to make women want to take me home and care for me, protect me, nurture me, perhaps even let me win at arm wrestling.

Yet at times I must acknowledge that several personalities reside within this body—all tenants in this high-rise apartment building that we'll call the *Casa del Me*. Those of you who have been waiting for the metaphor will be glad to know that we're well into it now.

Yes, each of us is an apartment building sheltering many personalities. We're serious at some times, silly at others, conservative about some things, liberal about others, capable of having great energy or of lying inert on the sofa so long that we sprout roots and develop a craving for Miracle-Gro.

Here are just some of the tenants living within my flesh-toned walls.

In Apartment 114 lives the Gloom family. Yes, like most people, I have a pessimistic side that is triggered by the ominous headlines of modern life: crimes, drugs, disease. When the Glooms dominate my personality, I mope. I despair. I wallow in self-pity, even though wallowing violates the terms of my lease. To cheer up, I read my organ-donor card.

But just across the hall from the Glooms are the Happy-Go-Luckies. If these two families looked at the same slice of dry bread, the Glooms would see crumbs, the Happy-Go-Luckies would see croutons. When the Happy-Go-Luckies are in control, I stop to notice only the good in life: smelling a rose, hearing the measured breathing of a sleeping child, seeing my worst enemy get cornered by an insurance salesman.

In Apartment 204 is Mr. Reckless. When he is in control, I wake up on summer mornings wanting to buy a motorcycle. Ah, to feel the response of the throttle, the wind in my hair, the entomology on my tonsils! But next door, in 206, Mr. Cautious pounds on the wall and shouts, "Oh, I don't think I'd do that. You're just having your mid-life crisis. Do you wanna scatter several of your favorite teeth across the expressway and have to gum your croutons? Go back to sleep, fool."

In a penthouse head-high atop the *Casa del Me* lives Mr. Logic. He is analytical, objective, philosophical. He ponders the great issues. Why are we here? What is true happiness? If the wages of sin are death, how much can you sin and just get real sick?

Lower, in a warm and bright apartment at the heart, lives Mr. Emotion. When he is in control, which he usually is, I am romantic, sentimental, impulsive. I cry at movies, I rhapsodize at sunsets, I form emotional attachments to inanimate objects: cars, houses, furniture. I once hauled a worn-but-beloved easy chair to Goodwill. As we parted, I made it promise to write often. Oh, I got a postcard from it now and then for a while. And then nothing. Finally I heard that it had run off with a tawdry little foot-stool from Encino who was just after it for the loose change behind its cushion.

And in a dimly lit apartment somewhat below the head and heart live the Hormones. Boy, the building was a lot quieter before *they* moved in, back in my teens. They decorated their bachelor pad with Farrah Fawcett posters and lava lamps, stocking English Leather in the bathroom and Elvis in the record cabinet. Then the Hormones would stay awake all night, howling and twitching and calling up lady hormones to ask them to come over and play Clear Up Your Acne.

Yes, each of us is full of divergent personalities. Although this makes life very interesting, it has its drawbacks: I just found out that my metaphorical apartment building is being torn down to put up a metaphorical parking lot.

I just hope they don't use a literal bulldozer.

The most-traveled man, bar none

In case you are ever asked this on a quiz show or are just plain nosy, the most-traveled man in history was Jesse Hart Rosdail, a teacher from Illinois.

Rosdail visited 219 of the 221 countries and territories that are classified as such by the United Nations, who ought to know. He visited every part of the known world except the French Antarctic Territories, whose major export is frostbite, and North Korea, which won't allow anyone in anyway.

But then Rosdail wouldn't allow North Korea into *his* house, so it was a standoff.

It may have been the disappointment of having never reached those two remaining places that killed Rosdail. Anyway, in 1977 Rosdail died, going at last to what Shakespeare called "that undiscover'd country from whose bourn no traveller returns," while his luggage went on to Chicago.

I just wish that in his travels Rosdail had moseyed down the hall here and past my desk. Because there is one very burning question that I would like to ask of such a wondrous wanderer, a man who had seen so many of the marvels of this wide world: "After traveling 1.6 million miles and staying in countless hotels around the world, how many of those tiny bars of soap do you have at home?"

Some people do that, you know—take home those little bars of hotel soap. Certainly not you or I or anyone we'd be likely to know, but some people do.

They can't help it. It's a compulsion. Like gambling or eating peanuts or picking at peeling skin.

On any given day, thousands of tiny bars of soap are tucked into corners of suitcases, hurtling across the country at 32,000 feet in the cargo bay of jetliners. In the event of a mid-air collision, hundreds of passengers will be fatally lathered.

And after all, if you have petty larceny on your mind, those tiny bars of soap are less fragile than hotel stationery and less bulky than hotel towels or Gideon Bibles.

Besides, if you steal a Gideon Bible, the Gideons will hunt you down and drop the ten plagues of Egypt down your pants.

And you know that all those frogs, lice, flies and locusts are bound to ruin your crease.

Counting certain parts of Oklahoma, I am only about two hundred foreign countries behind the late Rosdail, and I have yet to stay in a great big burly hotel that didn't stock itsy-bitsy baby bars of soap.

It's like staying in the Ken and Barbie Hilton.

I wonder if in his far-flung travels Rosdail ever found a hotel that stocked man-sized soap. Why, Darth Vader could sing "Old Man River" in the shower while lathering up with one of those little sissy soaps and he would begin to sound like Alvin and the Chipmunks.

It's just too bad that Rosdail never got to the French Antarctic Territories even if only long enough to pose for a snapshot with a snowball. And it's too bad that he and North Korea never reached an understanding. If they had, he might be with us yet.

It seems to me that he could have gone over and had a good look-see at North Korea, checked it off his list and returned home — a satisfied man at last.

Then, as part of the bargain, North Korea could have left a light burning, locked up and came over to *his* house and stayed a while, seeing the sights, posing for pictures standing in front of Rosdail's Impala, touring his rumpus room, chipping off pieces of his fireplace as souvenirs, maybe taking a half-day side trip around his backyard.

Of course, North Korea probably would have checked out after a day or two, going back home and taking with it all of Rosdail's little bars of soap.

Are you down for the count?

Do you ever feel insignificant?

Do you have days when you feel like a zero, like Citizen Cipher, like Charley Nobody of 3510 Nowhere Lane, a grain of sand in the beach party of world history, a bubble in the dishwater of life?

Well, you aren't far wrong. Let me tell you how many folks have trod this tired old earth. If you were to start counting them right now and count as fast as ever you could and even skip supper, you would not be finished by Christmas Day.

Of 1991.

Let me put it another way. If you were to throw a dinner party and invite every person who has ever lived, you definitely would have to go next door and ask to borrow some chairs.

About 69 billion, to be exact.

That means that the 4 billion persons now living are just 6

percent of the total. And 6 percent sounds pretty puny, doesn't it, until you realize that most of those 4 billion will be at the mall with you this weekend.

Some demographers arrived at this total of 69 billion through a complex algebraic formula. This formula uses lots of fractions and exponents and is based on the rate of population increase, the average life expectancy and such. And strangely enough, if this formula is held to a mirror and read, it is also a pretty good recipe for spinach quiche.

Sixty-nine billion people. I think it behooves us at this time to ponder this imponderable, to put the individual into perspective.

Of course, of this 69 billion total, untold numbers were our earliest ancestors who evolved as primitive tree- and cave-dwellers and lived out their simple, squalid lives in simple squalor — unknown and unknowing, having no concept of art or science or how to write a really sincere thank-you note.

But if you were lucky enough to be one of those prehistoric ancestors, being among the first people on the block, you *were* somebody back then. Yes, sir! The individual had significance. A prehistoric person could rise up semi-erect and look around and grunt, "I *matter.*"

When a few of these people died, the world population plummeted, and there were dire predictions of extinction and calls for people to go out and have more babies. But way back then, no one was even going steady yet, and so that sort of thing just had to wait.

(Creationist version: When Cain slew Abel, the world population fell 25 percent. Suddenly there weren't enough people left in the whole world for the first family to get up a foursome for bridge.)

But alas, things are very different now. Now you are but one of 4 billion. We are born, we strive, we get the car paid off, and we die. It's enough to make you wonder if people will remember you a million years from now. Or when you get home from work today, for that matter.

Think of the relatively few people who have transcended their own time. Moses. Galileo. Columbus. Shakespeare. Edison. Joan of Arc. And yet, immortal as these few are, would you recognize Joan of Arc if you saw her shopping at the mall this weekend?

Probably not, unless she was buying an asbestos body-stocking.

Yes, it can make you feel pretty insignificant. Of the past and present population of the world, you are but one sixty-nine billionth. And if that figure is converted to a decimal, it produces a number that can be rounded off thus:

.00000000001.

But, hey! Look at it this way—that makes you a one among zeros.

Don't you feel better now?

I thought not.

Rand is grand, but Gandhi is dandy

In these troubled times, when crime is up and employment is down and inflation is just sorta squatting, let us take time to review the great philosophies.

After all, there are many views of life. The optimist looks at a jug of wine and calls it half full; the pessimist calls it half empty. While they argue, the hedonist says, "What's the difference?" and drinks it down. While he is passed out, the opportunist gets a deposit on the jug.

Modern philosophy, of course, can be traced back to Plato. As Emerson said of the immortal Greek, "Plato is philosophy, and philosophy is Plato. Or is it the other way around? I get so confused."

Some philosophies had quite humble beginnings. Friedrich Nietzsche's first philosophy was based on onion dip. "All truth derives from onion dip," he liked to say, "although you can get pretty close with a really good sour cream and chive." He eventually went insane while contemplating his hand and wondering why he had five fingers but only four spaces in between.

Here are some others:

—John Stuart Mill's utilitarianism holds that actions are right in proportion to how much they promote happiness. He once used this reasoning to try to convince a coed from Bryn Mawr to spend the weekend with him. She just blushed, giggled and hit him over the head with Immanuel Kant's ukulele.

—Existentialism, as advocated by Jean-Paul Sartre, teaches that existence precedes essence, that man ultimately defines himself and is only what he makes of himself. Once, as Sartre and Ayn Rand were playing croquet, she asked Sartre to explain this philosophy. While Sartre was talking, distracted, Rand took the opportunity to toss his ball behind a tree trunk.

Later the two great thinkers would argue bitterly over the concept of good and evil, with Rand conceding that while good is better, evil makes for a more interesting diary.

—Hedonism embraces pleasure. A hedonist devotes his entire life to wine, women and song. And he excels at all three, singing slightly off-key only after he sits on his corkscrew.

—Stoicism is the opposite of hedonism, embracing self-denial and indifference to pleasure. Thus a stoic also devotes his entire life to wine, women and song, but only in towns where no one knows him.

—William Paley reasoned that there is order in the universe and thus there must be a cosmic intelligence to account for this order. Paley used this teleological argument to prove the existence of a God, although the existence of Paley's Aunt Phoebe made him wonder if that God is always paying attention.

—Determinism is the belief that everything that happens is the result of antecedent causes. There are two kinds of determinism. Hard determinism holds that people are not free and thus not morally responsible for their actions. Many of the Watergate defendants came down with hard determinism as soon as they read about it.

Then there is soft determinism, which is simply hard determinism with some of the air let out of it.

—Ontological dualism is the theory that reality consists of two different states of being. But scholars disagree on what these two states of being are. The philosopher says they are mind and matter. The teacher says they are ignorance and knowledge. The psychiatrist says they are mental health and psychosis. The patient, Morty R., says that if we're talking about *his* psychosis, he and the llama are very happy together, thank you.

And the hedonist says, "Will you guys shut up! I've got a hangover."

The philosophies presented above do not necessarily express the views of this columnist. He is a disciple of benign idiocy, which combines the classic teachings of Mahatma Gandhi and Porky Pig: As you go through life, harm no one and b-dip b-dip b-dip, that's all folks!